WITHOUT FANFARE

THE STORY OF MY FAMILY

BY

SUSAN BURNETT OF KEMNAY

Published by
Kemnay House Publishing
Kemnay House
KEMNAY
Aberdeenshire AB51 5LH

Typeset from author generated discs by
Reflective Images, Pitcaple, Inverurie.

Printed by
BPC – AUP Aberdeen Ltd

ISBN 0 952 3979 94

CONTENTS

ILLUSTRATIONS

DEDICATION

To my cousin, Bunty, and all the other
brave Burnetts who have gone before.

I mention my cousin, Bunty Swan, the eldest daughter of my Uncle Doodie, Air Chief Marshal Sir Charles Burnett, because she really inspired me to make some record of our family by her extreme courage and cheerfulness when she was dying of cancer. I felt that her bravery and fortitude were perhaps indicative of this family of ours and that she was being "true to type". She laughed when I told her this but said it was an excellent idea and that she was just sorry that she would not be here to read it. Her last words to me were "Off you go and write your book."

So – many years later, this is the Story of the Burnetts of Kemnay, our ancestors, as I have come to know them from their own letters and papers and letters written to them by their contemporaries.

Family Tree of the Burnetts of Kemnay

THOMAS, 1ST. of Kemnay ~ 2ND Son of James Burnet of Craigmyle.
d. 1689 m. Margaret, only child of John Pearson of Edinburgh.

- **THOMAS, 2ND. of Kemnay** 1656–1729, m. 1713, Elizabeth d. of Richard Brickenden of Inkpen, Berks.
  - **GEORGE, 3RD. of Kemnay** 1714–1780, m. 1734, Helen d. of Sir Alex. Burnet of Leys; m.2. Janet Dyce of Disblair
    - Helen 1734–1810
    - **ALEXANDER, 4TH. of Kemnay** 1735–1802, m. 1781, Christian, d. of John Leslie, Prof. of Greek at Aberdeen, & of Christian, d. and heiress of Hugh Fraser of Powis.
      - George b & d 1783
      - Helen 1784–1864, m. 1805 Dr. James Bannerman Prof. of Medecine in the University of Aberdeen.
      - **JOHN, 5TH. of Kemnay** 1786–1847, m. 1814 Mary, d. of Dr Charles Stuart of Dunearn, Fife.
        - Mary Erskine 1815–1890
        - **ALEXANDER GEORGE, 6TH. of Kemnay** 1816–1908, m. 1849 Letitia Amelia d. of William Kendall. d. 1855; m.2. 1877 Anna Maria d. of Ebenezer Pledge. d. 1885; m.3. 1893 Emily Julia d. of Joseph Burch. d. 1908
          - Letitia 1850–1936
          - **JOHN ALEXANDER, 7TH. of Kemnay** 1852–1935, m. 1877 Charlotte Susan d. of Arthur Forbes Gordon of Rayne
            - **ARTHUR MOUBRAY, 8TH. of Kemnay** 1878–1948, m. 1921 Muriel d. of Col. Henry Andrews Speed & widow of Seymour Langham
              - **SUSAN LETITIA, 9TH. of Kemnay** 1922–
              - Jean Muriel Moubray 1926–
            - Lettie Muriel 1880–1966
            - Charles Stuart 1882–1945 Air Chief Marshal
            - Thomas Leslie 1885–1940
            - Robert Lindsay 1887–1959 Admiral
            - Irene Dorothy May 1893–1982
          - William Kendall LLD 1884–1912
          - Amelia 1855–1941
          - Ebenezer Erskine 1877–1951
          - Alexander Douglas Gilbert 1879–1962
          - Henry Martyn 1881–1915
          - Octavious Winslow b & d 1882
          - Stuart Alexander b & d 1883
          - Frances Mary Stuart 1884–1976
        - Christina Leslie 1818–1866
        - Charles John 1820–1907
        - George 1822–1890 Lion King of Arms
        - Stuart Moubray 1824–1893
        - Henry Martyn 1826–1881
        - Erskine William 1828–1848
      - Elizabeth 1788–1806
      - Christian 1789
      - Lamont 1791
    - Anne 1736–1782
    - Jean 1739–, m. Alex Dunbar of Boath.
    - Elizabeth 1740–1807
    - Mary 1747–1802
  - Anne 1717–1787
  - Elizabeth 1721–1723
- Andrew d. 1726
- Rachel 1679–1732

KEMNAY

IT ALL BEGAN with Thomas – the three hundred year old story of the Burnetts of Kemnay. Like most families, it has had its share of modestly outstanding characters. One very definite characteristic is an inability to throw things away and if it were not for this fortunate trait, I should never have been able to get to know my ancestors at all. Besides keeping all letters and documents, the early members of the family wrote numerous letters and kept those they received in return, and in some instances copies of the letters they themselves had written. The first Thomas had not developed this habit, according to the evidence of the Kemnay archives, and as his position as the first Burnett[1] of Kemnay was of barely a year's duration, it has been impossible to capture even an idea of the sort of man he was. His father, James, was the immediate younger brother of Sir Thomas Burnet of Leys, the first Baronet, and in 1608, when barely nineteen, he married Elizabeth, daughter and heiress of Thomas Burnet of Craigmyle and Tillyhaikie, the grandson and representative of William Burnet of Craigour, Campbell and Tillyhaikie, who fell at the Battle of Pinkie in 1547. James was able to add to Craigmyle large properties in the parishes of Kincardine O'Neil, Skene and Fetteresso and seems to have become as considerable a laird as his brother at Crathes. James and Elizabeth of Craigmyle had four sons and two daughters who survived, apart from the usual sad series of infants who died very young. The second son was our Thomas who was a Writer in Edinburgh, which is how a lawyer was designated in those days. He married Margaret, the only child of an Edinburgh merchant, John Pearson, and they lived in Parson's Close where he owned what is recorded as being "tennement and lands". Three of their children survived infancy: Thomas, born in 1656, Andrew, and the youngest child, Rachel, born in 1679. Rachel never married and always remained in the care of her family. There are many references to her as she was left in the guardianship of her eldest brother. Andrew also became a Writer in Edinburgh and married his first cousin, Jean, from Craigmyle.

1 *The name Burnett evolved from the pre-Norman conquest name of de Burnard. The prefix 'de' was dropped, making it Burnard and then it became Burnet. The extra 't' came and went, as the spirit or spelling moved the writer, for a hundred years or so until they decided on the double t – thus enabling the English to mispronounce it!*

THOMAS

The second Thomas, my great-great-great-great-great-grandfather, was one of the most interesting of my ancestors. When he had finished with the customary tutors, he went to Holland and studied at the University of Leyden. There was a healthy trade between the two countries at this time and the University was not then the rather odd choice it might seem to-day. In the early days it was easier to travel by sea to the Low Countries from Aberdeen than by road to the south. Thomas developed a liking for the Netherlands which eventually culminated in his gravestone being imported from there to a countryside shot through with granite! After completing his studies, he returned home and was admitted to the Scottish Bar. There is no record of his having practised as a lawyer but he soon became known in the literary and political circles at home and abroad, particularly as a scholarly man with a quite reasonable grasp of the philosophical ideas and political opinions of the day. Meanwhile Thomas's father had decided it was time that he became a man of more substantial property so that he would have some fixed assets to leave his son Thomas when the time came. In 1688 he bought from Sir George Nicholson, a Lord of Session, under the title of Lord Kemnay, the lands and barony of Kemnay and the "toun and lands of Craigerne." Sir George had purchased them but four years previously from Thomas Crombie.

The Barony of Kemnay was a modest estate of some four thousand acres but most suitable for a second son of a second son and a Writer in Edinburgh. Unfortunately he did not live to enjoy his new home and possessions for very long as he died the following year and was buried in the church at Kemnay on 19th February 1689 beside his wife Margaret, who had died the previous November. Thus did the responsibilities of the inheritance descend upon the somewhat reluctant shoulders of Thomas, second of Kemnay. He was certainly in no mind to forsake his chosen way of life and settle down as a laird so he engaged a Factor, James Marshall, also a Writer in Edinburgh, to manage his affairs. The reason for appointing an Edinburgh lawyer to act as Factor for an Aberdeenshire estate seems to have been solely that James Marshall had been well known and well thought of by Thomas's father, who had, in co-operation with a certain Provost Binney, raised Marshall "from the first seeds of educatione to any degree of capacity and whom I myself thought whyle I was in Scotland Honest and Diligent."

James Marshall's first recorded act for Thomas was in September 1689 when he paid 13/4 to a "Blacksmith when Andrew Burnet and James Marshall returned from Berwick from conveying the laird of Kemnay" and presumably seeing him off on his journey to London, and spending 4/- (scots, I hope) for a "Padlock to the Laird's Cloakbag." Never having practised in the profession himself, I wonder if Thomas realised how much money he was going to spend on every little detail of expenditure. James Marshall's "Accompt Book" makes very interesting reading and is most informative. He lists every single thing, as you will see from this extract:

Accompt of the Charge of James Marshall's Journey to the North:

		£ s d
Item	Expenses at Leith	2:00
"	for passage to Burntisland	4:00
"	for Charge there and a Boy to carry out my Books etc. out of the Boat and to seek a Horse	5:00
"	one Night's Quarters at Kennoquhay [Kennoway]	1:01:00
Item	horsehyre from Burntisland to Dundie Water syde being 22 myles	2:04:00
"	to the Lad and Charges there	2:06
"	for Passage to Dundie and to a Boy	2:06
"	to Dinner there	7:00
"	at Arbroth [Arbroath]	3:04
"	for Charges for 2d. Nights Quarters Douket [?]	16:00
"	horsehyre from Dundie to Monross [Montrose] water syde	2:01:00
"	for Passage there and a Boy to carry the Cloakbag to Monross	2:00
"	Charges there	7:00
"	the North Water Passage	2:00
"	Charges at Stonehyve [Stonehaven] for Dinner	8:00
"	Passage to the Cassie end	:08
"	horse hyre from Monross to Aberdeen	2:18:00
"	3d. [third] Night's Quarters at Aberdeen	15:00
"	payed for my Horse att Brush having gone there to crave Lentush [?]	

"	horse hyre from Aberdeen to Kemnay be way of Drumb [Drum as in Thumb!] being 15 myles	1:10:00
"	to the lad	1:06
"	payed out for Ale at Kemnay besides 2 Firlots of Malt that was brown	16:08
"	being 3 nights at Moniemusk I left drink Money	12:00
"	by the Way from Kemnay to Aberdeen for Ale	:10
"	Charges in Aberdeen that Night and in the Morning	1:01:00

The Cassie end is a misspelling on James Marshall's part: he meant the Causey end or, more correctly, the Causeyport. In later entries he refers to the "Cassie port". The only coast road to Aberdeen from the South from Stonehaven was the Causey Mounth. According to Fenton Wyness in his book "Silver City by the Grey North Sea", the road south of the Causeyport was fraught with difficulties and danger as this part of the road was frequently under water and sometimes quite impassable. The Magistrates of Aberdeen secured an Act of Parliament authorising them to "big and causey" this stretch of road and to levy a toll which was collected at the Causeyport. It appears from James Marshall's accounts that the Toll charge was 8d per horse.

Besides attending to estate business, James Marshall's other task was to see to the care of Thomas's sister, Rachel, then aged only ten. Now that the poor child's parents were both dead, Thomas had arranged with the Lady Corsindae to put Rachel to school in Edinburgh. The Lady Corsindae, or Aunt Corsindae as she was referred to by the family, was his father's sister, Mary, who had married Alexander Forbes of Corsindae. After her husband's death, her only child, a son, sold Corsindae to the Duffs and bought a property near Southampton. Aunt Corsindae went to live in the Burnet "tennement" in Parson's Close and was, no doubt, very glad to have Rachel's company. James Marshall paid her regular sums of money for Rachel's board. I am glad the little girl had some kind aunt to look after her but first Rachel had to be brought down from Kemnay and this is the story of her journey as told by Mr Marshall. First of all she was accompanied to Aberdeen by a "lad" and the following morning she and James Marshall set off.

		£	s	d
Item	for Passage of 2 Horse at the Cassy end		1	04
"	for Dinner at Gilliebrands and Horse Corn		9	00

Gilliebrands is still marked on the Ordnance Survey Map as a farm house.

		£ s d
Item	Charges at Stonehyve for Supper and 1 Nights Quarters for 3 people and 2 horse	1 : 17 : 00

The lad obviously continued to accompany them and I wonder who sat pillion! They stopped at Benhoukirk, which I have not been able to place, for horse corn and dinner and crossed the Northwater of "Eresk" (Esk) before crossing the Montrose water. They slept that night at the "Doucat" which was obviously an inn and next day had dinner and purchased horse corn at "Geordie Crammonds". I had great hopes of locating Geordie Crammonds but other than its being this side, or rather north of Broughty Ferry which was the next crossing, I have not managed to pinpoint this hostelry. The cost of hiring horses from Aberdeen to "Brughtie" came to £9. 4/-, the distance being forty-six miles by his reckoning. The third night was spent at Ferrieden and the next day they dined "within a myle of Kirkcaldie" and journeyed on to "Bruntisland", another forty-four miles where they spent the fourth night in anticipation of crossing to Leith the following day.

		£ s d
Item	for Passage at Bruntisland to Leith haveing payed for a Lass who had a care of Rachel at sea being Stormie Weather and she and I both sick at Sea	12:00
"	spent at Leith	4:00
"	to a Man who carried Rachell out of the Boat	1:00
"	to a Lade that carried out the Baggage out of the Boat and went up to Edin. to get a Coach there being none in Leith	3:00
"	payd. to the Coachman for Coach hire	1:08:00

The next item of expense was 13/4 for two pounds (lbs) of plaiding "to Rachell to make her ane undercoat and for a pair of stockings to her besides the red pair that was taken out of the Chist at Kemnay" and he paid seven shillings "for a Skirt Violet and Green frog makeing" so what with the new shoes he had purchased for her before leaving Aberdeen she was well equipped with new clothes to start school, the charge for which came to 13/4 a quarter. He adds at the bottom of the list that he had bought "half a pund of reasins to her at Abdn.

to eat by the way and half ane unce of whyt Candie – 5/-". I cannot believe they could have lasted for four days but it is nice to visualise Rachel munching away at her goodies on the road south!

Aunt Corsindae was paid £1.10/- for putting Rachel to school. Marshall went north to Kemnay at least once a year, sometimes stopping at different places. On one occasion, after having what must have been a very good dinner at Coupar, the following entry reads – "to charges at Churchaldie", however the next morning he actually left "Kirkcaldie"! The stormy crossing he experienced from Kinghorn to Leith put him against long sea journeys so he altered his route and rode further round the coast and took the shorter crossing from Queensferry. James Marshall's "Compt Book of my Intromissions wt. Kemnay", besides being very illuminating and amusing, has been an invaluable record. Apart from the Kemnay estate the "Tennement" in Parson's Close had also to be administered. In old Thomas's day, he had occupied most of the house himself but had let the "undermost storie" to one Alexander Anderson, plus a "sellar" for £50 a year, and the "laigh house" to Agnes Stuart for £12. She occupied it for several years but other tenants came and went and at one time the "Master of the Flanders Coffiehouse" leased the third and "Cape stories" and Agnes Stuart's ground floor for the princely sum of £72. "Cape" is an old Scottish word meaning the highest part of anything. "Parson's Close", actually "Pearson's Close", had been named after a John Pearson whose son, David, was a lawyer in Edinburgh. Then it became known as "Knox Close" after a George Knox and later as "Burnett's Close" after Samuel Burnet, a brewer and prominent citizen but no relation to the Kemnay Burnetts. It was demolished by fire in 1750 and is now the site of the City Chambers. In 1695 James Marshall had to spend some considerable time in Inverurie "to take Instruments against the Magistrates of Inverury and Kintore requiring them to provide Captain Hamiltoun's troup of Dragoons with peits and not to suffer them to oppress the Tenants of Kemnay."

II

In 1694, when the "Craigmyle Affair" began in all its complexities, Thomas questioned Marshall's handling of his business. This "affair" arose out of the very complicated matter of the inheritance of Thomas's cousin, Alexander Burnet of Craigmyle. This is so often the source of great unpleasantness and frustration in families but when the main character changes his mind, in this case twice, and does not put pen to paper, the only result must be a lengthy and disagreeable legal fight. Sir Alexander had no male heir, just three daughters – Isabel, Anna and Margaret – and it was the settlements he made that gave rise to considerable litigation. First of all he settled his lands on his daughters – there were only two at this time – provided that they married Thomas and Andrew, the sons of his uncle, Thomas Burnet. The date of this first will was 1686 but two years later Sir Alexander entailed his lands on his own male heirs (who, as has been said, did not materialise) with the remainder passing over his bachelor brother successively to his eldest uncle, by this time of Kemnay, and male heirs of his body; or to his second uncle, James Burnet of Monboddo, and his male heirs; and failing that to his third uncle, Robert Burnet of Criggie and heirs male. In the same year, while in Edinburgh, Sir Alexander made "an obligation", his uncle Thomas having offended him in some way, to annul the entail as soon as he got home and "to tear" his uncle's name from it. A few months later, however, the offending uncle died and Sir Alexander went home and lived a further six years without amending or destroying the entail. His "obligation" was found with the entail upon his death but no later entail or will was discovered. There followed years of legal battle. Cousin Thomas of Kemnay held that to refrain from cancelling the entail signified that his cousin had changed his hasty decision and that he, Thomas, was the rightful heir and he applied to the Court for sight of all entails made by his cousin on heirs male. Being biased, I think Thomas was right – after all he did know the law – but Uncles Monboddo and Criggie were out for all they could get, determined to make the most of the early changes of heart, and being on the spot, they were able to prevail upon the Law Lords to refuse this request. A decision in favour of the daughters was given, with Monboddo (needless to say) their guardian! Thomas considered he had been very badly treated and in a lengthy letter from London to his kinsman at Crathes, Sir Thomas the third Baronet, he complains bitterly and tells how:

> I had written to Monymusk and Mr. John Burnet [no relation] about this Tyme to entreat them (in conjunction with Yourself) to tak such exact Account of Mr. Marshal's Actings in my Affairs whatsoever as they thought fitt. I never had any Answeir. My coming to Scotland was most resolutely determined about the Tyme I received Information of Craigmyle's Death; But hearing whow unnaturally I was passed by, this Blast of Unkyndnesse did beat me back more than any Storme could have done.....Since that Tyme the Alterations of the Climat and Weather seasing upon me I am become much changed in my State of Health which does not permit me to ramble much more back and forwards even though it were bot to Scotland. My Melancholy and Hypocondriaque Temper hath contributed much to this bodily Indispositione. And ill Treatment from some I reckoned upon for my best Friends heth riveted that uneasie natural Temper which I endeavoured all maner of Ways to root up.....I lyk Scotland well, and wish it well more than any other Place, Bot I should be false and disembling if I said my Love to it were from the Maner of Living in it which in no Wayes suits my Humer.

A word by way of excuse for Thomas here would not be amiss. Kemnay, when his father acquired it, was situated in bleak and cheerless surroundings. No improvements had been carried out and no trees planted so it was open to all the prevailing cold winds from west, north and east. Knowing it today, and having seen it in its prime, it is very difficult for me to imagine the forbidding mansion house and exposed position, since nowadays we enjoy the shelter that Thomas never knew. In his letter, he goes on to say how great is his esteem for his cousin at Crathes and how he acknowledges the honour of being descended from his family. He writes how it was "natural to expect the Succession of his [Craigmyle's] estate in the greatest part, with his Daughter" forty-four years his junior. Thomas was thirty-eight years old at this time, had lived most of his life in London or on the continent and had no idea of "countrey life" and even though he was "upon the Place would committ the Care of All to a Factor. Iff my little Estate were bot looked to with modest Care and Skill I think I would find it almost all One of being here or there." He goes on to ask Sir Thomas to look into the management and to discharge James Marshall fairly if he considers he had managed the land honestly. His "little Estate" was to suffer again more than once in later centuries from the mismanagement of factors.

A word here in James Marshall's defence would not be in-apt. Every act. letter, petition or what you will concerning this wretched "affair" is noted in his accounts. Admittedly Thomas paid for every little detail: the number of pages each letter or petition consisted of is written down and the whole business cost him a pretty penny. When he returned to Scotland and had time to examine Marshall's books, Thomas could see for himself and indeed he accepted all the accounts and signed them as being in order and Marshall remained in his employ until 1709.

The Craigmyle case appears to have upset others as well. Andrew Burnet's behaviour had caused his brother annoyance and sorrow:

> I never knew a Brother manadge to ane other Brothers Mynd bot we all knew and Andrew manadge for ane other Thomas of our Name to his Sorrow and Ruine. I am greived exceedinglie for his Cariage to his Aunt Corsindae wherof she lamenteth to me bitterly. We are certainly fallen into the last and worse tymes.

Did James Marshall write to Thomas about Andrew's actions or did Aunt Corsindae report his lamentable behaviour? We can perhaps read between the lines of the following letter written in March 1697 by Jean, Andrew's wife. The wretched Craigmyle business made everybody touchy and suspicious.

> Sir 8. March, 1697
>
> I am sorry I should be constrained against my Inclinations to give you the Trouble of these Lines that yourself may vindicate Me of the Aspersions Mr. Marshall has laid to my Name and my Husbands by forging to Himself Acalumnions bye saying to Sir T. B. of Leyes that both of us have written to You that he has been acting a separat Interest of his owne judging by this to excite him to forsake your Interest and raise a Discord and Jealousy amongst us all. And had not Lyes misbeleeved so unworthy a Representation wee had

surely all split as without Doubt Mr. Marshall designed led by Envie and Malice that any should be concerned but himself and thereby his Negligence be discovered. Sir you may believe I do not write this out of Malice or Revenge only I take the Freedom out of Conscience and Deuty to advise you of such injurious Dealing for I know had your Business been honestly lookt after in the beginning it might have been difficult befor this Tyme for Sir Charles Maitland himself confessed that Mr. Marshall had been spoke to and brought over in the beginning for which Cause I earnestly intreat you maybe so kind to yourself not to suffer Mr. Marshall's being further concerned lest that affire be postponed and neglected as much as formerly. All your Friends heir have thought it proper that I should take your Sister Rachel to the north which I have very willingly complyed with it being very agreeable to my Inclinations only I should be sory if I thought it disagreeable to yours. My Heart I hope shall ever be preserved from toufnes [?] beyond the Force of base Temptation I am sorry I cannot testify my Deuty in that sense I both wish and ought yet I request the Credit of a most serious and sincere Acknowledgement of your undeserved Caracter I shall be very much pleased if you doo me the Honor to understand of your Health and Welfare by a return of this when you shall be pleased

So wishing you ever Prosperity I remaine
your most affectionate Sister
and obedient Servant J Burnet

my Husband gives his Love
and good Wishes but defers
his own writting till the next.
Excuse the ill writt being in
my Way north from Leith.

This letter was addressed: Mr. Burnet Esquire Att
Madam Barhams In Park Street
Westminster Opposite To Mr. Wilsons
By the Royall Corbssitt, London.

Maybe it was Rachel's removal by Andrew's wife from Aunt Corsindae's care that caused the latter to lament bitterly. Rachel by this time was eighteen years old and had been eight years at her school in Edinburgh. Whatever she may have learnt there, she certainly never wrote anything for posterity and there is only the odd mention of "the doctor to Rachel" and various medicines in her accounts. In any event Aunt Corsindae eventually followed her north and looked after her either in Aberdeen or at Kemnay where she died in 1700.

I must own that I find it a great relief that Thomas did not marry his cousin's daughter. Besides her being so very much his junior, the families intermarried quite often enough and a daughter of a somewhat odd father would not have improved the character of future Burnetts of Kemnay, some of whom were pretty odd anyway! Thomas's eventual bride was not in any way related, was beautiful, much loved and revered by her children and showed great strength of character and ability to manage the affairs of the family after her husband's death.

III

Family feuds are most distasteful and I find myself agreeing with Thomas that his life among eminent scholars and his standing in royal courts would have wooed lesser men than he. How much more civilised was the style of living at the Court of Hanover! A clever man and one with a marked leaning to melancholy, how he must have shrunk from contact with the petty jealousies and underhandedness of some of his own kith and kin. He counted amongst his friends some of the most notable personalities of his time, the most outstanding and possibly truest friend being Wilhelm Gottfried Leibniz, the famous German mathematician and philosopher. The correspondence between the two men is extensive and dates from 1698 when Leibniz was in the service of the Duke of Brunswick Lunneburg. He wrote with some apprehension about a report of a "conspiracy against the King [William III], and every precaution must be taken for the safety of his person which is valuable beyond words. We hope, however, that God....will confound his enemies and that France will finally settle for peace. Perhaps she deludes herself that this will break up the Grand Alliance, but I believe she is mistaken, and we in Germany are taking steps to ensure our security."

In a lengthy postscript he finishes with a little bit of humour:

> I forgot to tell you of a dispute between some scholars, who asked me to be arbiter of their discussion. One took exception to the fact that on the coinage of England there is the inscription, William III By The Grace of God, and on the reverse, King of Great Britain, France and Ireland, since he is not the third King of Great Britain of his name but the first, being III of England, II of Scotland, I of Great Britain. The other replied that the usage had to be that authorised in the Public Arts, which called him William III. For my part, I said on the point that the argument of the first wasn't bad, but that nevertheless one might justify the English not only by the authorised usage but by reason: since he is William III in England, they have the right to describe him on their coins, even if they add his full title afterwards. But I added that I thought the best thing would be to leave the number blank, not only because of the objection, but also so that people did not become accustomed to distinguishing him by the number, since it would be more appropriate someday in History for him to be known as William the Great. I summed it up in this couplet:
>
> William First, or Second, or Third?
> Ask not, Critics, Great's the Word.

Another correspondent was John Locke, and there was also considerable communication between himself and his cousin Gilbert Burnet, Bishop of Salisbury. His standing in the select court circle of the Electress of Hanover, to which Leibniz had by this time transferred his services, is confirmed by the tone of the letters from Sophia which are most affectionate and show she obviously valued his worth. In 1700, when Queen Anne's one surviving child died, the succession to the British throne by the Hanoverians became more than just a possibility and Thomas was charged with secret instructions from the Electress to carry to certain leading men in England. The culmination of all this was of course the Act of Settlement in 1701. Sophia was a grand-daughter of James I and VI (Perhaps we should give him his nickname to please Herr Leibniz – "The wisest fool in Christendom") which made her the next in line to the British throne after Anne as all Roman Catholic claimants were automatically disqualified. The French King, Louis XIV, recognised Anne's half-brother, James (the Old Pretender), as the heir to the throne and this caused a great ferment and was the immediate cause of Queen Anne's declaration of war in May 1702. It was a good six weeks before this declaration, however, that Thomas crossed over to France on his way back to Hanover. He was staying with friends in Paris before continuing his journey. Here is the account of what happened next in Thomas's own words to Leibniz, translated from his French which became more and more anglicised as he got more and more annoyed and vexed.

> Geneva – this 5 November 1703
>
> Very dear and esteemed monsieur,
>
> I cannot express adequately the desire I have to hear news of you, and principally of your health after the interruptions in my replies to your letters over a period of more than twenty months past; For my part, I had been unfortunately hindered from writing - freedom to write, or indeed undertake any correspondence whatever having been taken from me for more than fourteen months while I was kept under close imprisonment in the Bastille at Paris, without knowing why, to-day any more than the moment when this disaster overtook me. It was during that period of peace which lasted about six or seven weeks before war was declared against the English. Nor could I imagine what particular suspicions they entertained of my actions or my intentions, for they accused me of nothing despite the fact they interrogated me about everything, even to the extent of wishing to know my secret thoughts and conduct over more than fifteen years previously. They wanted to know far too much, and for my part, I did not want to tell them anything more than I considered relevant. To tell you all that I suffered in this prison would be a long story. It suffices at the present moment to tell you that the manner of proceeding towards me – viz. to seize a foreigner, in his bed in peace time, to keep him in close confinement, to accuse him of nothing, nor even to examine him for a year, and finally, after God knows how many supplications, prayers and requests from myself inside and

> my friends outside to have justice, to have the doors opened on my behalf without a word of apology for the wrong that had been done to me, or any reason given for having used me so, or any reprimand whatever for any particular of my conduct in France. It was certainly in spite of them – one could do more in honour of an innocent person, and a very demonstrable example of the regular justice of this country and its ministers for I am persuaded that the King himself is not at all informed of the millions of disorders and abuses in these prisons. They wanted to conceal and make a mystery of the reasons for my imprisonment, but I noticed myself that they insisted on these two points in particular, seven or eight times during my interrogation – viz. my relationship with the Bishop of Salisbury and the honour of being given such a good reception at the Courts of Hanover and Berlin and doubted no more that they were expressing hatred and envy towards me on account of these two points; I [suspect] if I had gone to St. Germain they would have treated me with greater tolerance.

Thomas goes on to say he had "nothing very much to write you about this place [Geneva] in respect of the sciences or art" but nevertheless continues for several pages on the three or four persons worthy of description and always remembering Leibniz's "maxim when you told me that you do not despise even little things". He mentions the Public Library in Geneva just reformed by M Turatin to whom honour is "due for the fine order and reform of the public library in this town, which by the beauty of the vase [?] the clearness of the light, the order and arrangement, the choice of books, and principally for the beautiful view and prospective on the lake, has something of that mixture of the agreeable and the useful that is superior to the majority of libraries of comparable size which I have seen."

He bemoans the loss of some books by the "present Archbishop of York" which he left in the hands of M Dupin in Paris and

> ...which were never given me back again as he was unfortunately in exile at Charetault when I came out of prison. But I should like for preference to take them to you along with some others which I have borrowed here in the town if I were not confined here by the ravages of war which do

> not permit me to leave this little spot of earth where I am and which I regard at present as the only country of rest. The roads are not safe, nor free to return to you nor to England, by Italy, by Germany, by France nor by sea, and having already suffered at their rough hands (notwithstanding that they did not add humiliation to physical suffering as they will do to several others) I should rather be held prisoner by the Turks than fall into the hands of those people who have so vaunted the civility of the French...I should much like to know Monsieur, if M. Locke is still well. There is a person with whom I am especially intimately acquainted who has written in his defence against the author of those letters addressed to him, which appeared at different times a little while ago and to which he never deigned to reply. I sent them to you in a packet...he [Locke] is a very young author of whom I could say much more to you...

There follow accounts of two conflicting stories concerning German troops sent to the help of the Duc de Savoie at Piedmont and the claim by the French to have lost only two men from the engagement although "there had been brought back seventeen cartloads of wounded French soldiers." He begs Leibniz to give him the pleasure of receiving news from him and "If you address your letters to M. Mavin, merchant of Geneva, or rather in the mail-bag of anyone who is writing M. Loubierre, the Governor, or M. Normandie, counsellor, or any other person here except the Resident in France, I am quite well known by everyone....you will give me extreme pleasure if you can let me have news of you as soon as possible and fill me with favourable designs regarding the advancement of the sciences, and interest in the republic of letters which you always take to heart. Many things will be quite new to me, in that I have only had three letters from Scotland and none from England."

This letter which takes up eight pages of foolscap in the translation eventually ends – "I should like to write to you more freely and at greater length on many matters...I can add no more than my perseverance in my attachment to the interests of the Electoral House, and my vows and prayers for the health and prosperity of Her Most Serene Highness the Electress in particular, As also for the health and perpetual prosperity of His Prussian Majesty, his illustrious daughter also, I wish all that I could ever express.

> I am, very dear and very esteemed Monsieur, in inviolable friendship, your very obedient and obliged servant,
> Burnet de Kemnay."

In the following months Leibniz replied from Hanover:

> As we were awaiting news from you from England, I was surprised to receive it from Geneva; but I am well pleased, as it gives me hope of seeing you before you return to your island. I at once informed the Electress, who was happy to hear that you were in a place of safety. But I can well see that you are unaware of your own history when you do not mention gratitude either to her or to the Queen [of Prussia], who have both worked so hard for your deliverance. I can tell you both how you came to be put in the Bastille, and how you got out of it. But in exchange you must write to us in detail everything that has happened to you. I wrote you a fine long letter but don't know whether you received it. However there was nothing in it which could harm you if it was intercepted. When I had received no reply for some months, I asked M. Brosseau, our Ambassador at the Court of France, to find out if you had perhaps returned to England. He found out and replied that you were in the Bastille, but the reason was unknown. I did not delay in informing the Electress and also the Queen, begging them to interest themselves on your behalf, but they had little need to be asked. I wrote about the matter too to the Bishop of Salisbury, who answered that he would try and persuade the Queen [Anne] to exchange you for someone. However several attempts having completely failed (we got a lady at Berlin who is known at the Court of France to write, but she received no answer), I asked M. d'Alefeld, the Danish Minister in Berlin (where I was myself then) to write about it to M. de Meiercron, Minister of his master the King at the Court of France, to get him to talk to the Marquis de Torcy, and the Queen also spoke to M. d'Alefeld in my presence. That envoy acquitted himself with zeal, and M. de Meiercron on his side spoke to the Marquis de Torcy, who said he would find out about the affair. Someone had told the Secretary of State that you were known to have evil designs, and were mixed

up in suspicious activities, having come to France also without a passport; the lieutenant of police, learning this, had put you in a place of safety: in a word, your business was not at all clear. I was still in Berlin when this report arrived, and at once drew up a little memorandum in reply, where I said that one part of the report was slanderous and it looked as if the rest might well be too. For I myself knew for certain that you had come to France before the rupture for reasons of health, at a time when passports were not in use at all, and your character was too well known in our courts for there to be any possible suggestion that you had malicious designs against the Government and the State. We also got M. l'Abbé Polignac and M. de la Rosiere, who knew you in Berlin (or the latter, at any rate) to give you a good testimony; and the Electress wrote to the Queen [of France] on your behalf, who took up your interest, along with M. de Polignac and M. de la Rosiere. The last named wrote to me about you and told me of his intention to help. At last I learned of your release from the Gazette, and the Queen had already learned of it from M. l'Abbe Polignac. When M. de Torcy had received my memorandum, he had had the affair gone into, and there was nothing to be found against you. It was learned only that certain spies who haunted Paris taverns had thought they were doing themselves a good turn by denouncing you, and the lieutenant of police had believed them too easily. The same thing happened to you as is reported of a scholar who had put some Greek words in a letter. They were taken for a cypher, and he was left for some years in the Bastille without his situation being investigated. Eventually, at the insistence of his relations, the case was examined, the error discovered, and the doors opened to him as to you.

Thomas was very fortunate in his friends; otherwise he might have languished in the Bastille for even longer. Leibniz goes on to thank Thomas for all his information regarding the scholars he met in Geneva, and to tell him in exchange what books he had been reading. He was not over-enthusiastic about Mr Locke, however, remarking that there are a good many things on which "I do not agree at all." But not wishing to offend, he adds, "However, it must be confessed that there are innumerable fine ideas in M. Locke, and when he supports truthful opinions he sets them out in a great and fine manner."

A letter from Her Serene Highness in reply to Thomas's letter of gratitude for her endeavours on his behalf reads:

> La nouvelle, que vous m'avée mandée, Monsieur, touchant votre elargissement de la Bastille, aussi bien que votre heureuse arrivée à Geneve, m'a été d'autant plus agréable que Je suis ravie de vous savoir a l'abri de ceux, qui vous ont traite avec tant d'injustice. Je vous suis cependant fort obligée des sentimens obligeans, que vous me tempignée a ce sujet, et en même tems fort aise d'avoir ou moyen de vous marquer a quel point je m'interesse pour vous. Vous me devée pas nonplus douter que Je n'embrasse encore volontiers les occasions qui Je presenteront de vous donner des preuves se mon estime.
>
> Votre tres affectionée
>
> Sophie Electrise,

There is also a reply from the Queen of Prussia:

> Les remercimens que vous me faites, monsieur, surpassant de beaucoup le plaisir que j'ai pru vous faire en contribuant par mes offices a votre elargessement et cela d'autant plus que c'est aux Contes de Madame, que vous deves principalment attribuer votre liberté. Je ne laisse cependant pas de me rejouir avec vous de vous savoir si heureusement sorti de ce labyrinthe et me reserve de vous en feliciter de bouche, quand Je vous verrai l'ete prochain a Litzebourg, ou Je vous invite d'avance. Au reste vous devés etre persuade, que Je prendrai toujours part a ce poura vous rewarder, et que J'aurai une joye particuliere de vous obliger dans les occasions qui s'en presenteront,
>
> Sophie Charlotte.

IV

While Thomas was stagnating in the Bastille, life in Scotland continued in a mundane fashion. At Kemnay the Baron Courts were held regularly. Our Baron Court Book records sittings from 1688 to 1707 and show the date on which "Mr Thomas Burnet has granted to the said James Marshall full power to doo and exerce all and sundry things sicklyke and as freely and in all respects as he myt do himself if personally present whereof He [sic] the said James Marshall doth hereby Nominate and appoynt James Crem in Auquhithy to be Baron Baylie to the lands and Barony of Kemnay toun and lands of Craigearne with power to him to decide and determine all matters, debates, questions and differences betwixt the said Mr. Thomas Burnet and his tenants of the Lands and Barony foresaid And to punish all delinquents and Criminalls within the said lands and Barony And to do all other things wch a Barron Baylie has power to do by Lawes and Acts of parliament."

The courts were usually held "within the maner place of Kemnay" but on occasion at some other house such as "at damadillie in James Laws chamber" or other Highly respectable "dwelling house." The courts were conducted by the 'bailzie' as it was sometimes spelt, the Clerk of the Court and the Ground Officer, and dealt with thieving and fighting "to the effusion of blod", slaughtering each other's sheep and eating same and on more than one occasion "killing eating and recepting of hares black fish smolts truts and wylde foulls of game" belonging to the laird. The courts were "continued upone 24 hours advertisement or sooner iff neid beis."

James Marshall's accounts are also an invaluable source of information as to Thomas's travels. On receipt of a letter from the laird, Marshall entered both the date he received it and the amount he had to pay for delivery. The charge for letters from London, whither Thomas went in 1689, was 5/-. The following year a letter received from Holland cost the factor 13/-. Thomas was en route for Italy at the time and Marshall's replies had to be sent to Venice. The next Spring saw him back in London and in 1693 he travelled to Italy once more and spent some time in Venice and in Genoa before journeying to Berlin by way of Amsterdam! In 1694, the year of Craigmyle's demise and resulting 'on-carry', Thomas was in Hamburg and a very bulky packet that "Inclosed the Consultation for raising one Avocation of the Curatorie of Craigmylles" cost £6. 7/- to despatch.

Another interesting entry of October 1691 notes that £1. 9/- was paid to Mr Fraser "of a herauld for one draught of your Armes blazoned." It cost me rather more!

In 1700 repairs were needed to the Edinburgh property and £75. 8/- was paid to "Deacon Nizbett for building up the Lumms when they were like to fall." An accumulative account, I hope.

At Kemnay, Rachel did not enjoy good health and perhaps the reason may be found in this Chemist's bill:

Accompt to Laird of Kemnay To Geo. Burnet Chemig:

& Apothecary in Abdn	£ s d
Beginning Ap.	7 : 17 : 02
Item two Doses of a purgativ bolus	1 : 05 : 00
" powder of Zedoarie once	12 : 00
" two doses of purgativ pices	1 : 04 : 00
" five drach. of a Supporating oynment	3 : 00
" Tamarinds 1 once with whyt pott	7 : 00
" Syrup of Pale Roses 2 onces glas	11 : 06
" purgative ingredients	1 : 03 : 00
" Gargarisms bottled.	1 : 02 : 00

To mention but a few items.

According to Mr Culpeper's "Complete Herbal" the Damask roses which "are of a pale red colour and of a most pleasant scent" can be used to make a syrup by "infusing them twenty four hours in boiling water, and then, after straining off the liquor, adding twice its weight of refined sugar to it. This syrup is an excellent purge for children, and there is not a better medecine for grown people of a cositive habit." It sounded so refreshing, but I ought to have guessed!

Thomas's health was not improved by his incarceration in the Bastille and in 1705 he had gone to Pyrmont to take the waters there. A letter from the Electress' Secretary, M Gargan, gives us this information – the only letter written in English:

> The Elector hath asked me if I had heard from you since we came from Pyrmont and I answered that I had not, therefore I pray let me know how many dayes you have drunk the waters and how they agree with you and when you will be here.

> The Duke of Cel is at Hesen House and will stay Severall dayes yet.
>
> My Ld. D of Marlb: hath forced the French Lines in Flanders and will soon be the master of Brussells Loraine Mechelen and all the open Townes he goes to besiege Antwerp I am
>
> Sir
>
> yr. most humble servant R. Gargan.
>
> M. Burnet
> Gentilhomme Anglais
> à Pyrmont

From there Thomas returned to Hanover but the year 1707 saw him back in London again on the Electress' business. A letter from M. Gargan is addressed "A Monsieur Burnet de Kemnay, ches Mr Philips a la boule d'or dans fontaine Cour dans le Strande a Londres". (M. Leibniz adds "pres de Bedford House " on his envelope!) This note contains the Electress Sophia's thanks for the news he has sent and assures him of her good health.

The following year Thomas allowed himself the luxury of attending to some of his own personal affairs and of visiting his family as this time he is entitled "M. Thomas Burnet Seigneur de Kemnay en Ecosse." This letter contains rumours that have been rife of French preparations of naval and military aid for an expected uprising in Scotland in support of the Stuart cause.

> Je suis ravi d'apprendre par la dernière lettre que vous venés d'écrire a S A E; Madame la continuation de votre bonne Santé, et que vous respires presentement le doux air de votre pays natal..... Les lettres de France nous parlent d'un grand Soulevement en Ecosse, et qu'il y a deja 3 corps de [militaire?] en armes a la tête desquels se doit trouver le Duc d'Hamilton et plusieurs autres Seigneurs qui n'attendent que le Pretendu Prince de Galles, pour le declarer leur Roy...

As Queen Anne's health deteriorated, Thomas found himself mostly in London, keeping the Electress up to date with developments there. M. Gargan writes frequently in reply and in the August of 1710 was extremely worried that if the Duke of Marlborough resigned his command at the conclusion of the current campaign, it would be a grave loss "aux interets de la Cause commune." This time Thomas's address had changed a little, or rather Mr Philips had moved his abode: "Ches Mr. Philips dans Clare street proche Clare marquet a l'Enseigne des 3 Lions noirs Lincolns Infelds a Londres" and Thomas has marked on the back "Received at London about 3 a Clock afternoon with a Letter to My Lord Sunderland."

The correspondence between Thomas and his great friend, Leibniz, continued, covering general matters of literature and philosophy and the suppression of atheism. The last letter that we have from Leibniz is dated 17th March 1712 and has a request – "A translation of my *Theodices* is on hand I should greatly like to know what English scholars think of it." That Thomas treasured Leibniz' friendship is without question and he must have grieved deeply when the latter died in 1716.

In 1710, when Baron Bothmer was sent as Envoy Extraordinary from the Court of Hanover to that of Great Britain "on a very critical Occasion, he was instructed to communicate in every Thing relating to what he was charged with at the Court of London with Mr Burnet, and Mr Burnet was desired by Her Electoral Highness to give Baron Bothmer his Advice and Assistance in a letter wrote by the Secretary, sealed with the Electress' Signet and accompanied with this gracious Declaration of her Intentions 'S.A.E. m'ordonne de vous bien remercier pour sa Personne, et pour les Interets de cette Maison Electorale dont Elle vous temoignera dans l'Occasion sa reconnaissance par des Effets...."

The situation in London changed almost from day to day as the Queen tried to decide on her course of action regarding the succession. Thomas had no doubts as to the legitimacy of Sophia's claim to be Queen Anne's rightful heir and we can only be sorry that she predeceased the Queen by a very short space of time as her son, George, was not popular with the British nor did he, on his part, care very much for the prospect of residing in England. The Electress would have seen that her wishes regarding Thomas Burnet were carried out. She had made it known in all quarters that Thomas had served the court of Hanover with zeal and fidelity "The Electress expressing her entire satisfaction in his Services, and wishing for an Occasion to carry her good intentions into Execution, that she wrote a letter to my Lord Sunderland (Secretary of State) in which she desires her good Offices in procuring some Mark of favour from the

Court of England to Mr. Burnet which she is pleased to say, will be very acceptable to her and all her Family, who interest themselves in him. But this letter was not delivered till the Day before that Lord was removed from his Employment (Resigned the Seals), and it was not at that Season a Recommendation at the Court of England."

Alas, in spite of many prods to the royal memory both from London and Hanover, no recognition was ever given to Thomas in his lifetime. In the words of his grandson, he "did not live to receive those Rays of the King's Goodness His Majesty was so gracious as to signify he intended for him."

V

During his sojourns in London Thomas had met the Brickenden family from Inkpen in Berkshire and in 1713 he married Elizabeth, the beautiful daughter of Richard Brickenden. Thomas was fifty-seven and considerably older than his bride. There must have been great hustle and bustle at Kemnay getting the house prepared to receive the new mistress. One can perhaps permit a short flight of fancy and picture Aunt Corsindae and Rachel giving orders to the servants to have everything scrubbed clean and maybe even engaging a maidservant or two. At any rate the first purchase made by the new Lady Kemnay was for a great selection of brushes:

a bissom brush	¼d.	a washing brush	12d.
a chimnie brush	12d.	a sowes head brush	11d.
a scrubing brush for shoos	11d.	a Spanish bissom	2d.

Another necessary item among early purchases from the Blacksmith together with numerous fire irons was a "heater for a Smoothing Yron 2lb. weight."

Thomas acquired a town house in Aberdeen "upon the Green" and this they occupied in the Winter if they had not journeyed down to London instead. An expedition into Aberdeen was not one to be made very often as the roads were practically non-existent. The Aberdeen road from Kemnay ran by Castle Fraser and over the Gallows Hill to Skene and to Inverurie one went by Aquithie to the ferry at Haughton; there were no bridges over the Don above Aberdeen. It would be 1720 before a meeting of Aberdeenshire landlords unanimously agreed that "the whole highways and bridges within the County should be repaired, amended and built with all convenient diligence."

Once he had taken the formerly dreaded step of living on his "little estate", Thomas set about arranging his library there. The catalogue, written in his own hand, which has been bound for us very kindly by the University in Aberdeen, makes interesting if depressing reading. There are so many entries in the margin "lost". No doubt other books shared the same fate as those he left in Paris. I think Thomas would approve of the library today although he might regard some of the later additions to it as too frivolous!

Thomas had gathered quite a collection of pictures and portraits during the time he was a frequenter of foreign circles. A catalogue of "Pictures belonging to the Deceased Thomas Burnet of Kemnay" was drawn up by his widow in or about 1729. The inventory reads: "A Madonna – a mad woman – The Last Supper – Seven Dutch pieces – a head of Dean Callet by Holbane – his late Majesty King George – The Princess Sophia his Mother – the late Queen of Prussia his sister – The Present Queen of Prussia his Daughter – 2 copies of the present Queen of England – King Edward VI upon wood – 1 for my Brother unfinished – a Dutch man at his morning draught – the late Kemnay his own picture – his Ladys – his Sons." The pictures of the Madonna and the mad woman and the seven Dutch pieces are no longer here, neither is the head of Dean Callet (I wonder if it was by Holbein?). The Dutch gentleman with a pipe in his hand and drinking from an enormous glass goblet through which you can see his face, together with the Last Supper and Edward VI, are obviously some of the earlier acquisitions. The various royals could well have been added at a later date as were the portraits of his wife and son. The two copies of the then Queen of England are of Caroline of Anspach, wife of George II. These purchases shed light on another aspect of Thomas's character and he no doubt enjoyed hanging the mementoes of his former days where he could appreciate them.

As was the custom, Thomas entered important events in his Bible once he became a family man and the first of these entries reads:

> In the year of God 1714 my sone & first borne George Burnet was Christianed about two houres after his birth which was the 29 of September about 5 of the clock in the afternoon att Aberdeen in the house of Thomas Burnet upon the Green there, who also with his wyffe and Mrs. Sarah Merre were

together as witnesses to the chyldes baptisme by Doctor Andrew Burnet phisician and minister of the Ghospoll in that city. (The doctor was no relation.)

A sister, Anne, was born three years later in London in the Parish of Saint Anne's, Westminster, and a second sister's birth was "on a Sunday betwixt eleven and twelve o clock in the forenoon being the 12 day of February, 1721, And was baptised by the name Elizabeth upon the twentysecond day of the same month being Ashwednesday & Leip year in St. James parish of Westminster." How could 1721 have been a "Leip" year?

It was in this year while in London that Thomas had portraits painted of his wife and son and heir. They were done by the Dutch-trained artist, René Auguste Constantin, who worked mainly in Germany where he was well known and where Thomas had no doubt come across him. George, aged seven, is standing proudly in a scarlet jacket with a parrot on his right wrist. With his red curls and penetrating eyes, he has always dominated the old dining room where the portrait hangs beside the one of his mother and below the dark and sombre one of his father.

The year 1721 was one of considerable expenditure. On their return to Aberdeen after the portrait painting and the birth of Elizabeth, there are accounts for many purchases including

		£ s d
Imprs. to Cash		3 : 03
to ditto	ale & Brandy	2 : 04
" "	sugar	8
" "	Entertainment	7 : 00
		£0 : 13 : 03

1721 Acpt. 14. Laird off Camney Dr. to George Mowatt

	£ s d
20 door naills	8
1 lb candles	4 : 06
1 lb loose shugar	10 : 00
½ lb Tea	3 : 00 : 00
1 lb Candi broun shuger	14 : 00

Portrait of Elizabeth Burnet
by R.A. Constantin, 1721

Portrait of George Burnet
by R.A. Constantin, 1721

1 lb kitchin shuger	6 :00
1.2 lb loafe shuger	5 :00

and one not so "illl writt":

Sept. 13 1721 Accompt The Right Honourable the Laird of Kemnay
to Patt Gray Wright

	£ s d
To upputting a Bed in your uper flatte with tows & canvis	16:00
To ane Dail[2] for the head of Do. bed wt. workmanship	16:00
To ane Dail for the bustin peice wt. sawing & workmanship	1:00:00
To half a Dail for the footboard of Do. bed wt. workmanship	8:00
To Upputting another Tow to bed in your Laigh room	8:00
sum is	£3:08:00

In December of the same year

	£ s d
Washing the stair head room	2:10:00
Plastring below the Corners of the same room For the Chimney and the Foot of the Wall Plastring betwixt the Baking and Corners of the Hall and for plastring & laying the Chimney for the Stair and dressing another Chimney	3:15:00

Earlier that year Elizabeth had a lot of different sorts of cloth dyed by William Alexander Dyer. "Sarg" and other "stuff" and wool had all been dyed "blew" and, no doubt, was the material used by her dressmaker, Elizabeth Anderson, to make the following:

	£ s d
4 holand shirts	2:08:00
linen to Mr. Georg and Miss Agnes is	1:01:00
2 shifts and 2 blew frocks to Miss Betsie	16:00
9 Stocks making	4:00
for buttins to the Shirts is	5:00

2 *A Portion or Part of.*

"Miss Agnes" must be Anna and poor wee "Miss Betsie", just under two, is the subject of Thomas's next entry in his Bible: "upon the 11 day of Aprile 1723 by the mercifull and good God was called from this miserable world into a better state about 5 of the clock in the afternoon & was buried at the Church of Kemnay." At a time when child mortality was very high, parents may have been more resigned to the loss of their little ones.

The following is a rather curious apothecary's bill:

	£ s d
It. ane vomet	6:00
" 24 bottles wt. dyet drink	16:16:00
" 1 dozen off purgativ pills	12:00
" ingredients for a fomentation	16:00
" 18 bottles of wt. sherry	17:12:00
" ane pott off oynment ayasm	19:06

No doubt the sherry was medicinal!

A receipt for a proportion of money for "defraying Charges etc., anent the Wells & Publick Lights of Streets from Whitsunday 1721 to Whitsunday 1722: £3.12/- scots" shows what extra one had to pay for the luxury of having a town house. These receipts recur monotonously! In July 1723, Thomas, remembering the more elaborate dress favoured at the royal courts, made an extravagant purchase of:

	£ s d
2½ yairds fine scarlett Cloath att 17s.	2:02:06
1 paire Taickine Shoon	3:06
6 drops scarlett Moyhaire, 2½ yairds louprine	
6 bigg Scarlett buttons and 3½ drops lining silk	

and Elizabeth squandered £1. 7/3 on a "fine Hatt" with 3½ drops of Silver lace and a silver button to it. Shades of her brother, Beau Brickenden.

The same year Thomas rented a "lodging and furniture lying on the North side of the Castlegate at £11 a years rent sterling money." A much more upmarket dwelling house than his one on the Green, and being on the north side, they would have had more south facing windows which we would consider a great improvement today but whether they considered sunshine as much as we do now is, of course, a matter of conjecture.

Thomas also turned his attention to the garden at Kemnay and 1723 is the first year there are records of money spent in that direction:

a not of the seeds for the laird of Kemnae Garden

			s d	
2 pund		whit pease	1:00	
2	"	croun pease	1:00	
2	"	turry beans	¼	
3 ounces	of	onions seed	12:00	
2	" "	leek seed	10:00	
1	" "	parsneeps seed	3:00	
1	" "	carrots seed	4:00	
3	" "	spinnage seed	9:00	
1	" "	lettuce seed	16:00	
½	" "	radishes seed	1:00	Alexr. Catto.

Certainly quite a variety of vegetables. Patrick Adam was the gardener and he appears to have been paid "£36. scots money full and complete payment from Martinmas 1721 to Whitsunday last" which was two and a half years' wages. At least all the servants, as well as the family, had plenty of vegetables to eat!

Andrew, Thomas's brother, according to the number of very varied receipts, was a man for smart clothes and fine accoutrements. He patronised Geo Cooper for his swords, sword hilts etc and was pretty often at his tailor, a James Milne, who made more than one "sute of fine cloathes" to him with all kinds of extravaganza - drops of silk, special "twiddling at 11/- to lyn the britches" and pockets to them as well, "scarlett westcotts" and still more drops of silk. At the same time his elder brother was economising with Wm Lyall Taylor who charged 12/- "for letting out the breast and dressing your daughters stays." But Andrew was not satisfied and bought yet another suit of fine clothes and this time added a "Jocky Coat" (great coat) with lots of buttons, hair padding, binding and stay-tape. A lot of good it was to him as only a few months later Thomas's Bible tells us that Andrew died "on the 16 day of June, 1726, in the house of his brother Thomas, and as God would have it in the same bed as George Burnet was born upon the Green in Aberdeen, and was buried in Drum's aisle there." (Church of St Nicholas). Andrew and his wife must have used the old house on the Green. There is a curious account in connection with his funeral:

John Carnegie Litster In Aberdeen & Present Master of
the Litsters Mortifications
for hanging a Pall to Mr. Andrew Burnet£24

A Litster was what a dyer was named and a pall, of course, was a death cloth. A Dyer and Undertaker's no doubt combined very satisfactorily. Andrew Burnet was buried as he had lived – in great style. This bill is followed by another for Elizabeth from an Alex Christie of "Things furnished to the Lady Kemnay from 30th May to Aug. 1726" which starts with some Black Ribbon, for the funeral I am sure, but continues with some cherry coloured ribbon the following month and frivolous things like "paper patches" and English shoes and gloves and silk handkerchiefs, a "hatt" and an Ivory Comb! There is a rather lovely account for the June of the next year – "a fether Bede weighing 5 ston of ould fether weight at a croun per ston is £15.13/- els of new tikin att 14 pence and all is 10:10:00 et al."
In January 1729 a new kitchen grate was bought weighing "11 ston & 12 lbs. is £3.2/6". Thomas also bought a new shoe scraper, for all that mud at Kemnay, but his last and most extravagant purchase was through his London agent, George Catanach – a Sedan chair no less – "The Street Chair you ordered me to buy – those who had more knowledge in these affairs thought it a very good one. I paid £17. 10/- for it." With the chair came a bundle which contained "4 yds. superfine drab cloth at 19/6 yd." along with other materials and a little note "Please my Compliments to the Lady Whitings, the Sadle her son ordered is not yett ready, but Shall Come by Next Occasion." Thomas was not above helping his friends with their shopping! I am sure the street chair was very nice to use in Aberdeen in the winter months: all the nasty cold winds straight off the North Sea and not so many buildings then to offer shelter.

In his final entry Thomas almost enters his own death in his Bible. Dated 19th July 1728, he noted down "Remarquable passages of Scripture" which he had often meditated upon during his life "and now in a dying condition commend to my two childrings for quiet reading as the best Legacy of divine Instructions for Lyfe & maners that I can leave." Most of his recommendations are for the Psalms but there is a passage from Job: "He disappointeth the devices of the crafty so that their hands cannot perform their enterprise." Is that relevant to his treatment in the Bastille? I had rather expected "O put not your trust in Princes".

The following year, on the 26th February, Thomas Burnet died at the age of seventy-three years; considering his "bodily indispositione and melancholy and hypochondriaque temper" he lived longer than might have been expected. A great man in his way and one who most certainly left his mark on history. He was buried in the church of Kemnay and his gravestone reads:

SACRED TO THE MEMORY OF THOMAS BURNET OF KEMNAY

WHO AFTER MANY PEREGRINATIONS THROUGH MOST OF THE

COUNTRIES OF EUROPE RESTS HERE IN THE HOPE OF A

BLESSED RESSURRECTION

GEORGE

When Thomas Burnet's first child, his son and heir, was born on 29th September 1714, it was obvious that he would be baptised George after the first of the Hanoverian kings of Great Britain. Born in the year of George I's accession, he was named after the monarch so that he might always remember his allegiance to the House of Hanover for whom his father had laboured so assiduously, and for favours bestowed upon him and the invaluable assistance the Electress and family unhesitatingly gave when he was in dire need. That George always retained this loyalty to the royal family will be apparent as his story unfolds.

George was only fourteen and a half years old when his father died and his sister, Anne, nearly eleven. Conscious always of his failing health, Thomas had made provision for the care of his children:

> I, Mr Thomas Burnet of Kemnay, considering the obligation all Parents are under To name Proper People as Tutors and Curators To such of their Children as are under age – Therefor I have named and appointed and hereby Name and appoint Elizabeth Brickenden my Spouse, Both Tutrix and Curatrix to George and Anne.

What malaise Thomas suffered from during his life we can only guess at but there is no doubt that when he died his family buried him with all the honour and respect that they considered his due.

> To the cost of Kemnay's Funeral £995.16/- scots
> £60 which Kemnay appointed to be given the Poor at his burial, and which was given accordingly
> £20 sterling allowed the Lady Kemnay for her mournings

Eventually in 1730 "By the expence, Layd out, in bringing forth Kemnay's Grave Stone, and placing it upon his Grave in the Church of Kemnay £18.17/-"

Thomas had made a Codicil in his will leaving his wife the house and garden in Aberdeen, and family life continued in the same manner as it had before his death. In 1727 Thomas had engaged a young Dr George Lamont to be tutor to his son. George Lamont had graduated Master of Arts at Edinburgh University privately on 24th May 1723 and it may be that Thomas had made his acquaintance through his brother Andrew Burnet or else he had come to know him after his arrival as a doctor in Aberdeen in 1727. After graduating at Edinburgh, Lamont had studied a considerable time in the medical school of Drs William Graeme and George Martine at St Andrews and on 11th July 1727 "there being a desire proposed to the University in name of George Lamont, Master of Arts, that they may be pleased to confer upon him the degree of Doctor of Medecine and there being also produced an ample certificate of his learning and skill in medecine signed by Doctors William Graeme, George Martine, William McFarlane and Adam Murray, doctors in medecine and this being considered by the University they agreed that the said degree should be conferred upon him and his diploma given out communi forma."

When one wonders how a young doctor would have the time to be tutor to a young boy as well as following his profession, one must remember that in the eighteenth century things were very different from today. Doctors were not consulted so regularly as they are nowadays and in some cases not at all. A great many people had their own cures and herbal medicines or consulted an apothecary and a young doctor may well have had the time to engage in other pursuits. George became devoted to his tutor and remained so to the end of his days. In his turn, Lamont was to have a great influence on the boy and must have derived much pleasure from teaching such a bright and intelligent lad. George developed a great love of nature and beauty and possessed a very lively imagination. The choice of a young man as tutor was a very wise one for the only son of an elderly father. In fact George Lamont was to have a profound influence upon the whole family.

II

The year after Thomas' death, young George enjoyed an expedition to Edinburgh and the south of Scotland which George Lamont had arranged for him. They travelled down by coach and returned on horseback. The careful Lamont kept a strict account of their journey and expenses.

> List of Traveling Expences wherein my Son and I bare equal Shares began on July 17/1730." (His calling George 'my Son' shows the great fondness he had for the boy.)

	s d
That afternoon at Stonehaven	2:04
That night at Laurenkirk	7:06
The next Day at noon at Glamis	1:04
For seeing the Castle there	2:06
That night at Coupar Angus	5:06
The next day at noon at Perth	3:06

I think they always had dinner at noon. They slept that night at Falkland. I like the wording of the next entry – I know so well what he meant:

and have paid the post-master at Aberdeen for going out o' the Town

	£ s d
in a coach forgot in its place	1:06
Crossing the Kinghorn the 4th day	3:00
Coach hire from Leath to Edr	2:00
Carrying the Baggage upstairs there	8
Paid the coach for carrying us south	2:00:00
To seeing Holyrood House	3:00
Two Assembley Tickets is	5:00
Seeing the Castle	2:00

They spent a week in Edinburgh and paid their Landlady £2. -/2 for their board and lodging. At the end of the week they took a coach to the stables where they were to hire horses for the road to Moffat. George discovered that he had left his greatcoat at their lodgings so a porter was dispatched to retrieve it which cost him an 8d tip! Once on the road they stopped for a meal at "Lintown" (Linton) and slept that night at "Brughton" (Broughton). The following day they arrived at "Tweedybrayfoot" which presumably is at Moffat as the next entry is the cost of "the horsehire to Moffat £1. 4/4 To given the man that rode with us 1/-." I imagine the man had to take the horses back to Edinburgh again.

	£ s d
To a Tavern for a supper and a nights lodging to George and the Dr.	6 :06
To bringing the Baggage from Edinburgh	3 :06
To washing at Edr. forgot in its place	2 :06

To the Barber and Boy there forgot likewise	2 :06
September 10 paid our Lodgings at Moffat	
for six weeks at 6/6 per week	1:19:00
and spent there in meat, drink, fire and candle	
Tea and sugar in that time	7:00:00
To seeing a Ball there and his supper	6 :06
To another Ball	2 :06
(Moffat was obviously a whirl of gaiety)	
and washing for that time	1:00:00
and given the maid when we came away	5 :00
Likewise to An. Sloan a horsehirer	1 :00
to a brush, a nife and forke	2 :00
to bating the horses and man that morning	2 :06
We left Moffat Sep. 10 at Dumfrese that night	
and part o' the next day	8 :00

They saw some churches there and spent the next night at Dumlanreck. Before leaving the following morning they visited the Castle and Gardens which cost them 3/6 (scots, I hope). I wonder if young George's imagination was inspired by seeing other established gardens to plan his own creation at Kemnay. They journeyed to Leadhills and from there to "Bigger" and dined at Lintonbridge the next day before arriving back in Edinburgh. "September 13 paid Horsehire for this circuit from Moffat to Edr. with what was given the hirer £1.11/-" They returned to their lodgings and the next day saw their hiring yet another coach "out of Town to see six fine seats and our two dinners – £1.5/-

	£ s d
A Coach a nother day out o' Town and seeing three	
more Seats and our dinner	9:00
To a fortnights washing at Edr.	5:06
paid in our Land-lady's bill there for a	
fortnight's Lodgings and Board with what was	
given the servants when we came away makes	2 :15:08

On 28th September they bought cords for packing their baggage for home and hired a coach for Leith where they had dinner before crossing to Kinghorn where they spent the night. The next day they dined at "Cowper o' Fife" and proceeded to St Andrews which, of course, could not be omitted. They spent a day and a half there and visited the churches and "one of the Colledges" (no need to ask which one). They then crossed to Dundee and retraced the old route taken by James Marshall many years before – Arbroath and Montrose – but varied their progress slightly by having their dinner at "Bervey" before arriving at "Stonhive" for the night. "We came home to Aberdeen the next day being the Second of October haveing been away eleven weeks and one day." The total cost of this tour was £34. 5/11. George had made several purchases of his own which amounted to £5.16/10 but still prevailed upon his mother to buy him some new riding gear: "Imp. for an hunting saidle to your Son wt. braidle, cruper, strup leathers, irons and girth £1 and 1/2 yard of green cloath for an Housen 8/-." No doubt he used it when he returned to Edinburgh the November of the same year when "Colin MacLaurin rec. from Dr. George Lamont three Guineas when he entered George Burnet of Kemnay to my Class."

III

Dr Lamont was not the only one to keep meticulous accounts. Elizabeth looked after the family affairs with a careful eye for detail. Alexander Downie was the estate factor and between the two of them it is possible to reconstruct a credible picture of the responsibilities of a laird at that time. The receipt of rents from tenants was only one small matter; he maintained their houses and buildings and also that of the minister and the church.

The 1730 accounts read:

	£ s d
Payd for paynting the houses of Kemnay and Auquhythie	9:00
Payd for paynting the Kirk and workmanship	6:00
Payd John Lunan for Glass work within the house of Kemnay	2:06:00
Stipend to the Kirk Session	366:15:00
Rent upon the Rigs in Parkhill allowed the Minister for grasscroft	12:00:00

£9:4s:0d scots advanced for the Communion Elements in June being 6 Pynts of Wines and four great loaves

Recpt. from Francis Downy, Minister of the Gospel at Kemnay, stipend from George Burnet and Elizabeth Burnet his Mother 263 lbs scots and 25 ½ bolls Meal and 13 ½ bolls Corn."

It is not much wonder that George was later to refer to the then incumbent as "my minister".

Other items in the receipts include vast plantings of firs to supplement the peat used for fires which was then beginning to give out:

	£ s d
Payd for 26,000 firrs and Planters wages	64:08:00
Payd John Silver for 10,000 young firrs planted in Leschangie at 2/- sterling the 100	12:00:00
Payd the Gardner for planting the said firrs and to 4 men with him @ 8/- the day to the Gardner and a groat to each man, They being 8 days at work in all	9:12:00
For 600 young ashes furnished at £3 scots the 100. Planted in Leschangie Park and other yards and a Days wages to the foresaid men to plant them is	19:04:00 scots

Another reason for planting so many conifers was that they were grown amongst the hard wood trees to make them grow straight. Once the hard wood had grown up the firs were then cut out. The planting of so many ash trees makes one question the reason behind it - the old superstition of their potency against witches or their virtues as firewood.

The entry in the accounts of "£6 for Protestations taken against Inverallochy in the moss of Leschangie" shows that life had its ups and downs with the neighbours too. Charles Fraser of Castle Fraser was George's nearest neighbour and was known as Inverallochy because of his estates near Fraserburgh. These accounts are all entered in the ledger entitled "Account betwixt the Lady Kemnay and Master Burnet of Kemnay her Son containing the Lady Kemnay's Haill Intromissions as Curatrix to her Son. 1727–1732", from which date it appears that Elizabeth had already taken over a considerable amount of the estate work from Thomas during his last illness.

George had got his new hunting saddle so now it was sister Anne's turn to have some money lavished on her and Elizabeth decided to buy a spinet. For this type of extravagance it was no use looking in Aberdeen; one had to send to London or Edinburgh. It was customary amongst the more comfortably off to secure an agent in the south to look after one's interests and Mr McColme was the

Burnets' agent in 1731. He had a brother in Aberdeen which was very convenient especially when mistakes arose:

> Aberdeen, August 20, 1731. Madam, I had a letter from my brother in London wherein he advises me that he received £5. 14/- sterling which your Ladyship sent to him to pay for the Spinet. He says it should have been 3/- more. viz. five guineas for the Spinet, five shillings for bringing it here and 7/- for the Case about it. He paid the whole and asked me to get the 3/-, which your Son has paid me. My brother offered his humble Service to your Ladyship and your Daughter. Your most humble Servant,
>
> Quinton McColme.

There are entries for Assembley tickets and other entertainment which George enjoyed when in Edinburgh and he lost his greatcoat again – this time on the road to Kemnay! – which involved the Crier so there was the cost of the Crying thereof and a tip to the man who found it.

Here is a letter written by George, aged seventeen and still at school in Edinburgh, to The Lady Kemnay to be found at her Lodgings in the Castle Street of Aberdeen:

> Edinbur., March the 22d 1731
>
> Dr MADAM
>
> If any thing can excuse the frequent trouble I put you too by my writing so often it is the ardent desire I have by that means to show that respect & obedience which so well becomes me to a Lady who has ever been so indulgent & careful of my interests abouve what I ever deserved or am afraid will be ever able to requitt. I have sent by the post a new Tradgedy viz Euridcie I know it would be no Recommendation to it for to speak of its success at London which has been prodigious for the Author is reconed to have made two thousand pond by it in the Space of a fourthnight it's done by one Mr. Mallock the Author of that little song which used to please so much I mean William & Margaret if it would be no presumsion in me to give my opinion of a thing which I hope you'll be so kinde to peruse

> I should its sweet agreable piece and deserved part of the incouragement it mett with since I sent Dr Martins Bill north I have gott some things from him I have allways a very ill cough accompanied with a shortness of Breath which makes me very certain that this air has a bad effect upon me which I could not have believed if I had not felt it Im affraid I have troubled you too long allready therefor I conclude Your ever dut: & aff: Geo: Burnet

There must have been other letters as Elizabeth has written on the outside "Kind letters of George's when at Edr: wherein is no business." His English, spelling and punctuation did improve!

IV

In the summer of 1731 George Lamont and Elizabeth announced their intention of getting married. Their banns were called:

> That Dr George Lamont Dr of Medecine in Aberdeen and Mrs Elizabeth Burnet Reliet of the Deceast Thomas Burnet of Kemnay Esq have had their marriage purpotest three severall times proclaimed in both Churches here and no objection given is testified at Aberdeen the thirteenth of Septr 1731.
>
> James Bailyie
>
> Received also for the Poor £20.12/- scots by JB.

The Burnet relations threw up their hands in horror and removed George and Anne to Crathes. Heaven knows why they made such a fuss; Thomas had been dead two and a half years and many people remarried quicker than that in those days. George Lamont came from a very good family so there could have been no fault to find on that score. It is possible that they did not care for their English cousin and would find fault with whatever she did. They can have had no just cause, to quote the marriage lines, or they would have objected when the banns were proclaimed. Their actions were unforgivable and only caused hurt to the children and their mother. We have George's own words in a letter written much later to George Lamont:

> ...You know very well how dear you was to me from the

> first Time I was acquainted with your Worth, I respected near as much as a Father, I loved you more, & if I did not receive the account of your marrying my Mother with a Transport equal to that more than filial affection I had allways bore you, would you wonder that so young a Creature should be so far wrought upon by the Company he was then ever in, as to appear in some Things what he should not have been; tho' it was never in the Power of all the officious Malice that was employed to make me what they desired. Interest was likewise employed, That never had, I think, it never will have great influence upon me. Indeed it is enough to count it, but I am not made for that – I say Interest was brought in, I was a Thousand times abused for a Fool and a Simpleton that ever consented to give up my Mother's buying a House in Aberdeen that was by the Disposition to go to her Heirs, I know intended so by my Father...

Presumably the codicil was contested by the relations. The result of all this unpleasantness was that Elizabeth made a new Will leaving everything to her husband to the exclusion of her son and daughter and all other kin. George Lamont in his turn willed everything to his wife's grandson. Where did poor Aunt Rachel come in all this upset? She was a woman of fifty-three at this time and presumably was able to follow her own inclinations, either residing at Kemnay or with her sister-in-law and George Lamont in Aberdeen where the latter continued his medical practice for several years. One letter from George to his mother, written from Edinburgh in 1731, very upset that he had not heard from her, is all that tells us that he continued at school there for another year. George returned to Kemnay in 1732 and one of the earliest accounts for that year comes from a wright in Aberdeen, one William Crystall for undertaking –

"Acct. Mr. Burnet of Kemny
To William Crystall wright 1732 May the 12
To an Coffin for your Aunt being Enamled green within £25. 4/-"

Poor Rachel – I hope she had some happiness in her short life.

The following year George married his cousin Helen Burnet of Crathes. Helen was accomplished and beautiful and her qualities were celebrated in verse under the pseudonym of Peggy:

> Kind Kemnay's seat, how beautifully placed,
> With shady woods and flowery gardens graced;
> See how the feathered choir extend their throats
> By Nature taught - hark how they swell their notes.
> Yet when fair Peggy, mistress of the grove,
> Joins her sweet voice to sing the praise of love,
> The birds sit listening to the wondrous song;
> The river calms and smoothly glides along;
> The gentle zephyrs with her tresses play,
> And from her balmy breath steal sweets away.

Which is rather overdoing it, but also tells us that it was written after George had done a great deal to improve the situation of the surrounding policies. Indeed, a vast amount of work and improvements had to be carried out before it was fit for George's bride.

V

George's "improvement" plan for Kemnay began as soon as he returned to Kemnay from Edinburgh in 1732. Several items of furniture were repaired and the same William Crystal in Aberdeen who had supplied the coffin for Aunt Rachel was called in to do major joinery repairs which included the making of a "large Chist of Wainscott drawers, 3 large Sash wondows and a large Naprie press." The work must have been quite extensive as it all took up "400 man days work at Kemnay" and came to the tidy sum of £322.11/14. More sophisticated items were required for the young and lovely new Mrs Burnet and for these George sent to London. At this time the London agent for the family was one George Cattanache and early in the January of 1734 he wrote:

> ...Sir, this chiefly serves to bring you a bill of lading and invoice of goods aboard the Unity, Captain Cruickshank, who is sailed, amounting to £138.11/- Sterling. I daresay everything will give you content, for they are all made by the Best Hands. I am worst pleased with the mahogany Table, but the Maker assures me the Colour will mend. If you don't

approve of the Crystal Chandelier I have agreed with the man to take it back, upon your note.
Your humble servant George Cattanache.

	£ s d
Fine crimson mounted Bedstead	12:10:00
A large mahogany Table	3:00:00
Four fine Sconces, carved and gilded...16 gns.	
Two Chimney Glasses to match	11:00:00
Crystal Chandeleir	2:10:00
Fine walnut tree Cabinet	15:10:00
Welve walnut tree Chairs	9:12:00
A silver Teapot	9:06:05

The sconces and chimney glasses are still here at Kemnay as is the fine walnut tree cabinet but there is no sign of the crystal chandelier. Did George not approve it, I wonder? Neither is there any trace of the walnut tree chairs. An old diary mentions that much of the dining-room furniture was sold after the rebellion in 1745 when the years of extortion from Government levies and the Jacobites, together with late springs and the bad farming years experienced in the north east during those troublous times, reduced many a laird to penury or something very close to it. On the other hand, various Burnets at various times were not above making off with smaller, more moveable pieces!

George also bought new clothes for the new life on which he was embarking and the making of a suit of clothes cost him 3/-. A dressmaker, Elizabeth Hankinson, was engaged for the new Lady Kemnay and her bill of 1733 reads:

	s d
To the making of a black and white Chinese night gown	4 :00
(a 'night gown' was an evening dress not a nightie)	
For five yards and a half of Scotch cloth to line it	5 :06
for ferrit for the Apron and Buttons and Laps	6
to the making of a yellow damask Night Gown	4 :00
for new pleating a grey lustring Night Gown and taking sleeves out of the tail	4 :00
for Scotch cloth to line the body	4 :00
for making a flowerd Silk Night Gown	4 :00

Once again the more sophisticated things had to be ordered from London or Edinburgh. Several pairs of "mixed silk Hose", a suit of "satteen lined with blue shagg Velvet with rich gold spangled Buttons", a fine beaver "Hatt" with a blue feather, a pair of furred gloves, two pairs of black garters, whalebone, stay heads, hooks and eyes and so on. Never before had such finery been seen at Kemnay. The men, of course, wore wigs and a "light bob wig" cost two guineas. A vivid picture is conjured up by reading these accounts. New servants were engaged to run the house and new livery for the men servants alone came to £30. Animation and bustle took over the house once more. The year 1734 saw the birth of the first child of the marriage, a daughter who was named Helen after her mamma but always referred to as Nellie by her father. The following year, on the 3rd July, the fourth laird was born and was baptised Alexander after his maternal grandfather. Another sister, Anne, was born in 1736, Jean in 1739 and a fourth girl, called Elizabeth after her grandmother, was born in 1740. Above stairs the nurserymaids and nannies must have been kept very busy. George was a devoted son, husband and father and also a dedicated laird and farmer. He found the demands of the estate, his tenants and the home farm took up much of his time but he always wrote graphic accounts of life at Kemnay to his Mother and the good doctor who had moved to London in 1737.

VI

On the 12th June 1740 George Lamont became one of the "Physicians Extraordinary" to the household of Frederick Lewis, Prince of Wales, eldest son of George II. Dr Lamont readily acknowledged his wife's influence as the widow of Thomas Burnet of Kemnay which introduced him into these royal circles. In a letter to his mother, George expresses his joy at the doctor's good fortune. George's letters convey such vivid pictures that there is no point in marring his story by précis so I make no apology for offering them to the reader verbatim.

> Dear Madam, The pleasure of your long wished for letter came at last I am very sorry you had so good a reason for not writing. Those quick and strong sensations which subject you to such accidents, as you mention, allways accompany good Souls, who feel everything in the extreme. While the

inferior rank of Mortals rather seem to sleep thro' life in apathy and ease. And here I can't help expressing my dislike of the Philosophy of Zeno and his followers. Stoicism tho' much in vogue in the learnedest age of antiquity, and graced with such disciples as Cato, Cicero etc. instead of elevating debased human Nature. For could a man be found devested of all Passions, to whom every thing was indifferent, alike good or evil, I could see no difference twixt him and an Oyster, save his performing more various Motions, which might be oweing to his being a more complicated Machine. True Philosophie is not for extinguishing but regulating the Passions, well knowing that they were all given us for certain and determined ends and purposes, only villianous when pushed beyond those. To prevent which God has given them and subjected them to a Judge, unerring and impartial in his decisions. I mean conscience which, if deeply attended to, will not fail to guide us right.

I am heartily glad to hear of the Dr.'s Preferment, and am glad that for once, at least, in a degenerate age, modest Merits has not passed unobserved. I was indeed afraid his Modesty would have been a great bar to his Fortune. I should be glad to hear he has gott a little better of it, by the Traffick and Commerce of the busy world. As to the Dr.'s Letters as you mention them, I sometimes complaine of them to himselfe as too laconick; but I remember he never liked writting which does not at all surprise me as I had rather do anything than write. I don't know if you remember Invercauld's eldest Daughter as she was but a Child, when you left this place, and a homely one too, tho' she is realy now in every way a fine Woman & has an agreeable softness and delicacy in her Manner and Conversation. She is just married to an ugly old stupid Fellow not rich neither & much against her Liking. You must know the Sacrifice is made to her Father's Vanity to be alliyed to the Chief of ten Names, the great laird of Mcentosh which entitles him to be followed by a great many nakid Highlanders with empty Bellys, Dogs, Swords and Pistols. God knows when we had a Marriage before, that cerimony is quite out of Fashion, which is in a great measure oweing to the counterbrand Trafick carryed on by unfair Dealers who alone make any

> Thing of their wares. The fair Traders are forced much against their Wills to keep their Goods till they're much damaged by Time & in the end would be glad to lett them go for little or nothing. I wonder they don't petition for a Tack to the smugling Act in their Favours. Notwithstand most of the Legisture are suspected of having a Share in this underhand Trade. Whatever sway Cupid has here, Bacchus is all powerfull, you'd think the Tutilar God of the place by the continual Libations that are made. This putts me to minde to thank you for your kind caution about drinking. There is little more than usual on account of Elections here which you know are carryed on in a different manner from what they are in England; as to myselfe tho' I can't say I never drink yett it is seldome that I think I may be called a sober man [Presumably he means "tee-total".] I can't take my leave without telling you that your happie turn in writing, your agreeable and entertaining Pen as it vastly raises my Desire to hear from you, makes it as the same time very easy for you to gratify me. Pray tell the Dr. that I beg to hear from him if it should be but three lines...
>
> PS. You will receive a Kitt of Salmon by the first Ship Goes from this place. I would have fain sent it by a sloop that it might have come more easily but they durst not take any but to the Fish Mongers at London who freights them

The fish was salted but even so I cannot help wondering what state it arrived in! It appears to have been sent off quite regularly so must have been all right.

The Farquharson of Invercauld mentioned was John 9th of Invercauld who took part in the 1715 Rising and was long a prisoner in the Marshalsea. His Gaelic style was Mac'ic Fhionnlaidh, and it was said that he could put five hundred clansmen in the field. His first wife was Isobel, daughter of Sir Alexander Burnet of Craigmyle, and was in fact the eldest daughter, destined to marry George's father, Thomas, in the intricate "Craigmyle affair" referred to in the story of Thomas. She died without issue and so did Invercauld's second wife, Christian Menzies. The only children came from the third marriage to Margaret, daughter of Lord James Murray of Dowally. The second child of this marriage was Anne who married Angus Mackintosh of

Mackintosh, 22nd Chief and to whom George refers. Later, during the '45, she was styled "Colonel Anne" for her prowess in heading her husband's clansmen, which somewhat contradicts George's description of her - or perhaps five years of marriage had altered her.

Kemnay, 14 September 1741
Dear Madam, We are just now cutting down our corns and have a pritty good Appearance tho' I think it will not be sufficient to bring things to the old Footing. God knows when we have had a sad Summer here, the scarcity was so great as to border on Famine we never had less than three or four Beggars at our House in a day...I'm to try to live in Aberdeen this Winter & have taken a House there for that end. If I can live as easily as in the Country I believe I'll continue to go in every Winter any Thing of a Town being fully more comfortable than the Country in that Gloomy Season, tho' I am sure I feel it as little as any body. I'm sure as long as I have good Books I defye the Winter to weary me. I'm sure I have wearyed you by this Time that are used with the Doctor's short letters - a Quare of Liliputian Paper would serve him a long time. My sincerest Wishes are with you Both I realy am what I am bound to be with all Duty etc, etc.

Geo. Burnet.

Aberdeen, 30th November, 1741
Dear Madam, If the Paines a Thing costs has any Share in enhansing the Merite, your agreeable letter has a Thousand Times too much for me. The natural Beauty that drops from your Pen makes them relish highly with me. I came to Town with my Family about a month ago I have not been long enough to form a Judgement how I'll like it, but one thing I'm sure of is that the Price of every Article of Expence is double what it used to be. I'm certain that if you was to be in Abdn. now you would not know it, the great Number of new and fine Buildings both Private and Publick such as a large Hospital and Infirmary a Bedlam a Corectionary and a Workhouse for the feeding & keeping to labour such idle Vagrants as used to infest the Streets. I say this with the Finery of the Inhabitants and their Improvement in modern

Politeness or the Art of spending with Taste & Delicacy & Killing those cruel Enemys Time & Thought might well make you think it a different Place.

'Pamela' has long made a great Noise, yett I never read it, tho' we had it here just as soon as it was published, as we have all Books, and Pamphlettes, as I took it by the Title to be a Book of meer Amusement & it's long since I've given up reading all such. I don't know but that I may now be tempted to it, by the Pleasure it seems to have given you. We have had lately in this Town an odd sort of Creature that you must have heard of he made so much noise in the World, the famous Mr Whitfield...I know of no subject to write on that could give my letter any Merite. I resolved it should have that of being wrote the next day after I gott yours. I beg to make my compliments to the Dr. whom I salute. All my little children join with me in offring their Duty & Affection, pray accept these often from Dear Madam your most affectionate Son & Humb. Ser. Geo. Burnet.

And to Dr Lamont:

Aberdeen, 22 Feby, 1742.

Dear Sir, I receive the Accounts you give me of my ever dear Mother with a real and poigniant pain. I swear to you my bosome at this moment swells with sighs – the only alleviation I have is that I hope the value you sett on her makes you magnify the danger she is in. I pray God it may be so and that she may soon gett out of the ill state her health is just now in & you may long and happily enjoy eachother without being disturbed ever with the Fear of parting. I can't help thinking here how idle it is to wish for long life to those we love if we mean anything but our own Satisfaction or Advantage – in this we follow Passion blindly, for reasone would talk another Language and would ask us on those occasions: If human Life was so agreable with so few real Pleasures many real Paines, continually at war with, or hurried along by, Passion and Apetites jarring and in discord, continually hunting after what we call Pleasure, which tho' we imagine still in view is allways out of reach, yett we as boys do Butterflys, still pursue the flying, fluttering

> thing. Thus we go on unto the very verge of Life, seeking what is not to be Found in this state of our Existence. But thanks to Heaven we have a better Hope, an elevated and unbounded Prospect! and now my Imagination leads me beyond this little point of space, thro' all the wide expanse of Worlds, & consider this Life as one link of the infinite Scale of my Existence in which I may already have made a considerable Progress tho' I'm not conscious of it & in which I'll be advancing, according as I merite Thro' all the ages of Eternity. There is something in this infinite Progression most immensely Grand! - Something that expands, enlarges, cheers the human Soul which hurryd by the thought of pain would leave this case of clay and soar aloft. As it's thus stated, says reason, you do your Friends mighty favours to wish them stay? yett still we wish to keep them and vainly think it's love of them. The only thing that gives me uneasiness in this System is (don't laugh now for I'm serious) that I'm afraid friends will be parted for ever, when they happened to launch out of this Life twenty or thirty years before us, they might gett two or three Worlds before us and we never able to overtake them. You'll wonder what has drawn all this from me why I'm just come from seeing a Friend who I think is dying & has thrown me into a reverie. You may say that my dear Mother would be glad to see me. I only wanted to know it would be acceptable to have that pleasure some time ago, if the Winter had not been so far spent I should have choose that time of year being the idlest for us Country Folks. My Wife and Sister desires with me to present our dutiful and affectionate compliments to my Dear Mother, pray tell her, often tell her, how much her health and ease concerns that of, my dear Doctor, yours in the most affectionate manner GB.

George did not wait until the Winter months to go and visit his mother, and, having been assured by Dr Lamont that she was indeed very seriously ill, he left for London after he had seen to the planting and sowing of his spring crops. His next letter to Elizabeth on his return to the north is dated 23rd June 1742. He begins by saying that he fears uneasiness on her part as when he left her in London he had promised to write whenever he returned home

...which indeed I have kept for this is the first Post Day since I got to Aberdeen on Monday night the fourteenth day after my Embarkation so long did our ill fates keep us on that detestable element the Sea what with calms cross winds & misty weather, as for the Sickness, I had nothing worth speaking of, slept as well as ever I did in my Life, eat & smoked in the ordinary manner, but then the Company consisting of a West India Tea Captain drinking and roaring & belching forth his odd uncouth ridiculous kind of knowledge every moment, an Aberdeen's burger not three degrees above an idiot yett for our curse thinking himself wise, but for our Comfort drunk & quiet by twelve in the forenoon. A Recruiting Officer that would do nothing but swear & sing baudy which occasioned a continual war betwixt him and a zealous Disciple of the Church who was continually denouncing the Judgements of God & emphatickly describing the pain of Hell the first of which he made no doubt was predestined the Officer to feel. In the Cabin on each side of the Door by way of Supporters were placed a street Whore & overgrown Baard [probably 'Bawd'] who constantly kept up a very fast dialogue. Such company, very little room & other unavoidable Inconveniences you may be sure made us very glad when the Bonds of our Union were dissolved & indeed I parted with the "Charming Peggy" (our Ship) with great pleasure & wish my Successors who ever they may be have a greater relish for her charms that what I had. As to the Master of our Vessel no man could be more civile or do more to please us. I am now at home, found all well & am very happie...

Having seen his mother obviously quietened his fears for her and on her part she must have enjoyed his racy account of his journey. He inherited her sense of humour in the same way he inherited a capacity for serious thought from his father. His sequel to the journey in the "Charming Peggy" followed in August of the same year.

Although your good Sense may condemn this Letter as void of Subject, perhaps of Sense, yett I know you have good Nature enough to excuse everything, when you think how considerable my Motives for writing to you are, why no less than the hopes of employing your Thoughts on me for a while, and showing you that you possess mine. I Believe my Last to you, Madam, I told you what had happened a Shipboard but nothing after my Landing, you see how I'm putt to it when I'm forced to speak so myself of myself, however I'll go on and tell you that we arrived before Aberdeen on Sunday in time of afternoon's sermon, which we immediately intimated by the discharge of five pieces of Cannon, this tho' very agreeable to our Friends gave great offence to some of the Godly and no doubt gave roome for some of those Charitable Reflections they usually bestow on the rest of the World. But it brought most of the Town down to the Shore when we were conveyed up to Town with as sincere a Welcome as some Princes from their Summer Expeditions. It would be impossible for me to describe the insatiable Thirst everybody expressed for News, or to tell of the ridiculous Folly of People I was but barely acquainted with, in asking for my private News and most foolishly imagining that I knew and would disclose the most hidden Arcana of State. I was forced to gett the last Newspapers in my Hand which allways presented to any of those curious inquirers that attacked me. which at last putt an end to their Folly and my Persecution. When the Private Subjects came on I found Mrs Martha Udny the reigning Topick of Conversation and the agreeable and innocent Amusement of every Teatable. I swear I do not exaggerate when I say that they tore her unmercifully and with as much seeming delight as Crows do Carrion. There you might see a Prude, great in her Selfe Sufficiency, declare that she was sorry for the Reflections that were brought on the Sex in general by such vile Steps, the Lady (added she charitably) deserves whatever happens since no Fellow could have presumed to have such Proposals had not she descended below the Dignities of her Sex. But She thanked God, there were some Women who knew how to keep those Creatures at a Distance, bridling up upon this with an Air that signified Behold this example in me. To which you'd hear the Coquett answer That really those Ladies that affected much Reserve in Publick were apt to govern with a slacker Reign in Private. She then modestly observed that she for her share was resolved allways to indulge herselfe in inocent Freedoms, which nobody would censure...with that she asked the Gentleman's opinion that satt next her with such a familiar squeeze of the Hand as brought him over to her Side. The discourse was next taken up by a sweet blooded Virgine of fifty who said she thought nobody had a Title to Censure what way People disposed of themselves that were come to Years of Descretion, and that her Regard for Mrs. M. kept her from crediting the Storys that were talked tho' behoved to say she gott her accounts from very good Hands and they really contained things so loose and unguarded that Mrs. M. was very lucky to gett so well off at last. She begged to be excused from naming Particulars on Account of her Friendship for the Lady. She was here interrupted by an old Religiosa who after having had six Children by each of her two former Husbands had in her Grand Widowhood married a brawny young Levite, That as to the Things being a Secrite or not it was but a small Matter, since such Abominations could not be hid from God, that it was such Crimes as these (too frequent alas!) that drew down the vengeance of an offended God on a people, as no Inordinances were so hateful to His Eyes as those Carnal Sensualitys and her Charity bred in her much Fear about the Future state of such People, since Christ became not Flesh for Such as indulge themselves in the lusts thereof but for the Elect only, and thus ended a Conversation in which were many instances of Friendship, Good Nature and Charity. I have just received a letter from the Doctor who I find is gone to Tunbridge. I pity you much, Madam, until he returns again only he tells me of one Thing that gives me as much Pleasure as any Thing can do, that you are just now very well. That you may allways along with Health enjoy all the other Blessings of Life shall all ways be the sincere wish of GB

For one who disliked writing. George certainly made a very good correspondent. In the Autumn of 1742 he turned to Pranks and Politics. It was just at this time that he stood for election as the Provost of Inverurie. This was strongly resisted by the Earl of Kintore, his reason being that as there had never been a Provost of the town before, there was no earthly reason why there should be one now.

Aberdeen 7th November, 1742.

Dear Sir, I have not heard from my dear Mother since I saw her & not from you God knows when, have you forgott me? I am just come into Aberdeen for all Winter...I had a great struggle lately with my neighbour the Earl of Kintore about Inverury, however in spite of opposition I was elected Provost which was what my Ld. wanted to prevent. He since threatened a Law Suit to reduce the Election under the pretence that it did not appear that ever they had chose a Provost since that Right was granted them by Charter. My Ld. consulted Lawyers on this head and laid the same before a meeting of his Friend [?] who gave it their opinion that there was not sufficient Encouragement given to begine a Lawsuit so there is to be none. I believe I shall be able to stand my Ground there at Inverury without he resolves to give a great deal of money which they say he is advised to & resolved on against next Year as his Honour & Interest is thought concerned in the Question. If he will Bribe high he must have it for I cannot afford that.

There has been great confusion amongst the successors of Calvin in this part of the World. There was a scheme given into the last General Assembley proposing that on each Ministers paying yearly the sum of four pound, if ever he should leave a Widow she should be entitled to an annuity of £20 sterling as long as she continued unmarried. A great many that are married of the Ministers are against it & all those that never intend to marry. My Minister whose Zeal is allway, tho' moderate, greater than his Wisdome is quite frantick at the Proposal. He made a bold and elaborate speech in a Church Indicature which he seldome does. The force of his Argument lay here that as the £20 a year would tend towards pampering the Flesh at the same Time under paine of Forfiture thereof apply only lawful remedy the Lord in his Infinite Mercy has thought fitt to allow to satisfy the cravings of the Flesh, viz the Marriage Bed, it was not to be doubted but that those Pensioners would be guilty of gross Carnalitys & by stretching forth their Legs to strange Nations [?] would pollute those Habitations that Ministers of the Gospel had vouchsafed to visite. I must tell my Mother a piece of

Diversion I had with him lately. – He came to my House to ask my Commands for Aberdeen where he was bounding tomorrow morning God willing. I takes it into my head to spoil his bounding. I begune a story of the Surgeons lads at Aberdeen having lately taken up a great many fatt People. Fatt People? says Downie, his eyes stareing with wild Astonishment. Yes sir, says I, & particularly a milk Woman remarkably fatt who was just snatched up by them and her two milk stoups left with five Mutchkins in one & three & two gills in the other. Strange! says he was such a measure, naming the quantaty as I had done, the exact thing that was found in her stoups – precisely, says I, Humph – rejoins Downy (wonderfully confirmed in the truth of the story by the measure of the milk) I have realy heard that the Doctors make use of human Tallow in composeing of their Drugs I cannot pretend to say (say I) what use they make of the fatt but this is a melancholy Truth that I tell you & no longer than the other day Mr Burnet of Leys (whom you know is very fatt) had gone into Town but hearing how Things went in Town with fatt People took his Horse and returned with the utmost precipitation. O strange! (says Downy) he had reason, a wise young man! but pray ye tell me will no notice be taken or stop putt to such Enormity? Why realy. (replied I) Mr. Downy, I'm in great hope it will be the subject of a strict Enquiry as this Provost is very fatt himselfe. O, (says he) I take you now and your Conjecture is not ill-founded that if they be allowed to go on they might nippe up the Provost himself & so leave the Town Provostless. To conclude Downy putt off his journey to town & run up & down the country speaking this story. Pray tell my Dear Mother that I long to hear from her & present my best respects. Lett me hear from you often in Winter I'm sure you might tell me the news thats Town talk. You need not mind however little News you have to write & little piece of Witt or so. I am ever my Dear Sir with tenderest Regard & affection yours etc. etc., G.B.

VII

The Winter of 1742–43 brought a share of ill-health to the family. George wrote to Doctor Lamont in February:

> I would have wrote sooner after I gott your last if it had not been for my Wife's illness who still remains in a very dangerous condition. You may be sure it gave me the utmost Concern to hear that my dear Mother had been so bad and was not then entirely recovered, for God sake lett me know how she does. Excuse this short Line which I have but the good reason for my humblest Respects and best wishes to Dear Mama and you…

A letter to Dr Lamont written on 24th May has a mysterious enclosure:

> enclosed you have a letter for Judge Burnet and Packet containing a silver box in which is enclosed a Burgers Tickett for him – a neat Piece of Work, you can lett my Mama see it – a greater compliment as they never gave any but a wooden box before. I wrote you that my Wife had been very ill but that she was better she's now relapsed and I am much affraid is in Hazard. The cold you mentioned to me in one of yours some time ago is come hither & siezes allmost everybody but is not mortal, tho' very uneasy in the meantime. I have been down in it these four Days, tho' I be gott up this Day I am not well tho` I think in the way of being so. My sister[3] Mollie, Sir Alex. youngest daughter that I told you was so pritty is just going to be married to the present Provost Alex. Aberdein, a merchant in this Town who was but young when you left this so you'll not know, is a sober industrious sensible Man wourth £70,000 or 12,000 Sterg. which is a great Deal in this Place. However you must know I had a terrible work to persuade Papa because he was not come in good Family you know the temper of the man. Pray lett me know when ever this comes to hand with an account of how my Dear Mama is I'm quite ashamed that I have not wrote her…

3 *His sister-in-law. Mary, known as Mollie, married Alexander Aberdein of Cairnbulg. 'Papa' is his father-in- law, Sir Alexander Burnet of Leys.*

Dear George – this was true as he then wrote again to his dear Mama and such a letter must have made her smile, however poorly she was feeling.

> Dear Madam, I'm extremely concerned that all my letters to you should have occasion to regret your illness and that all my Wishes for a good and continued state of Health should be in vain. It is not in this Period of Existence that Virtue is rewarded...[after some moralising George explains that his reason for so doing is because there is very little news]...News I have none. Politicks is now a most melancholy Subject, and realy a man would need have a good deal of morality to speak upon it with any Patience, and lastly what is as prevalent as any of these Causes this is a most misty gloomy Day. We have had the finest May ever seen in Scotland, the warmest sunshime and the softest showers this Country looks as well just now as it can,. If it holds this way we shall have a very great Cropt. I fancy you will by this Time be gott out to your sweet lovely Abode in Knightsbridge, You have there a Wholseome Air, a smiling and extensive Prospect mixed with Towns Houses, Spires, Open Lawns and shadowy Trees, surrounded with a very deep Verdure it would be a fine place for Study or Retirement, when either glutted with the Pleasures or fretted with the Disappointments of the World: but it has somehow a dead kind of calm and stillness that would not suit me – And indeed I believe when the Doctor is not near you your chief Amusement will be thinking when he will. In my last to the Dr. I wrote my Wife's sister, Mollie, was just going to be married. She has had a whole Company of Lovers, no less than two Baronets, a Squire, a Captain and the present Provost of Aberdeen who is to be the happie man. I don't believe she was in love with any of them but I think she has made the most prudent Choice and I hope she will be happie with him I'm sure he 'll be to blame if she is not. I dare to be confident that if it be not a happie marriage it will not be her Fault, for I never knew a sweeter Girl, both as to Persone and Humour. My Sister and hers are both to have a Present of Green Silk Stockings which is the usual Joke when the elder Sisters are left behind by the youngest. They don't seem either of them to relish the Compliment. It

is not without a good deal of Reasoning that Sister Jeany is persuaded to receive them with tolerable civility, reckoning the very offer an affront & next to calling Old Maid, the most shocking Sound that can touch a female Ear.

> I make no doubt of the mighty Preparations[4] we have made and are making but we shall soon be as famous by Land as we were before at Sea and as we had before displayed the splendour of our Naval Power it was fitt to show our Force on Terra Firma; that all the World may know that the Strength and Riches of this Nation are only to be exceeded by the Wisdome and Integrity of those who steer its Helm...

Poor Helen does not appear to have been endowed with robust health and had been unwell for months. An extract from a letter written in the late Summer makes her out to have been very frail:

> My Wife is now greatly better & in a very fair way of recovering her Strength again tho' she is just now so weak that she could not stand alone and tother Day when she was carried down to the Garden to gett a Gap of Air in as warm a Day as ever I knew in July she was so fatigued that she fainted when she came into the House. I assure you I was sadly frighted for her but that is I think now quite over, at least I imagine so.

4 George refers here to the Battle of Dettingen in 1743 where George II, the last British monarch to command his army in the field, defeated the French. A short-lived victory but still, loyal Hanoverian that he was, GB was obviously mightily impressed with his sovereign!

VIII

1745

1745 dawned with all the traumatic chaos that writers of historical romances have glossed over with fanciful adventures. Civil war is grim and romance was very far from Aberdonian hearts especially those of Government supporters who had a very rough time indeed. George was not alone among his neighbours in his loyalty to the Crown; others included Lord Forbes, Lord Kintore, Grant of Monymusk and Paton of Grandhome. General Sir John Cope, commanding his Majesty's troops in Scotland, had set out from Stirling to intercept Prince Charles Edward's army marching from Glenfinnan where he had raised his standard in August. The Prince managed to elude Cope who then marched on Aberdeen and embarked his troops for Dunbar, taking all the Town's guns with him. On 22nd September he suffered a crushing defeat at Prestonpans. Aberdeen, now left defenceless, was occupied by a Jacobite troop on 25th September and Lord Lewis Gordon, brother of the Duke of Gordon, was appointed Lord Lieutenant of Aberdeenshire by the Prince. He collected all the Land Tax and in addition imposed a levy of £5 sterling on every £100 scots of valued rent – an infamous tax as £100 equalled £8. 6/8 sterling. George, who had been unable to send money due to his step-father, wrote:

> September, 18, 1745. Dear Sir, Our Civil Commotions have putt a stop to everything, and made it very hard to get money from any of our Tenants else I should have remitted you ere now; which I am not yett in a case to do; but if you'll be so good as draw upon me at a Month's sight, I shall know the same. The attempt of the Chevalier has raised bad Tumolts and Disorders and tho' few of any Note have joined the rebels, yett the small number of the King's Forces in these Parts puts everybody that wishes well to the present Government in great Alarm. By what we can yett learn of the number of the Insurgents, they don't exceed 2000, and I hope they will not grow. I do not think it safe to write particulars, as the Rebels are in possession of the Post Towns 'twixt this and Edinburgh – at least we are told so. On the 19th. General Cope with the King's Forces that had gone to

the Highlands to attack the rebels, and having missed them had come back by Aberdeen, embarked there, to the Number of about 2000 – for Leith, as is thought. There is said to be a body of Rebels to the number of 4000 to the south of us by 14 miles. What they intend to do, in which way they'll come, we know not; but people are concealing their most valuable Effects for fear of a Visite. I wish to God the publick Peace was restored. All Health and Happiness to you and my Dear Mother, to whom I hope my dutiful Respects and kind Wishes may be acceptable. I am ever, my Dear Sir, yours in the warmest Manner...GB.

Two months later, in December, a band of 700 MacLeods and Munroes attempted to relieve Aberdeen but were routed by Lord Gordon at Inverurie. Aberdeen itself was fined £500 sterling for encouraging the Highlanders and the County remained at the mercy of the Jacobites, who were bent on routing out anyone in the vicinity who had pro-Government sympathies and generally tyrannised the populace, as George's next letter tells us:

Edinburgh 23 January 1746. Dear Sir, I wrote to you whenever I came here, which is about twelve days ago, telling you of my Arrival and with what Difficulties I gott out of Aberdeenshire, after being hunted about for a good while by the Rebellious crew that were Masters of the Country; who have lorded most tyranically, and made me much the Object of their Wrath, as I had from the beginning of this execrable Attempt given them all the opposition possible in my private sphere by dissuading all my Friends and Acquaintances from taking share in a Design so wicked, so ridiculous, and so dangerous, and encouraging everybody to oppose their rigorous Extortions to the utmost of their Power. If this letter – as it had all the news that was then going has come to hand I know not. So many are stopped just now. I am very anxious to know how you and my Dear Mother does; it is so long since you wrote me. I wrote you in the month of November, desiring you to draw for some money. If you got the letter I know not, but if you had I would not have answered it though you had drawn; for these harpies soon drained us of every Sixpence, having extorted from the town of Aberdeen £1000 sterling and from the country £14,000 sterling. You'd be surprised that there was so much, rather than that they left some behind. You would be surprised at the Misery I and my Family have suffered. I am very sorry that I cannot send you money, but in my country we are all forced to live upon Credit for the necessaries of Life. God send better times – this is a miserable country. You will hear that the King's troops engaged the Rebels near Falkirk on Friday last. I am sorry to say that all the Troops behaved ill but the Regiment of Ligoniers, Barrel's, the half of Price's and the old Buffs – though the latter only kept their ground, not being engaged. What dragoons were engaged behaved pritty well. All the others fell into disorder and gave ground almost before they were charged; being seiz'd with a Panic unaccountable and shameful, for the Rebel army was repulsed and drove off the Field by the two Regiments and a half first mentioned. Then indeed the others thought fitt to rally and altogether kept on the ground for about three quarters of an hour, when they retired to Falkirk, where their Camp was tho' they stay'd there but a short time, for though it was near Dark ere they left the field of Battle, they marched that night to Linlithgow, leaving a good many of their tents, and burning some. During the action Captain Cunningham of the train ran off, which made the fellows along with the horses that drew the ten field pieces that were with them cut the Traces and make off with the horses; so seven of the Cannons fell into the Enemy's hands. On Saturday all the Troops came back to this place and neighbourhood. The numbers of the slain are not well known but it is thought to be about two or three hundred on the side of the King's troops and more on that of the Rebels. Both sides claim the Victory. People must judge of that by Consequences. Our troops it is true, came back a little quickly, but the Rebels retired to Stirling. The Officers allowed the troops behaved ill except those I have mentioned; but surely the other side behaved most scandalously in not taking advantage of the confusion an ill-grounded Fear had thrown them in and in being check'd and repuls'd by so small a Number. As the Soldiers are so ashamed of what has happened and are convinced from what they saw that the

> other side are not so formidable as they imagined, I am convinced they will behave like Men the next time. If they do they will put an end to the reign of these Ruffians. When the Army will march out again I cannot tell, though they talk of going this week and are recruited by Sempills and the Scots Fusiliers. I am very weary of being here. If I had not thought it would have been soon over and I could have gott Home, where I dare not yett sett my Nose, I would have come up to London which I will yet do if the Affair does not yett come to a speedy Close. I should have told you that a Court Martial is sitting on some of the Chief Delinquents. Mr Cunningham has cut his Veins, but is not yett dead. My most dutiful and affectionate wishes attend my Dear Mother, and I will ever be yours GB.

In the month of March a small Government force marched on Corgarff, a fortress on the upper reaches of the River Don in Aberdeenshire. Major Morris commanded 300 foot and the 100 dragoons were commanded by a Captain Alexander Stuart (from Dunearn in Fife) whose great-niece was eventually to marry George's grandson. That, of course, was in the dim and distant future and there is no record of the two men ever having met but it is interesting to know they were within a few miles of each other during those momentous times and a relief (?) that they were on the same side! The letters that Captain Stuart wrote to his brother, who was in Edinburgh, telling him of his exploits in the engagements in which he took part found their way to Kemnay nearly a hundred years later. George, having deemed it safe to return home, was busy trying to find forage for the Government troops.

> March 15, 1746. My Dear Sir, Pray let me know how my Mother and you do. God knows when I heard from you, tho' I wrote you three times of my being at Edinburgh in my Exile. I am now returned with the King's troops but I have not had a moment to write since you can't imagine what Work we have here in providing the King's troops in this poor Country. The Rebels are not yett dispersed, as we imagined they were by their precipitate Retreat North. They seiz'd Inverness with the Castle and oblig'd Lord Loudon with a body of 2000 of the loyal clans that he had to retreat

to Sutherland; after whom they sent a body who found the Passes so guarded that they thought fitt to return since which the Main Body has been in Moray: but a detatchment of the Rebels about 800 or a 1000, are on this side of the Spey about Strathbodie, within 14 miles of this. The main Body of the Royal Army is yett at Aberdeen, though four Regiments of Horse and 4 of Foot have advanced to Oldmeldrum and Inverurie. The Army cannot move from Aberdeen till the store ships come from Leith, who are expected every day – and indeed, the Weather being such for cold rains and snow mixed as I had ever seen at this time of year. If all the army were joined they will make with Lord Loudon, who comes from Sutherland by sea and joins them at Banff; and the Campbells being 800, at least 10,000 men – an army, considering how much they love and trust their General and how well he merits both, more than sufficient for treble the number of the Rebels, who at most won't exceed 5 or 6 thousand. Meantime the condition of this poor Country cannot enough be lamented. Exhausted and tax'd in a most exorbitant Degree by the Rebels, we find it the hardest thing in return to supply the King's army with porridge and provisions. If they do not get weather to move soon, this country will not be sown. Add to this the worst Cropt that has been these many years, which is more than we knew till tryal. Not one half of our Meal will be paid this crop, little or none of the money rent have we gott, and more than £100 sterling out of pocket by the Rebels. Lord have mercy on me. I am excessive uneasy besides my own needs not being able to remit you. As soon as it is possible I shall not lose a day. Please send me under a frank cover in College those letters from the Princess Sophia etc. to my Father, that I sent you. My best and most dutiful Compliments and Respects to my Dear Mother and you, and beg you believe me ever, Dear Sir, your most affectionate and most humble servant...GB.

PS This is dated the 15 March from Inverury in a great hurry, being plagued calling in forage to the army.

Just over a month later the Jacobites suffered the terrible defeat at Culloden that was to mark the end of the rising. According to Alexander Stuart "we have got a complete victory. Two thousand of the rebels were killed, a great many prisoners taken since, for hardly any were taken in action..." which may have given credit to the story of the fate of George's neighbour's son, Charles Fraser. He was wounded on the field of battle and as he lay bleeding upon the ground he spat at the Duke of Cumberland who was walking over the bodies that lay around. Cumberland ordered his accompanying officer to "shoot the dog" but he refused and so the Duke drew his pistol and shot Fraser himself. Stories of Redcoat Brutality were legion and no doubt some were fabricated but ugly incidents like this must have affected George's very strong feelings of justice and fair play. Considering all the work he had done for the Government cause, the following account also seems a shabby act. Lord Ancrum, now in control of Aberdeenshire, wrote to Sir Everard Fawkner in the June of 1746:

> I am persuaded that there is hardly one inhabitant of this country that would not rather conceal a rebel than inform us of them. Some examples that I have made of the houses that harbour rebels have made 'em cautious of receiving them. I must tell you what happened yesterday to a man that had been represented to me as one of the best affected here *viz* Burnet of Kemnay. I overheard him tell a gentleman that a non-juring clergyman in his house had said that he would not administer the sacrament to anyone who would hear King George prayed for. You may believe that I immediately insisted to know his name. Mr Burnet said that he could not betray a man who had been under his roof. I treated, I hope, properly at the time and as soon as he had gone out of the house wrote him a billet-doux which brought him to me in two hours, trembling, not hardly able to speak, more than to beg a thousand pardons and to tell me the rascal's name and place of abode. I shall endeavour to administer a bitter cup to him. [the clergyman]

The policy of attrition carried out by the Government in order to teach the Jacobites a lesson and the atrocities perpetuated in carrying out this policy sickened just and fair-minded men like George wherever their allegiances lay and the action of Lord Ancrum would not have surprised him at all. Earlier that year he had taken the unorthodox and brave step of writing to the Duke of Cumberland and trying to point out to him the likelihood of false tales being spread around for the purpose of self gain. He began his letter with a brief resumé of the facts of Thomas Burnet's allegiance to the House of Hanover:

> My Father resided long at the Court of Hanover and had the Honour to receive distinguishing marks of favour from that illustrious Family. He had just and true Notions of Liberty and the British Constitution which he thought wisely provided for in the Act of Settlement, and whyle he explained the British Constitution I learnt that this Royal Family were its most proper Guardians. These Principals so early laid have been so confirmed and rooted by comparing the arbitrary proceedings of former Reigns with those of the late and present King who have made the Law of the Land the rule of their Government that if I know myself I would at any Time venture my Life in Defence of His Majesty and his Royal Family...but [if] in a Country under such suspicions I should seem to plead the Cause of Rebellion which I from my soul abhor, I take the Liberty to convey to your Royal Highness the manner in which some of His Majesty's most faithful Subjects feel themselves impressed on hearing of the seizing of the Effects of such as are believed to have stray'd from their Duty.
>
> If the Laws of the Land are, or can be, totally suspended upon the breaking out of a Rebellion, it would follow that any suspected Persons, the most Innocent may be represented as such might lose Life and Fortune and be condemned before Tryal. If the Laws are in Force, can the Effects even of those believed actualy in Arms, or of those who by common Fame are thought to have been aiding or assisting the Rebels be seiz'd upon without, in some measure, holding them as convicted and depriving them of the Means of defending themselves at that Tryal any that has been once a British Subject, however unworthy of that name, may be thought entitled to.

> No doubt in times like these, Measures may be necessary which no Laws could have foreseen, or provided for, and Respect must alone be had to the main End of Government, the Good of the Whole, and no man that truly loves his Country would murmur even in his Heart if it were necessary to sacrifice his Property to the common Service, but they that would not might be sorry to see the Effects of suspected Rebels or their Favourers seiz'd upon without necessity until legal Conviction brought on a Punishment that would not be less certain for a short Delay. This seems the more reasonable as the Proof must determine wether Zeal for His Majesty or Malice brings the Information, and should it be the latter an innocent Man may be ruin'd and if a trading Man many that he had Dealings with him, tho' his Goods be restor'd, as Merchant's business frequently depends as much on his Credits as real Stock...Those about Princes speak so much the tutor'd Language of their Interest, that those who deserve them best are most diffident of the Praise they bestow; but did your Royal Highness know the Expectations formed of you by those who live at a Distance from the Hopes and Fears of a Court it would please you to think you had rais'd, you'd wish to live to answer them. I hope, in spight of the Difficulty I have found in expressing myself on such a Subject to your Royal Highness, the honest Purpose will appear,I am not insensible that this is above me, but affraid, from different motives, it might have been left undone by those it might better have become, I have ventur'd, if so that I have gone too far, I hope your Royal Highness will impute it only to that Fervour with which I am
>
> Sir...etc.,etc.

George confided in Dr Lamont that he had literally 'stuck his neck out' in writing to the Duke and in fact if he had not done so and sent the doctor a copy of his letter, we would not know about his action. His letter to Lamont is lengthy and touches several subjects but goes on to say that his natural inclinations, instead of encouraging him to seize opportunities which could better his position, seem to guide him in the opposite direction.

You might have thought that I had fine ones [opportunities] of making my Court when the great Folks were here, as I was well recommended to them, and introduced as one who had been driven from Home for his remarkable Firmness & attachment and indeed this got me a most gracious Reception from the D--- and I might, I believe, have been as much in Favour as any in the Country if I would have taken the Road that led to it, but I did not take it, my Heart led me a quite contrary one. I'm sure I may say my Heart for I perhaps yielded too much to its impulses! Affection and an honest Sentiment scorned to advise with Prudence --- I was vex's to the Soul at many Things I saw doing here. I was persuaded it was without the Knowledge of the D--- I begged of some of the Grandees to represent these Things to him, but all looked on with Fear & Trembling! and none would speak! Stung with Indignation at their sordide Souls! Zealous for the Service of the K--- and Country which I thought inseparably conected, and devoted to the Glory and Happiness of the D--- which I feared might be tarnish'd by such Proceeding, I took the Pen and wrote him the Suggestions of a Heart that was actuated by such honest Motives. I shall not say how it was received, but only that there was no Approbation signifyed. I have no Reason to think it mett with any. However I was then satisfied & can scarce repent that I did as I did; the letter was an honest one and does me no Dishonour. I may show it you if you desire some Time I only have mentioned this to show you why I could not make that Interest amongst the great Folk here at the time one might have imagin'd might have been made, at the same Time I believe I would meet with Assistance rather than Hindrance as I was acceptable enough but for the odd Way of thinking I had in some Things; all this I write only to you & my dear Mother to whose Discretion I could trust the Secret of my Life. You see this is a very great one it was going very far to take the Liberty I did; to seem to brag of it might ruin. But I need not I'm quite safe with you whyle I write with all Freedome. Pray represent my Love & Duty to my Mother in the most acceptable Manner & believe me more than my Dear Sir, your most affectionate & Humble Servt. Geo. Burnet.

X

Life gradually returned to normal after the '45 and George was able to devote his time to family, garden, estate and local politics. In 1747 his fifth and last daughter was born and baptised Mary. There was a gap of seven years between her and her nearest sister, Elizabeth. Nellie, the eldest, was thirteen now and young Alexander, twelve. George, according to one family history, was a strict disciplinarian but if one reads between the lines of letters and accounts, he appears to have doted upon his girls. True enough, he did send them down to Edinburgh for their education in the same style as Great Aunt Rachel all those years before, with just a manservant to accompany them but that was an accepted family custom and not deemed harsh as it would be today. Nellie was despatched at an earlier date as entries in account books show:

> To Nellie for all Small Things for one Year £2. 12. 6

There is no mention of "small things" for Alexander. A later letter tells us he was at school or college in London and he certainly went to the University at Leyden like his grandfather. Subsequent accounts read "To my four Girls Nellie Ann Betty & Jean for small Necessarys for a Year £10.10/-" Mary was seventeen years old before she was included in the account book. In January 1754 there is mention of a large sum being paid on Alexander's behalf which was obviously to finance his studies in Holland. After leaving school, the girls had a six month's clothing allowance of two and a half guineas. George produced the odd five guineas as a present now and then and all their excursions to Peterhead, Banff and Kinnaird were paid for by Papa. Jean was the only one of the daughters to marry and the entry for July 1763 reads "To my daughter Jenny for buying Wedding Cloathes, & a Chest Drawers & for drawing her Contract...£32." She married Alexander Dunbar of Boath. All the girls were said to be great beauties and perhaps fond Papa guarded them over jealously!

George was a very devoted son and kept in constant touch with his mother and Dr Lamont. The doctor in his turn informed his step-children regularly about their mother. Anne, George's sister, was living with them at Kemnay at this time. If only George had kept some of the doctor's letters, his 'laconick' letters as he was pleased to refer to them, for it was George Lamont who preserved all the correspondence from his stepson, and there are only two letters written by the doctor which came to Kemnay with his other effects after his death. As he played such an important part in the story of the Burnets, I include one here which he wrote to his wife which serves to enlarge our comprehension of him:

> Tonbridge. My Dearest, I wrote to you the day after I came here I am very uneasy to hear how you do, the greater Distance I am from you increases my Uneasiness. I am always in love with you – the more I see of other Women multiplys a ten-fold Degree, of all the Sex that ever I saw I never met with the like of you as to Manners, Sense, Person. They are all a Joke to you. I have been much affected with the Toothache since I came but this Day it is easyer. There are very few Company here and they don't appeal a great Deal more. I never saw fewer at this Time of Year. I beg you let me hear from you and don't neglect it and believe me to be
>
> Your most affectionate
> Loving Husband,
> Geo. Lamont

In the following letter George answers Lamont's queries regarding the political feelings in this part of the country.

> Dear Sir, It's a good While ago since I had the Pleasure of yours so long that you may be justly surprised that I never acknowledged it till now. I expected ere now to have heard from my Mother, I assure that I am very uneasy that I have not, as you told me in yours that her Illness had prevented her from writing till then: it makes me affraid that the same reason may subsist. Pray Heaven my Fears are groundless.
>
> You was asking about Elections, as I've but little Time just now it's with some Reluctance I enter on that Subject, because I'm sure I shall quitt it with more. In general there is a spirite of Libertie, Freedome & Independency in Scotland greater than has been known since we fought with England for the Freedome of the Crown; yett free from Licentiousness or any other Principle but the Publick Good, there is indeed a strong sense of grivances but at the same time a Resolution to wait patiently, and endeavour to gett them redressed in a

calm regular Parliamentary way – if that fails they (& I believe most of mankind) know no course but one, and that uncertain dangerous & much to be dreaded. Our Constitution has indeed hitherto gathered strength by such Strugles, but the Experiment should never be made but in the last Extremity, for one Effort made for Liberty and quashed by Power, might revert chaines for ever. Witness the Castilians once as free as we, yett by a number of concurrent Circumstances brought to the brinke of the Gulfe, at one fatal Blow were plunged into it – There is as many Instances of this Kind that it would be teadious to innumerate. I pitted on this because I can't help thinking that there is a great Analogy betwixt the State they were in just be fore their Fall, & ours just now. I wish to God the Comparison may stop there. – To returne I'm pritty well convinced that Scotland will at this next Election returne at least two thirds if not more, who have only the real Honour & Interest of Britain at heart. I hope this will in a great Measure consiliate us to the English who have had hitherto great reasone to complaine of us as a rotten part of the Constitution. Great court is made to Poverty, that professed foe to honesty, and money Post Pensions, & the whole Toy-shop of unrightiousness displayed, but I hope most people will dispise these rattles, sensible that its only in the common Good that the real intrest of every Individual is included. As to our County in particular you know I fancy that Sir A Forbes & Mr Wm Grant the Solicitor stand for it, & I fancy you'll see in the news papers the Resolution we came to about Placeman & the thanks & instructions we gave our present Member which were a pritty direct Declaration in his Favour & against his Opposite, he will undoubtedly carry the Election. His Mother is lately dead & had left her Son £3000 sterg; My friend Mr. Maitland Pitrichie stands for Abdn & that District against another plaiceman, John Maul, & I think will prevaile which I'm heartily glad of, as he's a Gentleman equal to & worthy of that sacrite Trust. I'm surprised what it could be in my Sisters that could make my Mother or you have such Notions of her, I'm persuaded she intended nothing to give Exception and believe me she's a very sensible good humoured Girl as you'd find out if you saw her. We have a very bad Prospect here. The snow has been very deep here a fortnight ago & came on above a Month since which is sooner than ever I saw which has done much harm to the Cropt. The Prices of Grain will undoubtedly keep up at the last Year's price which was double of the Usual and will distress the Poor most sensibly. My Tenants are pritty safe which is Luck both for them & for me. I shall be ready to answer your Draught after Candlemas but hope to hear from you once or twice ere then. I beg you'd let me know immediately how my Mother does for as she was to write to me as soon as she could I'll be very impatient till I gett one or hear that it is not owing to want of Health. Pray Dear Dr. what makes you allways so laconick with me, if owing to much Buisyness, which I hope it is, I shall be vastly pleased with the Cause. My Sister joins her best Wishes & Respect to our dear Mother & you. I am with the greatest Affection & Sincerity Dear Sir your Friend & humle. servt. Geo Burnet.

PS I wonder you don't lett me know more particularly about Mrs Gilberts & my Uncles wife how that Affair goes on. I wish you may make sense of this its wrote in such a hurry & Confusion (for the sake of takeing Opportunity to gett it franked) five or six merry Fellows laughing & roaring aside & hauling perpetually at me to join them. Aberdeen Nov. 4.

There are several references to the shipping of "kitts" of salmon down to London and this letter explains in part the methods employed to keep the fish which had several days if not weeks at sea before reaching London.

Dear Sir, I have Pleasure of Yours in which you tell me that my Mother and Uncle received mine, but I have not yett had the Satisfaction of hearing it from themselves which you made me expect...I have sent aboard the Unity of Aberdeen Alexr. Thomson Master (who is to sail to morrow wind serving) two Kitts of Salmon one for my Uncle; t'other for you, and I wish with all my Heart they may be good. I fancy they would have been more acceptable earlyer in the Year, but they can't be bad now at any Time but as a great Favour

from the Proprietors who are under Contract with the Fish Mongers at Lond. not to allow any to be sent up in that Way they used to be formerly. They were boiled and kitted[5] in the fishing House...
PS My Sister & Wife offer their Respects to my Mother her little Grandchildren pay her their Duty in their Prayers...

Elizabeth'a health did not improve.

St. John's Day, 1750 [27 December]
My dear Sir, I have this long time been expecting the Pleasure of hearing from my Mother and am extremely sorry that the same Impediment remains. I had much rather she had no Reason for it at all, than one that makes her suffer so much. I'm sure Heaven exacts of her a severe Capitation Tax. I don't know when she'll be repaid for so much Uneasiness but I conjecture it will be in the next World, for there are few if any Comforts in this Life that would compensate for such a perpetual Pain.

I have given over expecting any Good from P------t from what else it can be expected God only knows. I'm affraid it will be as impossible to restore that Equilibrium once so much boasted, and which was indeed the very Soul of our Constitution, as it will maintain the Ballance of E-----e which was kept up by our Forefathers at the Expence of so much Blood and Treasure & has been lately sacrificed to the Interest of a pitiful barren Spot of it. I need hardly tell you that I mean H------r has for these many Years been the important Centeer in which our foreign & domestick Affairs have turned. I believe this is now seen by all the Nation, and regretted by most of it, but I believe it has already gone so far as to render any Remedie doubtfull dangerous if not impracticable. I'm of Opinion the best Thing we could do would be to lett those on the Continent shift for themselves & content ourselves to be as Ulipes [Ulysses?] the last of whom Pollephemus will please to devour. For we can gett Nothing by any of our windmill Expeditions now but the Disgrace of hastening our own Downfall. Perhaps some would prefer a

5 *Salted*

sudden Death to a lingering Illness. But I hate the subject...Venit summa Dies et inevitabile Tempus Dordanis est. [?] I am just come home from St Pauls & have heard the Revd. Mr. Keith Minister there preach the wildest Stuff on the immaculate Conception & the way that the Dove came down, which you know signifies the Holy Gost, and gott her with Child & the great difference there must have been in the Womb betwixt a Conception by Procession & Generation I fancy by this little hint you conceive that he's an ass and that his Mother both conceived & brought forth an Incubus. Pray continue to lett me hear from you now and then. I wish my Dear Mother may be able to write one soon pray lett her know of my Wishes and Respects for her. I offer them most heartilie & conclude in praying Heaven that you may both see as many new Years as you can enjoy. I need neither tell you who I am nor how much I am yours I hope you know both.

The prayers of the family were not answered in the way they wished but doubtless in the best way for Elizabeth. She died shortly after that new year and was buried in St Pancras churchyard. George, who had been such a devoted son, was desolate and, one imagines, poor George Lamont even more so. George continued to write regularly to his step-father and was always most solicitous about his health and well-being. In the Autumn of 1750 his own wife, Helen, died on 21st September. I have found no letters about her death. If George wrote to the doctor about it, he did not preserve them: perhaps they opened old wounds; perhaps George never wrote. Later on their correspondence was resumed and it appears that Dr Lamont had given thought to young Alexander's future. George replies:

Kemnay 26 April 1751 My dear Sir, You seem to rest upon Physick as the most proper pursuit for my Boy, that makes me think I have omitted to tell you in the letter I wrote on that Subject that besides my own Objections, which were strong it was what he seemed not to inclyne, so that I must think Trade one of the quickest as well as the surest ways of attaining an independency. The Question is which is the most easy and expedient Method for one who cannot afford to spend much Money in trying Experiments. I have taken

> Means to have all the Advice I can. I shall upon the Whole come to such a Result as has the best Appearance of Success, and trust Providence for the Issue. I remember when I was in Bristol I saw one Mrs Fisher, a cousin, whose Husband was dead & left a large Fortune behind him made in the Business of a Distiller. He had Sons, I should be glad to know if they follow in the Business and then Alexander could be apprentic'd to them. It might be a great advantage to him to be brought up to a Business with a Relation who could be of great Use to him after his Time was out without putting that Relation either to Trouble or Expence...

He goes on to ask Dr Lamont if he could find out more about it. The relations were obviously on the Brickenden side. The letters do not relate the outcome of the investigations but we know they came to nought as Alexander had quite different ideas from either his father or the doctor and inclined more to his grandfather's life in the diplomatic world.

X

George missed the company and comfort of a wife and decided that a bachelor's life was definitely not to his taste. On 25th October 1751 he married Janet, daughter of James Dyce of Disblair. She was very much a country person and a most suitable choice. She settled into the Kemnay life and took a great interest in all things agricultural and horticultural and kept a diary in which she recorded details about the weather.

George was very much surrounded by women – a wife, a sister, five daughters – but he obviously enjoyed it. His father had left sister Anne an annuity, which George administered, of £500 (presumably scots). She is the Miss Annie of the following bill from a travelling tailor, aptly named Alexander Taylor:

	s d
To 17 days work in the house at 1/- a day	17:00
to making a pr. breeks to Mr. Burnet	6
to making a frock to Miss Betty	4
to two days work for Miss Annie	1:08

Material for better clothes was ordered through the agent in London but for everyday needs the home-grown flax was used. It was sent away for weaving and bleaching to Fettercairn by the housekeeper and a letter and bill from John Foulerton, Fettercairn reads:

> Madam, According to your Desire I have sent you the Lady Kemnay's Accompt. for weaving and if you can procur the Payment soon it will be a Favor, for I have occasion for Money about this Time. Your most obedient and humble servant,
>
> John Foulerton

	£ s d
To boyling 17 spindle of yarn	2:10
To weaving 22 Yd Linen at 2/- a Yd	2:04:00

Then it was sent to John Hogg the dyer:

> To dyeing 11 pound. 9 ounces Linen yarn deep Blew and 3 pound 14 ounces Sarge green £2:4s:0d

George and his new wife must have planned to refurbish one of the rooms at Kemnay – the parlour perhaps – and had asked the London agent for patterns of wallpaper.

> Shipt on board the Neptune Capt. Martin for Aberdeen for G. Burnet Esqr.

Pr. order of Mr. James Morrison Vizt:	£ s d
1 paper bundle It.	
1. 5 pieces of fine pencilled paper	
2. 5 ditto	
3. 10 pieces at 10s	6:00:00
12 Dozen of bordering	12:00
Commission	3:00
Charge of Shipping	1:00
Total	6:16:03
Deducted for money 1d pr. Yd.	10:00
	£6:06:03

Dear Sir London 16th October 1753

Some Posts ago my Brother sent me your order for paper hangings with a Cloath Paper Pattern. There being of late a paper manufactory sett up here, which is farr superior to any thing yet done in that way that it is like fine paintings to common daubings. My eldest son and I went and chose out for you (as above) 10 pieces in 2 patterns, judging You would much sooner approve of these than any thing of the cloth kind, especially as they're almost out of fashion here on Accot: of harbouring dust. This paper comes only to 11d a Yd. and it was lately sold for 18 and 20d. and some time ago for 2/6 a Yd. If I had an order for 25 pieces It will come at 10d. if for 50 pss & above at 9d. I have sent with your paper some other patterns for my Brother to show the Town and Country, to get more orders for it, for as the Manufacturer is a particular friend of mine he proposes that I should have the sale of it chiefly in Scotland, therefore would begg you will give no patterns of it, but as severals of your neighbouring Gentlemen or acquaintances may fancy this paper they may only apply to my Brother with their orders, the Amount of this parcels is £6. 6/3. which please pay to my Brother. I flatter myself this will give intear Satisfaction, as the figures & flowers are noble and well disposed as well as natural and the colours extremely strong lively & fine. Capt. Martin sails in 2 or 3 days and that Capt. Gordon is daily expected if you chuse yet any of the crimson paper or the blew on yellow please write soon, and it shall be carefully chose and sent by him. I shall be glad to serve you or Yours as Farr as I am capable in this place. I begg You'le pay my kind Compliments to your Lady and Family, I am

Dear Sir
Your most obedient
and most humle. Servtt.
Thos. Morison

PS. There are some noble designs going on in this paper for ornaments to large Rooms and chimney pieces etc.

And the receipt:

> Receivd: of George Burnet Esqr. of Kemnay for Acott: of Mr. Thos Morison the within mentioned Six pounds Six Shill: & three pence Ster: money Aberdeen Octob: 26th 1753
>
> James Morison.

One piece of the paper with its "extremely strong, lively and fine" colours was discovered in a drawer but, alas, the room that it was used in has been changed long since. It must have been very handsome.

Further accounts show that one of the daughters had dancing lessons for three months from a dancing master in Aberdeen who rejoiced in the name of Mr. F. Peacock, which cost George £1:10/-.[6] George also indulged in a glass of "claritt" and port and was not averse to a drop of French brandy.

	£ s d
To a hogshead of Claret	22:00:00
To a hogshead of Port Wine	20:00:00
To four Pints French Brandy	10:04
To four Pints Gin	1:04

Sherry and Malaga were other items and presumably they were considered more a lady's tipple. A Hogshead measured 52½ gallons which must have kept them going for a while but rum was bought in far greater quantities:

To one hundred and ten gallons fine Jamaica Rum	£52: 5: 00
Plus excise	3:10: 00
	is £55:15: 00

6 *In 1746 Aberdeen Town Council advertised for a dancing master of a "sober, discreet and moral character". A dancing master in Edinburgh recommended a Mr. Francis Peacock, also of Edinburgh, to be a fit and qualified person for the post. The Council nominated him as sole dancing master of the town and allowed him to charge seven shillings sterling monthly for each pupil. Mr. Peacock became a most respected citizen of the burgh and Peacock's Close off the Castlegate where he held his classes was named after him. An artistically gifted man, Francis Peacock composed music and painted miniatures. He lived to the ripe old age of eighty-four.*

That does appear to have been almost a two years' supply. Rum Punch was the "in" drink amongst the gentry at that time and perhaps the outdoor servants got a rum ration on cold days. After all it was an early form of central heating! George had other vices. One was tobacco.

> London 1760. Sir, I was favoured with yours of Post and wh. I would have answered sooner but no opportunity of an Aberdeen ship offered till now the Ship "Charles" Thomas Fraser Master. who now brings your Box of fine old mild Tobacco which for goodness cannot be exceeded in London. The box contains 33¼ pounds at 20 pence the pound.
>
> Sir, Your most humble Servant, Charles Donaldson.
>
> NB I seldom sell this fine Tobacco under two shillings the pound.

Another vice was the excitement of a game of chance. The family played cards and George enjoyed a gamble and bought Lottery tickets at fairly regular intervals. Always the optimist as this letter from his London Agent shows:

> London 27 November, 1760 Sir, I had the pleasure to write to you 3 ins. and then sent an Invoice of a Puncheon of Rum shipt for you aboard the Resolution, Capt. Cruickshank amounting to £50. 7/9 for which I shall soon be expecting remittance. I have since received the Favour of yours on 9 inst. and would gladly have complied with the contents had No. 2153, the Lottery Ticket purchased for you, come up to a prize, but I am sorry to inform you that, on examination, I find it has been drawn a Blank. I remain very respectfully,
>
> Sir, your most Humble Servant
> p.p. George Catanach,
> James Allardes.

George and his wife had social commitments and here is a bill of entertainment for the election of the Magistrates of Inverurie:

Michaelmas, 1757.

For dinner		Twelve guineas
For punch		Thirteen pounds six shillings
For two barrels of beer and a half		Eight pounds fourteen shillings
For horse corn		Nine shillings
	Total	Thirty-five pounds one shilling.

XI

Janet must have been a great help and comfort to George for in the same year, 1757, he wrote some good advice to George Lamont:

> Kemnay 6 Dec. 1757. My dear Sir, It will give me great Pleasure to hear you are well when this comes to Hand, as all here are and full of good wishes for you. I had a Letter from my Son dated Leipzig 6 Novr. he and Mr. Mitchell were in good Health and seemed to be in that flow of Spirits that Victory gives. There was scarce anything in particular, but that Mr. Keith did wonders!---This is the first Blow the King of Prussia has struck of any Consequence to Britain. This is really weakening our Enemies, and but for that cursed C....... the French might be driven out of Germany. And but for a certain Part of G......y which it is the Misfortune --- But stop! I dare not trust my Pen, nor need I say what every thinking Briton sees.

George then writes the very belated explanation of his feelings when Lamont and his mother married which I quoted earlier and goes on to say that he hopes to:

> ...maintain the Charitys of that Relationship Law had indeed adopted me into, but which I before claimed from the spontaneous & heartsprung affection I gave and received. There were a Table Clock & some Trifles that belonged to the Heirship moveable, that I gave up to my Mother & gott her Receipt that they should be returned at her Death...Speaking of Trifles brings it in my Head to speak yet of one that I would not have spoke to you of but that by your never mentioning any word about it, I was affraid it

> might become of too much Importance to me, if there was any Thing you had taken amiss about it. When my Mother was down here she askt, amongst other Questions, about my Father's fine brocade West Coat, I told it was too fine for my Course of Life, & had never been on my Back. She said it was a thousand Pitys it should not be wore & that if her Dr. had it he would wear it. You may believe that as I was glad that I had any Thing I could spare that you would like, I said you should have it with all my Soul. I know no way of Earth it would be so well bestowed – This was the precise Case upon my Honour, so that if you thought it wrong in me to send a Thing to you that was not entirely New, you see I was not to blame, my Mother took that upon her, & I could not suppose you would think I meant any thing less than a Token that I honoured far above the Value... Thus, dear Sir, it was given & has I hope been in the same Manner received. I will now boldly take upon me to tell you what I think is fitt for you, because it is what I wish. I shall be very sorry if it be contrary to your Inclination. I do therefore beg of you, my Dear Doctor, with all the Earnestness of an unfeigned Affection that you'll hasten to give yourself a virtuous and affectionate Friend. Your Ease, your Satisfaction your very Health requires it. The sensible and sober Life you lead, averse to the senseless tho' noisy Roar of tumultuous & inebriated Festivity, makes it the more necessary that you should have an agreable Companion, to sooth & sweeten those moments the severe Dutys of your Profession allow you to give to Repose & rational Self-Indulgence. And this can best be had by a She of good Sense & good Temper from whose Affection you will find those tender Cures for your Health, which every Day now will make more necessary & you will be too apt to neglect. For as we verge towards age, a thousand Ailments & Weaknesses come on that require both the Care & Indulgence of one full of such tender Solicitudes as I from my Soul wish you to find and fix for ever. Yours being as I am in the most affectionate manner...

From this one must suppose that Janet was indeed a guardian angel but Dr Lamont did not follow George's advice entirely; however, he did engage a faithful housekeeper, Martha Cripps, who looked after him until his death in 1789. He left her the sum of £20 and all his wearing apparel of every kind "as well as Linen and Woollen" and also during her natural life an annuity of £20 (sterling of course, as he died in England). Another letter written to Dr Lamont by George in the February following ends on what I find an amusing note:

> Now my dear Doctor forgive me if I pass some sensure on the Staleness of your news. We're near enough but not quite under the Pole, and I had the Lord's Protest that followed the Notion you write of sent me by a Friend in London ten Days ago!

George did not give up advocating the possibility of the doctor's finding "a lovely Widow" and I expect Lamont found this solicitude quite touching.

XII

George's marriage to Janet Dyce was a very appropriate one as they had so many similar traits of character. As has been mentioned, Janet kept a full and very descriptive diary which shows her to have been as avid a naturalist as George and a great one for recording all details of weather, garden and farm. I only wish she had inserted some family matters as well but we have to thank her for setting George a good example as from this time he kept two ledgers under the following headings: House Accounts – Beautifying Building & Planting – Day Labourers – Sundrys – Memorandums – Receipts, and they date from 1752 till 1770. They are fascinating to read and very informative both as to life in those times and for revealing other facets of George's character. The household accounts cover a multitude of different commodities from the purchase of "a swine, 11/-, and two sowes £1. 5/-": to "100 wt. Muscavade sugar 13/-. to 227 pd. Loaf Sugar at 7½d. £6.17/1½. to 55 pd. Powder Loaf Sugar at 8½d. £1.18/8. to Hops 32 pd. £1.16/-". The ale, I would imagine, was pretty powerful. Tea, at this date, cost 6/- a pound (much cheaper than at present) and the souter's account over a year for making and mending the children's shoes was £10.13/4. They must have done quite a bit of scampering around. Besides all the usual purchases of flowered lawn, ribbons and tartan, the house accounts also had to cover various journeys in and out of town, shoeing the horses, postages and so on. Janet had eye trouble and Doctor Rose charged three guineas to look at her sore eye – extortion! Repairs to the house are noted: "To Peter Mcay Sclater in Part Payment for poynting a Wing of the House at which he was three days 2/- and to his Boy 1/-". Janet must have discovered that it was cheaper to buy a whole box of tea instead of by the pound and one box cost them £4. 1/-. I should like to know what they required twenty-one dozen lemons for, for which they paid 15/-, the same price they had to lay out for a new bee hive. In 1752 George had purchased a chaise for £33. Among other miscellaneous items listed was a "Mahogany Floor Skreen" which cost 12/-. The price of a "piece of Cloth sent to me Son" was £3.16/- and he paid the cost of his servant's burial and "paid Mr. Angus for a Year's Subscription to Circulatory Library 10/6". In the account for Beautifying, Building & Planting are the mason's bill for harling the new dyke, a new orchard dyke and gate pillars and the cost of ale and refreshments to the workmen. There follows an account for Fir seed, Larich seed, Flower roots, Fruit trees, 600 Beeches and 15,000 more Firs plus Ash and Elm and a Garden roller. Besides the numerous bills for trees bought locally, a lot came from London and a considerable number from Holland. The entries for hardwoods add up to several thousand trees, mostly beeches , which seem to have been a special favourite. Larches were a novelty at this time and ash, elm, lime and sycamore, yews and chestnuts were among the others he planted. Trees were planted in the yards of tenanted farms as well and this was all included in the general programme of beautifying. With this enormous undertaking there had to be of necessity a lot of draining and the costs of "trenching" come to quite a sum. The new policy of enclosures led to the building of many walls which called for a vast amount of mason's work which included blasting of stone, cutting and dressing it to build new walls and gate-posts for different parks and the garden. Throughout these entries there are regular sums listed against "Drink money" for whoever was involved with the great work being undertaken.

This "beautifying programme" is considered by many to be George's greatest achievement and the one for which he is best remembered – the creating of avenues and walks, gardens and sanctuaries and the general improvement of the surrounding policies. He laid out a fine avenue of beeches leading straight down from the house. The present back door was then the front and only entrance and he planned a stately drive arriving at a circular lawn in front of

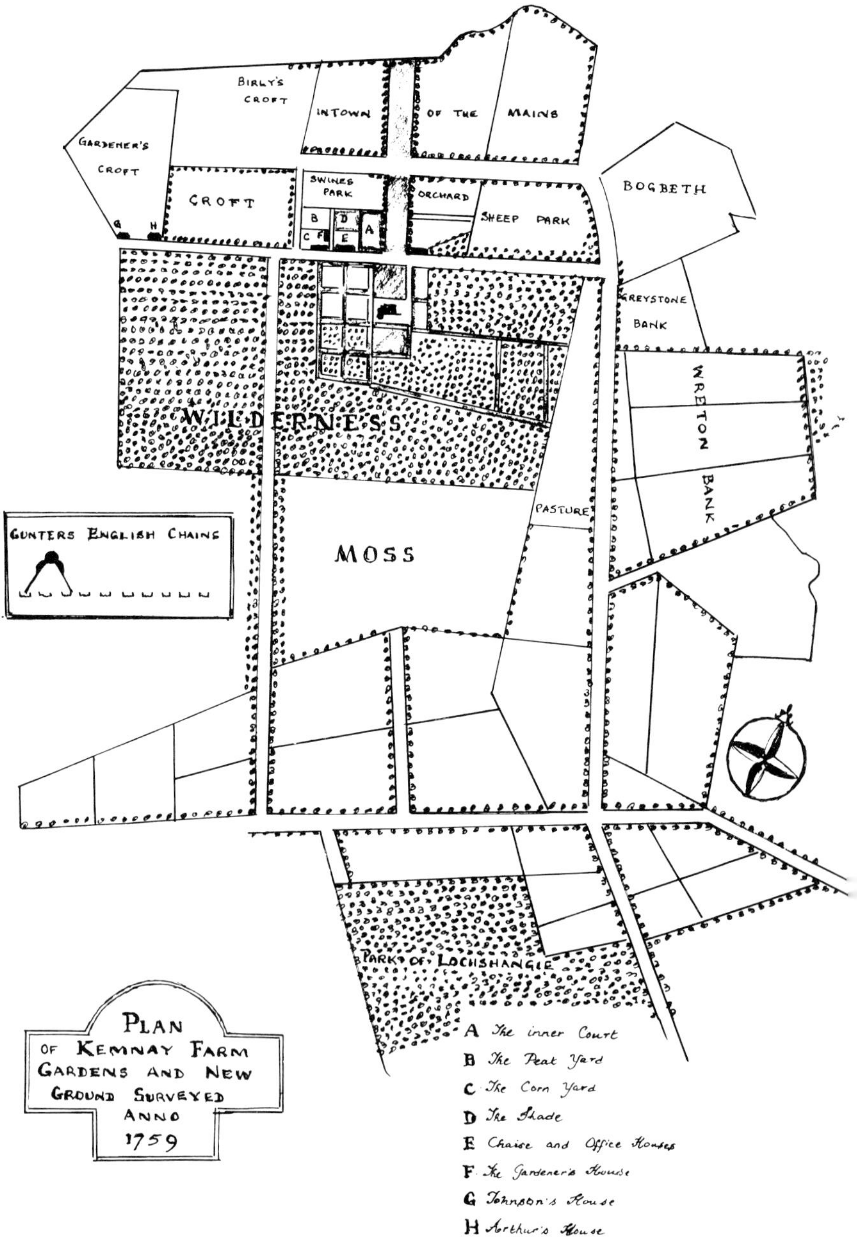

Map of Kemnay Estate, 1759

the courtyard. He was later taken to task, posthumously, by one of his London suppliers, for not having designed the avenue to take in Bennachie at its foot but of course George knew that the trees would eventually grow very large and any view of the mountain would be obscured! He named the land surrounding the house "the Wilderness", it was planted with the many different species of hardwood, laid out with numerous grass walks and paths, with every now and then, in a strategic site, a clump of yews to form a shelter and screen for a garden seat. He liked to plant circles of beeches and one enormous one of about fourteen trees, named "the Fairy Ring", formed a grand entrance to one of the roads through the Wilderness. This ring was destroyed by the gale of 1953 and it is my hope that future generations will enjoy the trees my gardener and I have planted on the site of the former ones as much as we, as children, enjoyed playing amongst George's beeches. As a matter of interest, George's gardener in 1756 was one Robert Walker. Two hundred and thirty years later my gardener, who has planted many trees in George's Wilderness, is James Walker. The land further to the south of the house was planted to firs only and was called the "Back Wilderness". In the Wilderness itself was the spring from which the house and farm were watered and which has been in use ever since. Nearby the Well was the Mossy Place, full of humps of sphagnum moss which is used in horticulture. In the walled garden fruit was a particular interest and George had nearly one hundred fruit trees lining the walls. These included nineteen varieties of apples besides cherries, plums, pears, greengages, apricots and quince. Other delicacies such as melons and "asparrowgrass" were enjoyed by the family. He had picked a wonderful site for the garden which lies on a slight slope facing south; it catches all the sunshine and warmth possible. It is no wonder that the landscape he created is what posterity associates most with George for one cannot even walk out of the house today without seeing the results of his master plan. Kemnay in its hey-day was the admiration of many and the beech avenue became one of the features of Aberdeenshire.

The Home Farm came in for much improvement and was made the example from which his tenants were encouraged to learn. New barns had been built from the stone blasted by the masons and there are accounts for "holing clay for bricks" which were used for interior walls. Very stony ground was blasted and the stones used for building dry stone dykes. There are accounts for all the different seeds required:

grass, bear, corn, turnips (red and white), white clover and flax. There are listed the sums paid out for shoes to the filly, twenty wedders at 5/-, nine geese from Al. Mitchell for 10/6. Paid Andrew Downie for a Two year old Bull £5.15/-.

There are frequent purchases of cows, sometimes "one for the house" and on one occasion he bought:

Autumn 1754 for the Plow at Bartholomew Fair[7]

	£ s d
Three Black Oxen the youngest of wh. dyed	10:00:00
One yellow	3:15:00
One Flecket	3:13:04
One Black	2:18:00
One Riget	2:10:00
One from Michael Fair Kinkell[8]	3:00:00
One from Peter Fair Strathbogie	3:10:00
One from do	3:00:00
One from A. Hunter at "	2:18:04
Deducting for one that dyed £3 wh. is	34:18:08

After the work on the Home Farm and policies had been completed, the improvements to outlying farms and crofts commenced. "To John Sutherland for 20 roods of trenching at four pence half penny being the first of the new Ground without the Inclosures 7/6" The account for blasting reads:

> "Agreed with James McPetrye for blowing at the Rate of seven pence pr. foot he furnishing Powder & Tools and given him in Advance 5/- is £10. 5/-". Thirty-six pounds of gunpowder cost 13/4. A keen agriculturalist, George was one of the foremost in the North East to advocate the new methods of farming. Old maps show his plans for rotating crops among his tenants and he introduced the planting of

7 *Bartholomew Fair - Bartle is a corruption of St Bartholomew. Bartle Muir, Kincardine O'Neil was where Bartholomew Fair used to be held on the last Tuesday in August (old style calendar) [ex Place Names in Aberdeenshire].*

8 *Michael Fair of Kinkell, last Tuesday in September (old style). Peter Fair at Strathbogie, Wednesday after the first Tuesday in July. (ex Aberdeen Almanac 1773).*

turnips in this area. He went into it quite scientifically and kept a record to show how cattle fattened on turnips as opposed to being grass fed. His record for the year 1768 shows the following comparison: "Profit on grazed cattle – £5. Profit on cattle Turnip fed – £25."

XIII

Kemnay 9 June 1756.
Sir, I hereby Engage my self to Enter your Service at Martinmas next and to serve you for one or two years thereafter as you incline upon Tryal diligently and soberly as a Gardener you paying me the Yearly Wages of Four Pound Sterling for Fee and cows grass which I am to take for my self and I possessing the gardeners Hous and Croft and being allowed Boll for my self and two lades as forman Gardiners I paying the usual Rent for the Croft
I am
Sir
your most obed^{t} Servant Robert Walker.

Thus did Robert Walker engage himself to George Burnet and the "Tryal" must have proved very satisfactory as he remained gardener at Kemnay for many years. George, it appears, was a kind and just master and a thoughtful one too.

There are frequent entries of "marriage presents" and cost of servants' burials, and indeed Robert Walker married shortly after coming to work here and received a wedding present of two guineas from the laird. Four years later another young man entered George's employment as an apprentice gardener, one Francis Masson. After finishing his apprenticeship, Masson went to work in the King's gardens at Kew. He later became the first of the Plant Hunters for that royal garden and it is lovely to know that his life's work was inspired by the example set him by George Burnet. He was an Aberdeenshire lad and his brother always kept in touch with the family. A letter from Francis Masson written to George's son after hearing of his father's death is quoted in Alexander's chapter.

In the Memorandum section of George's account book are all the agreements he had with servants and labourers. One interesting one is that of the blacksmith:

> 1754 February 17. Kemnay agreed that Wm. Sandyson be the only Smith within his Lands, and obliges himself to cause all thereon come to his Smiddy & Wm. Sandyson during the Time the said Obligation lasts, wh. is for one Year viz from Whit Javii & fiftyfive to Whit Sunday Javii & fiftysix, Obliges himself to Work all the Work that Kemnay has to do either as Laird or Tenant for no thing & to give ready & punctuall service. Geo. Burnet
>
> William Sandison.

As William Sandison remained his smith for several years apparently the agreement was to his liking. Another short term agreement from 1758 reads: "Agreed to give Pat Koinachsson for keeping my Sheep from lst. April to Mart. £5 scots. If he does very well I intend to give him £6." I hope he did. A very odd contract which requires some disentangling is this: "Jany. 28, 1765 Agreed with Ja. Deans to be my Servant for a Year from Whit. He is to keep an able Horse which is to be maintained by me all Summer and is to go all the Carriages as Carrier for the Rest of the Time that he's not going Carriages hes to work as one of my work Servants & is to have two Pecks of Meal pr. week and thirtysix pounds scots Yearly is to live on the Croft like John Duthies for which he is to pay the Same Rent that he paid & to have the Avenew for his Cow at six pounds Yearly."

George maintained his servants in clothing as well as food and each man is listed with items against his name. For instance Robert Bain got

	s d
Eleven Ells of Linen at 7d	6 :05
To making the same into 4 shirts	1 :00
To him 12 weeks at 1/6d for his Meat	18 :00
To a pr. of Shoes to him	3 :00
To him at Christmas	1 :00
To a Tickey Frock	5 :00
To Jacket Breeches	9 :04

and so on with the Christmas box appearing every year to each servant.

> Agreed with Geo. Moir to serve me as Groom for 2 Year at 30 Pound the Year.

Paid exchanging a Pair of Old Boots for a Pair of New that fitted Geo. Moir the new Groom 10/6d
Given Geo Moir Groom by way of Gratuity besides his Wages £1. 1/-

Geo. Moir must have proved reliable and efficient as he was chosen to accompany Miss Nellie to Edinburgh for which he had to be dressed very smartly in a new frock coat and handkerchiefs. He was given 10/6 on setting out for the big city. The contracts drawn up by George himself in his ledger are in no way so pedantic as those composed by a man of business. An early agreement, obviously drawn up by a lawyer, is a lengthy document with many repetitions and such ominous clauses as he must not "absent himself therefrom (his master's service) night or day without liberty asked and given under the taillie of one shilling sterling for each day's absence or serving two days for each day's absence.....and to conceal all his Master's lawful Secrets and not to reveal any part of his Busoness and to abstain from all carding dicing night walking and company keeping and all such evil practices..." All in all it would appear that George was a reasonable master and it is satisfying to see the entries for little presents and gratuities. His wages for Day Labourers came to a substantial sum and were what we would refer to as Casual Labourers today. There is no doubt it was a great help to some of the vast numbers of unemployed of the time.

Taxes, that bone of contention which many of the Scots in the eighteenth century blamed on the English Parliament and the Act of Union, took up a large portion of the landowner's income. George has them all labelled under the heading "Cess & other Publick Burdens" which for the year 1766 goes as follows:

			£ s d
Feb.	24.	Paid Mr. Reid Minr. half of Stipend from 1765	13:13:10½
	25.	Paid Collr of Cess Lam & Mart 1765 wt Rogue Money is	11:04:03
		Paid half a Year Duty & Windows viz Whit to Mart '65	1:03:00
Mar.	14.	Paid Divid Bartlet Tack Tiens Duty Cropt 1764–65	6:08:08½
		Minr. of Cluny for Cropt 1765	16:00
		Paid Collr. of Excise one Years Malt Duty from 24 June last	1:02:06

	Paid Mr. Reid for Communion Elements for 1766	1:13:04
Sepr. 1.	Paid Mr. Reid the first half of Yr. Stipend 1766	13:13:10½
	Paid Cess for Canlemas & White Sunday 1766	9:08:09½
	Duty on Windows from Mart. to Whit '67	1:03:00
	Forgot Plate Duty wh. was	5:00

Unfortunately just at this time there arose another crisis with ensuing expenses. I mean the complex case of the Crathes succession.

XIV

As has been seen, George had a very good relationship with his kinsman and father-in-law, Sir Alexander Burnet of Leys, the fourth Baronet. Sir Alexander was not a public figure but a kind-hearted and benevolent man of simple character and possessed of some peculiarities, one of which was a dislike of anything to which he was unused and another that was locally known as "a boodie fear" of ghosts. Helen had died leaving one son as had the youngest daughter, Mary, who had married Robert Aberdein mentioned in one of George's letters to his mother. Sir Alexander outlived his daughter, Helen, by eight years, dying at Crathes at the age of 80 in 1758. His eldest son, Thomas, had been killed by a splinter of rock in the course of his father's operations in draining the Loch of Leys. The second son, Robert, remained unmarried and the question of whether the family estates, saved from disaster by Sir Alexander through his wife's fortune and good management, should, failing Robert, go to Sir Alexander's daughters or to his brother, William Burnet of Criggie, had to be faced. Both the old investitures and Sir Thomas Burnet's entail of 1700 gave preference to heirs male. Criggie, prompted, it is said by his mother who was a lady of much vigour and character, endeavoured to resuscitate the entail of 1700, not to the extent of bringing the irritances into effect but to that of securing the succession to heirs male. After much very persistent litigation, the Court found that, in so far as the entail was not found among Sir Thomas's repositories at the time of his death, he must be presumed to have exercised his reserved power of cancelling it. Sir Alexander's views may perhaps be gathered from the fact of adjudications under which he held being taken to heirs of Line, from his opposing the revival of the entail and from the circumstances that, in bestowing the fee of certain parts of the estate, including Crathes and lands adjacent, on his son Robert in 1740, 1745 and 1746, he disponed them to him, his heirs and assignees.

In order to try and clarify a complex family matter as concisely as possible whilst at the same time retaining the relevant points which have bearing on the court case of 1759–67, I think it is necessary to explain some of the past history of the Leys family. I go back to Sir Alexander's grandfather, an earlier Alexander, the second Baronet. On his succession to Leys, the then laird of Brodie wrote in his diary:

> When I heard that the Lord of Leyis Burnet, being a sober, grave man, had a successor so profane, dissolute and naughty, my hart said 'What doe I travel for under the sun. How is it true of Solomon, men know not what shall come after them, whether a wyse man or a fool'.

The estate he inherited was burdened with debts and obligations and he was laird for just ten years, dying at the age of 26, leaving his wife and six children, the eldest of whom, Thomas, was still a minor. The guardians he appointed to have care of his children and estate were his uncle, Robert Burnet, an advocate, and Robert Burnet of Cowton and Muchalls. This second Robert Burnet is of particular importance. He was the fourth son of James Burnet of Craigmyle, whom the reader will, I hope, remember was also the father of Thomas, the first of Kemnay, elder brother of this Robert. He had over the years acquired a great deal of property and was a man of much substance and is generally referred to in family history as "Tutor of Leys": 'Tutor' in this case meaning guardian. His first wife had died without children and his second marriage produced three daughters, Helen, Agnes and Jean. Returning now to the young Sir Thomas, we find he married, whilst still under age and against his guardian's wishes, Margaret, daughter of Viscount Arbuthnot. The latter encouraged his son-in-law to raise a suit against his Tutor to account for rents and profits which ended very advantageously for Robert Burnet, it being found that a large balance was due to him. After a brief three years of his second marriage, Robert made up his mind that he was to have no son and that his inheritance was to become, by marriage, the property of the heirs of Leys. He entered into an agreement with Sir Thomas, obliging himself and his heirs to

Tree Showing Involved Relationships

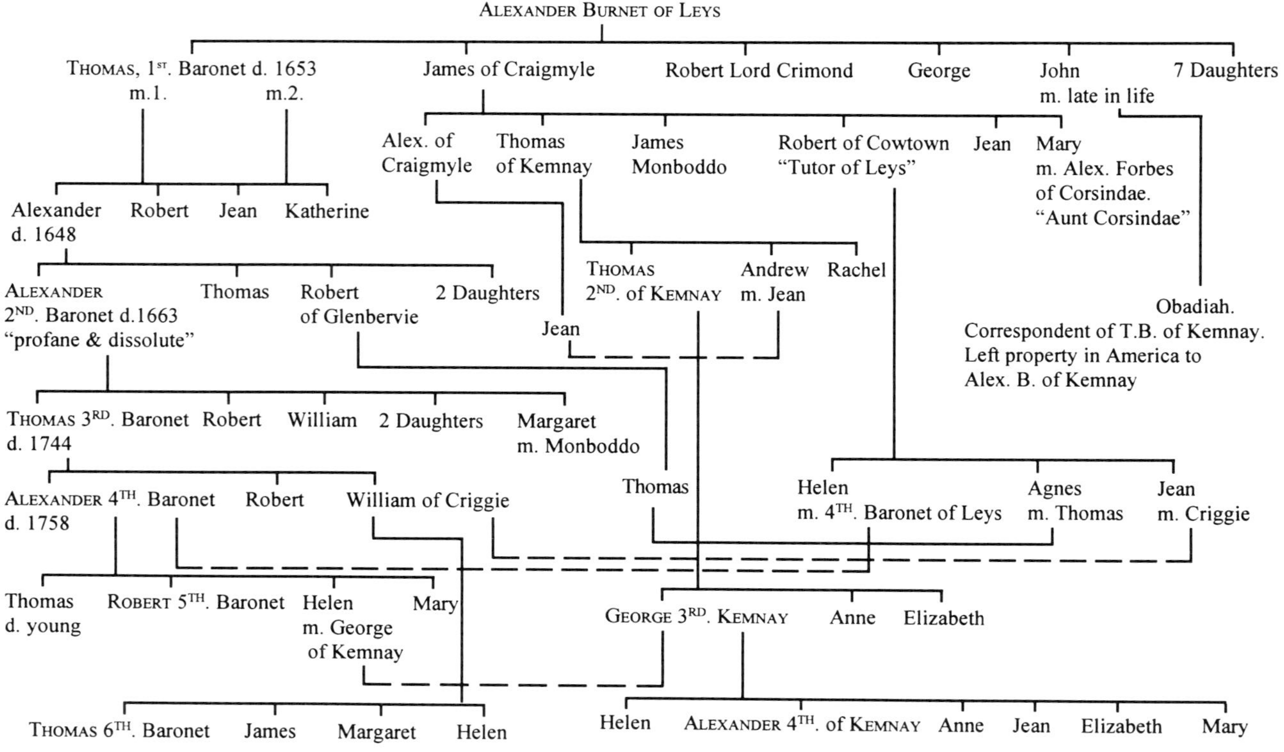

pay to Sir Thomas's eldest son and heir the sum of £60,000 scots as a marriage portion of his eldest daughter, Helen, at the age of fourteen years or sooner. The child was only four at the time. The second daughter was to marry at the age of eighteen, Robert Burnet, eldest son of Glenbervie, and the third daughter, Jean, was to marry Robert Burnet of Keir. (I could wish for fewer Roberts!) Sir Thomas's son, Alexander, did eventually marry, at the age of eighteen, Helen, daughter of the by then deceased Tutor of Leys, then fourteen years of age. Her share of her father's estate amounted to the sum of £7,000 sterling, a considerable fortune at that time. The second girl, Agnes, married her pre-ordained husband, Robert Burnet of Glenbervie but the youngest daughter, Jean, unable to fulfil her father's wish owing to the death of her pre-determined mate, married William, younger son of Sir Thomas of Leys, afterwards William Burnet of Criggie, and became the mother of the future sixth Baronet. How they inter-married! The family really was in need of fresh genes.

As far as Sir Alexander's marriage was concerned, he was very fortunate in marrying a lady as well endowed as the lands of Crathes were heavily burdened with debts when he inherited the estate and it was chiefly owing to his wife's fortune, together with that of his mother, that the family possessions were kept intact. The estate of Leys was saved but at the price of Muchalls and Cowtown.

As has been said, Sir Alexander, fourth Baronet, died in 1758. His second son, Robert, succeeded his father as fifth Baronet but survived him only a little more than a year and then the battle over the succession really began.

George, on behalf of his son, Alexander, who was at that time in Berlin, claimed succession and so did Thomas Burnet of Criggie, cousin of the late Sir Robert. Both were at Crathes for Sir Robert's funeral and history has it that each treated the other as his guest and was excessively polite! This, of course, could not last and one day George locked up the castle and carried off the key of the great door to Kemnay. The fat was now in the fire with a vengeance and a protracted lawsuit between heirs male and heirs in line ensued. One of Kemnay's suits was founded on Sir Alexander's title by adjudication. The £40,000 scots settled on Sir Alexander as a surrogate for Cowtown was payable to his heirs and assigns and these, it pleaded, gave the heirs in line a claim on the estates. A separate claim was made as to Standingstones, conveyed by Sir Alexander to his son, Robert, and conveyed by Robert to his nephew, Alexander, younger of Kemnay, his heirs and assigns. But seven days before his death, the back bond being unsigned, Sir Robert gave a mandate to his factor that the conveyance should be made absolute and the intended back bond should not be granted. The three cases were hotly litigated in the Court of Session and decided in favour of heirs male. Carried by appeal to the House of Lords, the judgement of the court below was affirmed with costs. George kept the key of Crathes which has hung at Kemnay ever since and Sir Thomas became sixth Baronet and had to fit a new lock! His possession ceased to be contested in 1766 and in 1767 he obtained from the Court of Session a decree against Alexander Burnet, younger of Kemnay, and from Robert Aberdein, Mary's husband, as the late Sir Robert's heirs of line. Standingstones was redisponed to him by Kemnay, reserving the Superiority. Thomas had married in 1754 Katherine, daughter and heiress of Charles Ramsay of Balmain. Their eldest son inherited Crathes and their second son became Sir Alexander Ramsay of Balmain.

Nothing tells us George's feelings about this wrangle and as it went on for so many years, he had probably got used to the fact that his efforts on his son's behalf were to be futile. He had much else to occupy him. His ventures into the scientific side of the new methods of farming had been successful and his garden was one of the showpieces of the country. He had inherited quite a fine library from his father and he added several very interesting volumes himself. "Eden or the Compleat Body of Gardening" gives week by week instructions as to the management of "Flora; or the Pleasure Garden", "Pomona; or the Fruit Garden", "Chloris; or the Kitchen Garden" and also a chapter entitled "The Business of the Seminary" and is a delightful book with lovely illustrations. Among others George patronised the Foulis Brothers, the famous printers in Glasgow. He did not only buy books on horticulture; there is a receipt for a set of Homer and "The Compleat Distiller" and "The Art of Making Wines" were no doubt often referred to. "Rules for Bad Horsemen" suggests either he or Alexander were not expert equestrians. Sometimes his orders for books were not very clear. His London Agent wrote:

> ...I suppose you must be under some mistake as to "Every Woman her Own Banker" as I have enquired at several Places but can hear of no such Book.

It turned out that the book he was seeking was titled, "Every Man his Own Broker."

XV

Sister Anne had left Kemnay and gone to live in London and, from the tone of this letter from her brother, run into debt. George appears very sanctimonious and rather lacking in his usual good humour:

> Kemnay lets his Sister know that he is not surprised that she is arrived at that State of Humiliation which he had often warned her that her Follies would conduct her. It is the last Resource of a Spendthrift but as it is the only one she has to take he wishes her a good Bargain. He returned her such Thanks as are due for an Offer she will have a better Opportunity of knowing the Value of when she comes to look out for a Merchant. The Remainder of her Portion shall be ready he will save so much a Year by borrowing from Another & be eas'd of a Burden on her Mind. He is no little more angry than he was before with his Sister, that he should just have satisfied himself with telling her that it was no Bargain for him if it had not been for the absurd Mention of Oeconomie in the Mouth of one that has squandered a great Part of what was one of the last Provisions made for a Daughter & in the Wane of Life tho' in the full of her Vanity and Folly declares herself not able to live upon a Remainder that must make the Whole of such as are every Way as good & I hope in many Particulars much better. He must add her concluding Insinuation would warrant Indignation to say that a continual Enjoyment of selfish Passions, neither leave the Feeling or Means of expressing grateful Remembrances.
>
> If this seems harsh, it is those Expressions of Kindness & Oeconomie she is not entitled to use that have drawn it upon her as to the Rest having said what he thinks becomes his future Behaviour to her will be such as he owes to himself.
>
> He has sent her £10 for her present Necessities. But his Sister would need to pay every Debt before she concludes such a Bargain & to know that if she leaves any behind her she must clear with her God about it, for her Brother, if he should chance to survive her, will take no concern as he shall let every Body know.

Unfortunately we are at a loss as to the nature of "the Bargain". Poor Anne! She must have inherited the Brickenden trait of living above her means. Her uncle Brickenden was often helped out of debt by the good Dr Lamont.

One of George's neighbours with whom he was on extremely friendly terms was Andrew Mitchell of Thainstone and he had undertaken to oversee the management of Mitchell's affairs while he was abroad as Ambassador to the Court of Frederick the Great of Prussia. George's son, Alexander, was secretary to Andrew Mitchell and had accompanied him to Berlin. The following letter conveys Mitchell's gratitude:

> Berlin, 4th June. 1768
> My dear Sir, I was favoured with your kind and friendly letters of 12th. and 16th. April which fully convince me of the zeal and warmth of your friendship and affection, you have alone fought the battle I do not know in what terms to thank you, if I could write my feelings on this occasion you would be satisfied.
>
> I heartily approve of everything you said and did at Banff and am entirely of your opinion, notwithstanding of which I send an extract of my letter to Lord Findlater of the 28th. May, in which you will observe that I have not named you because his Lrp. knew you was not of his opinion, and I write as from my self only hinting that I thought it proper to consult Troup etc. - though I consider this as money absolutely and unnecessarily thrown away; I am resolved to give it if his Ldp. upon what is suggested does not alter his opinion.
>
> I have no heart to look homeward in the present state of anarchy, and nothing worth writing from hence, the Russians will soon put an end to Polish Confederations as no forreign power takes any part, but it will not be so easy to extinguish the General Discontent and Disaffection in that Kingdom which however will hurt only themselves. Your Son has been a little indisposed, perhaps from eating too freely, and the Phisician thinks the Waters of Pyrmont may be better for his Complaint than any thing he can prescribe. I have therefore given him Leave to go to Pyrmont immediately and hope in a few weeks to receive him safe & sound as we

cannot both be absent at the same Time, I am to drink the Waters of Egra [Ezra?] here which have done good on former occasions.
My Compliments to all Friends and believe me etc. etc.
your oblig'd And. Mitchell.

There are several letters from Andrew Mitchell concerning his affairs and also with many references to local politics and the ensuing disagreements. Sir Arthur Forbes appears a choleric character and Lord Findlater seems to have disagreed with others fairly frequently, all the while remaining friends, of course! The gist of the next letter would lead us to suppose that Andrew Mitchell, who had been knighted in 1765, was preparing for difficulties in his re-election as the MP for the Elgin burghs:

Berlin, 18th February, 1769
My Dear Sir, The inclosed Letter to the Provost and Magistrates of Inverury will I hope give Satisfaction, and make them easy as to the Settlement of their Kirk. I cannot express to you what Pain this Affair has given me. Sir Arthur's Conduct surprised me, but as he has freely given up the Thing I think you should not only forgive but endeavour to forget what has happened...As to the Affair of Banff I am entirely of your Opinion as is our Friend Sir Arthur, but considering that Lord Findlater differed from us, I thought it proper to take Advice of Mr. Garden of Troup, who was of Opinion that if I subscribed one hundred Guineas for repairing their Harbour I acted very handsomely by them, and that they would think so too – I must therefore desire the Favour of you to pay One hundred Guineas into the Hands of the Provost of Banff for the above mentioned Purpose, if my Factor is not in Cash, let me know by return of the Post, and I shall send a Draft on Messrs. Drummond for the said Sum payable at Sight, and you will deliver the inclosed Letter to the Provost of Banff whose Name I do not know.

I have no News to write to you from hence – I am tolerably well, and your Son in so good Health he is very impatient and wants to go to Dinner so I have only Time to desire you to present my Compliments to your Lady and Family, and so assure you that

I am most sincerely yours etc.

And. Mitchell.

Needless to say that the letter on this occasion was written by the said impatient and hungry son!

The March of the following year involved George with a very unusual commission from his son:

Kemnay 10 March 1770

My dear Son, You will be surprised that you have been so long in receiving an Answer to your Bagpipe Commission: that you would have thought so easily executed. But I consulted so many Connoisures as involved me in Uncertainty; they made such different Commentaries on the Text of Mr. McInzie's Letter, that I found in the Multitude of Councillors there was. Polly [daughter Mary] and I had more than one Sett of Pipes, said to be the Thing wanted, the great McGrimmon must judge on Tryal. They are in Sir A. Mitchell's accounts charged 18 shillings & sent to Colin Donaldson to be forwarded by the first proper occasion; as it is more easy to send to London than to Leith from this, & an Occasion from the former to Hamburgh much oftener to be expected.

What passes at London I suppose you are as soon & possibly better informed than I am. Nothing, I am affraid, will you learn from that which can give any Satisfaction. O Temperat! O Mores! indeed!

You'd hear of the unfortunate Death of the E. Eglinton. Ld. Errol was elected in his Room. The Reason my mentioning which is, to tell you that the D. of Grafton, as upon other Occasions, wrote the Peers of Scotland, that as many of the Scottish Peers at Londn. thought Ld. Errol the fittest Person, he could not help giving him his good Wishes. Ld. Errol's Letter produced an Answer from the E. of Buchan so extraordinary that it was the Occasion of my mentioning this Election & is verbatim as follows:

'Lord Buchan presents his Compliments, the Earl of Errol is sorry to be obliged to acquaint his Lordship that as the Duke of Grafton has had the audacity, without the Participation of his Royal Master, to interfere in his Lordship's Election, by writing Letters to the Peers of Scotland among whom Lord Buchan has the Honour to be one; he cannot give Lord Errol his vote: Tho' he is very Indifferent about the Choice of the Peer, either now or at any other Time.'

This seems odd, it is so much so, that he had lately sent a Snuff Box with his Picture enriched with Diamonds, & embelished with Hymens Cupids entwined in most amorous Postures, as a Present to the Marishall College. It cost him 200 Guineas. Nor do I know, any single Circumstance that should have pointed out this University more than any other, whether he means to honour or to affront, or to show that he is m-d; for I shall expect to hear more about him.

But if Ld. B----- is m-d; what name will you give to the Sentimental Passion of Sir Archd. Grant & Mrs. Millar? for such each of this refined Couple declare the Passion to be, that is to unite them once in the Month of April. I don't know Mrs. Millar Sr. A. does. I hope they are congenial Souls, that as in this Life they are united, in their Death they may not be divided.

All the Family here are well & remember you with Love as well as

your affectionate Father,
Geo. Burnet.

Well, well! Such goings on in the Earldom of Marr!

In 1770 the Earl of Findlater died and George was particularly upset about the loss of one of his dearest friends. He wrote to Dr Lamont about his grief:

14. Jany. 1771

...When I wrote last, I forbore to mix the Sighs of a Heart in anguish with the Gratulations of the New Year, Sadly do I yet feel the Loss of my worthy Friend the Earl of Findlater. He so loved, he so trusted me – we were so United by Mutual Confidences and long Habits. He was at once possessed of all those Qualities that do Honour to the Head & Heart...that whyle I enjoyed many Advantages of his Friendship, I received the greatest honour in being distinguished by it above all the others. It gives me a melancholy sort of Pleasure to tell my Woes to my dearest, my best Friend. A Friend who I know has a feeling Heart. O were I but near you I might receive Comfort from your sympathising Tenderness & Your Cheerfulness might help to clear away the Gloom. May you & all you love be happy, & here the lovely Widow comes across. But how dare I think of her in such a gloomy Mood.

My dear Sir yr. affectionate Son & most obedient Servant,

Geo. Burnet.

My Wife & her Sister will have me tell you how particularly they remember you & my Girls too, O will not the dear Widow & You come here?

Troubles never come singly and on 28th January 1771, George's other great friend, and Alexander's benefactor, Sir Andrew Mitchell, died in Germany. One can be glad for George's sake that Dr Lamont outlived him or he would have been cast into an even deeper despair. His character seems to alter slightly after this time: there is not the same degree of humour and he is more prone to depression.

XVI

After the deaths of his two good friends, George became embroiled in the intricacies of politics. He felt that the vacancy created by Sir Andrew Mitchell's death would be ideal for his own son, Alexander. Intricate they certainly were and bear little relation to today's system of government. In order to make some coherency of the business, it is necessary to investigate the workings of the electoral formula of the times and whether any sense can be made out of such complicated and, at times, highly irregular measures, remains to be seen!

During the period 1760 to 1800, the House of Commons consisted of five hundred and fifty-eight members representing three hundred and fourteen constituencies, only forty-five of which were Scottish. These forty-five were composed of twenty-seven counties returning one member each; three pairs of counties, one county in each pair alternating with the other in returning one member; one burgh (Edinburgh) returning one member; fourteen groups of burghs, each returning one member. The burgh which concerns this story is the Elgin District which consisted of the burghs of Elgin, Banff, Kintore and Inverurie. Each burgh had a commander, patron or what you will but whoever he was, he more or less ordained how the votes were to be cast. Cullen was under the command of the Ogilvies, Earls of Findlater and Seafield. Kintore was commanded firstly by the third Earl of Kintore (who had so vehemently opposed George Burnet's election as Provost of Inverurie) and on the death of his brother, the fourth Earl, in 1761 the estates passed to the absent Earl Marischal and were administered for him by George Burnet who, of course, controlled the burgh of Inverurie. Elgin and Banff were open burghs. The old Earl of Kintore had said of them, "they depend on no particular person, but are determined some times one way, some times another, from different motives, and generally the candidate who gives the most money has the best chance of their votes." This explains quite clearly Sir Andrew Mitchell's gift of £100 to the Provost of Banff for the repair of their harbour! The Elgin burghs became vacant in 1754 when the sitting member, William Grant, was raised to the Bench and he offered his support to Andrew Mitchell on his vacating the seat.

After a considerable amount of argument and wheeling and dealing, Mitchell was elected in January 1755 and two months later made a donation of £300 to the Elgin burgh finances. But that was still in the future as at first Andrew Mitchell was member for the County of Aberdeen where he had been elected in 1747. He had attached himself to Henry Pelham and the Duke of Newcastle which gave offence to the Duke of Argyll, the "viceroy" for Scotland. Mitchell was appointed trade commissioner in Brussels and in his absence on the Continent, Argyll's hostility made his re-election in the next elections so uncertain that it appeared he would lose his place in Parliament. Newcastle insisted that he "must and should" stand for Aberdeenshire but after Pelham's death he was not anxious to oppose Argyll and persuaded Mitchell to withdraw his opposition to Argyll's candidate for the County. In Parliament Mitchell remained Newcastle's firm friend and ally. In 1756 he was appointed envoy to Prussia where, with Alexander Burnet as his secretary, he arrived shortly after the outbreak of the Seven Years War. He soon won the close friendship of Frederick the Great, whom he accompanied on most of his campaigns. In 1759 he was promoted plenipotentiary. Four years later he was angry and distressed at the withdrawal of the Prussian subsidy by the British Government but nevertheless obeyed his instructions at the price of losing his friendship with Frederick the

Great. Fortunately Alexander remained in favour. Despondent and with greatly deteriorating health, Mitchell returned to England in 1765, leaving Alexander in control of His Majesty's affairs at the court of Berlin. He attended the House and was reunited with his friends in the Rockingham administration who urged him to accept his re-appointment in Berlin. Andrew Mitchell was very reluctant to return, grieving over his lost friendship with the Prussian Monarch but in December 1765, on receiving his long-coveted KB and a pension of £500 for life, he agreed and returned to the court in Berlin in March 1766. Mitchell's ill-health dogged him for the remaining years in Germany although he was assisted always by the faithful Alexander and he became saddened by the conduct of his former 'hero', Frederick the Great. He died, a lonely and disillusioned man, in Berlin on 28th January 1771. His wife had predeceased him by many years and their only child, a daughter, had died when only a few years old.

On Mitchell's death, the vacancy for the Elgin burghs was contested by four candidates. The young Earl of Findlater was immediately besieged by many different people for his interest in the forthcoming bye-election but before giving his support to anyone, he made enquiries as to what Alexander Burnet's intentions were regarding the seat and was "assured that the Secretary of that Department had heard nothing of it and also that the Administration looked for your [George Burnet's] Assistance only in condition that your Son should be taken care of which was to be mentioned to His Majesty as Sir Andrew Mitchell's dying request." Having satisfied himself that Alexander was not interested, Findlater put forward the name of Thomas Lockhart, a young man from a Lanarkshire family which had produced numerous Members of Parliament since 1607. The Duke of Gordon likewise put up the name of his protegé, none other than his mother's second husband, Colonel Staats Long Morris. The other two hopefuls, Dalrymple of Cranstoun and Ross of Morangie, withdrew when they saw the colour of the opposition!

Not aware of this, George immediately wrote off to the Duke of Gordon, seeing the Findlater interest had been lost, seeking his assistance in securing the seat for his son. The Duke of Gordon replied "...it is not surprising to me that you should wish your Son to have succeeded Sir Andrew Mitchell in Parliament, but after having embarked for my friend Col: Morris I know you would not expect that I should alter my Plan." He went on to say that he expected

George's support and help for his Colonel. Lockhart, however, gained the support of the Administration and Morris withdrew and Lockhart was returned unopposed. The Gordon interest straight away began preparing and marshalling their forces to win the seat for Morris in the general election in 1774.

In April 1771 George received a letter from the new Lord Findlater:

> Yesterday morning I went to Ld. North by Appointment, who I made sensible of the Service you had been of to Government at different Periods, & I obtained Ld. North's Promise that You should be provided for as soon as any Pension or Place became vacant. My Ld. North absolutely refused to make any Addition to the Pension List, which he said he had long determined never to advise the King to increase. I have done everything in my Power for You & have got the most favourable Answer that could possibly have been expected. When there is any Vacancy among Scotch Places or Pensions I shall take Care that Ld. North be reminded of his Promise to me by some one of my Friends, as his Lordship paid me the Compliment of saying that what was to be done for You would be done entirely at my Request.

Young Findlater makes it abundantly clear to whom George will owe his pension. News of the eventual granting of this annuity to George was conveyed to him in a letter from Thomas Lockhart which rather implies that he was solely responsible for this munificence and looking for George's support in future elections! George replied, definitely on his high horse, and thanks Mr Lockhart for this

> ...Piece of agreeable Intelligence as well as for all the Pains you have had about it. At the same Time you must have the Indulgence to excuse me in explaining myself with some Freedom on your saying in yours that you expect to be enabled to assure Ld. North of my supporting you at the Genl. Elections; as I like to be explicit in order to prevent future Mistakes, I must say then, that tho' I have been much obliged to your Attention of putting my Ld. North's in mind of my Memorial, & of what he said at Lord Findlater's presenting it, yet you may remember you neither offered your Services nor did I accept them respecting Futurity – &

> tho' I shall be very Glad if Occasions so present themselves, as will permit to show you any Mark of my Good Will that you could wish, yet I am so far from coming under any Engagements what I want you should believe that I must in Relation to future Events, be determined by Circumstances that I can neither foresee nor suppose at such a Distance. I shall be happy if, in passing my Path, I shall fall in with yours.

As mentioned earlier, the Gordons were rallying support for Colonel Staats Long Morris in preparation for the next general election. Morris, from a wealthy colonial family, was born in 1728, a son of Lewis Morris, judge of Admiralty Court, New York and Tryntie, daughter of Dr Samuel Staats, a surgeon also of New York. He served in the French and Italian wars under General William Shirley, governor of Massachusetts, who sent him to England with despatches in December 1755. This brief visit completely altered his career as he met and married the eccentric Dowager Duchess of Gordon, who had long been seeking a personable young husband. She was the mother of six children and ten years his senior. After a short visit back to America, he returned to Scotland and established himself as the Dowager's consort at Gordon Castle. The English Chronicle of 1781 says of him: "He conducted himself in this new exaltation with so much moderation, affability, and friendship, that the family soon forgot the degradation the Duchess had been guilty of by such a connexion, and received her spouse into their perfect favour and esteem." Colonel Morris also appears to have made himself generally liked in the county.

In the meantime, Thomas Lockhart, who did not enjoy good health, was ill in London when nominations for the election were made and it was uncertain whether he would stand again or whether his place would be taken by Alexander Burnet. George, anxious still to secure the nomination for his son and knowing that the Findlater interest was most definitely in Lockhart, sought help from the Duke of Fife who was the Member for Banffshire. History does not relate what he said in his letter but he happened to be writing to Lady Findlater, widow of his old friend, at the same time. So intent was he on furthering his son's chances that he appears to have suffered from a mental aberration and got the letters mixed up. His note to the Duke of Fife was addressed to Lady Findlater and James Duff

(Fife) received his letter to the poor lady! She made a great how-de-do about it and took everything as an insult to herself, her family and the memory of her late lamented husband and George was called all the most monstrous adjectives a lady of her standing could muster. The first that George knew of his crime was the following letter from Fife:

Duff House, Oct. 23. 1774

Dear Sir, I wrote to you last Fri. but as I imagine that my letter may lay some days at Aberdeen I thought it best to write to you by Express. I informed you that the letter you wrote to me, by mistake you directed to Lady Findlater, the other for me was sent to her. Since Friday I have seen Lady Findlater and you cannot believe what Pain I feel for this very unlucky Affair. I do assure you at present that I have neither Candidates in view, but looks to nothing but what appears to me to be for your own Happiness and Interest. From the Engagements and long Habitts you stand in with Lord Findlater, and from the Interest that Government has taken in this matter I really feel that your taking a Part against them will Injure your Mind and hurt your Interest; which I do see to be the greatest Consequence to him and very clear Road to it, and this fatal step entirely shuts it up; I also fear that Lord North will resent it as I know he did interest himself very warmly for Mr. Lockhart. May I therefore suggest, my Good Friend, that the properest Thing for you would be to keep the City of Inverury intirely Clear of this Election and leave it to the other four Townes to settle the Member, indeed I have no earthly Motive but my Good Will to You, Proceeding from the Friendship you have always shown to me since I have had the Pleasure of your Acquaintance; I am certain if you do not go to the Election will entirely attach Lady Findlater to you, and will prevent any bad Consequences from Above. I hope you will forgive the Freedome of this Letter, which I am confident you will see can Proceed from nothing but Friendship to your Family. My best Compliments to your Son and all at Kemnay

...Fife.

The contest in the end was between Morris and Lockhart and the latter who "was very much indisposed and confined to his house in London" was not present at the election and was defeated. Morris stood again in 1780 and was returned but blotted his copy book by being absent from the House on too many occasions and lost the seat in 1784 to William Adam.

XVII

Janet Dyce's diary unfortunately is not in my possession and the typescript given me by her several greats great nephew is almost entirely given up to the weather and the sowing of crops and harvests with very little, if any, family gossip. On one occasion she mentions that one of the tenants "Jimmy Brownie shot a young Dear on Lochshangie" and I do hope her spelling was faulty! She also mentions "the new roof finished" but as there is no more information as to which part of the roof it was, it is not very helpful. The diary begins in 1758 and the weather conditions do not appear greatly different from our own times. Some of the types of fruit grown cause speculation as to the possibility of their hot weather being better than ours. I have chosen the following excerpts as being of a certain interest.

In 1768 June was solidly wet and July the same. August produced a fine week or two before a wet September which resulted in the "greatest overflowing of the River Don ever seen". The middle of January 1773 the "mercury fell so Low to be almost out of sight and a pretty loud Wind that day the next calm. 20th. from 8 to 10 o-clock a violent Wind Blowd down four hundred trees at Kemnay." At the end of the first week of January 1776 the snow started to fall but there had been a sufficient thaw for ploughing to start on 8th February. More snow followed and the drifts were so deep "no wheel Carriage could go from Kemnay to Aberdeen nor any Place round." Interestingly, the storm was "more severe in England and the snow lay deeper to the north and south." When the weather did clear "the Trees were most remarkably full flourished and every Shrub beautiful." A frost in May caught the plums and pears but the apples escaped damage. They cut a fresh cucumber on 26th May and that Autumn Kemnay had more apples than they could use and what they sold "yielded but 10 pence for two slicks of the corn peck." Janet tells us at regular intervals when and where the various ice-houses were filled and also mentions that they were able to have ice-cream with their strawberries!

The year 1779 seems to have been an extraordinary one. The snow did not last and January began with dry, frosty weather and sunshine "and on 18th. we filled our low Ice House from the water in the Wilderness". A thaw followed and the "mavis was singing strongly once more." A little more snow fell and hard frost with fine, clear, sunny days remained until the end of January when there was another thaw followed by a day of fog. Then they had a "month of fine warm mild clear weather, sometimes a little windy but no ways disagreeable. Anybody might have sown their Ground if they pleased after the first week of February." They themselves were not tempted to do this as they thought it too soon to start although they did begin to sow the oats by the 27th. "All the Flowers in the Pastures were blown as fully as if the end of April" and the cherry blossom was right out. March came in as it should with "loud Winds" succeeded by foggy weather but still warm, "the 7th. a little frost in the Night, the only touch of frost for a Month past. Grass Parks green and so long that the young Cattle were put out and left at Night. Rose bushes, gooseberry bushes etc. all green and some trees of Hawthorn." A field of turnips was in flower "and yellow all over". The remarkable "warm and mild" weather was interrupted on the 22nd March by three days of "loud Wind" from the south but no rain. The ditches were almost too dry. She mentions all the other fruit trees being in full bloom and the strawberries were also flowering and flowers were showing on the garden peas. The geans at Kemnay were in full flower but "the old ones at Castle Fraser so advanced the blossom was ready to drop at the least puff of wind." By now the pears were "set as bigg as peas" and cherry plums even larger. "17 and 18 Kemnay sowed his Bear" and then the weather changed on the 28th. The frost was "stronger" and snow fell on the hills with hail at Kemnay. On the following day heavy rain fell, the drought was broken and they had just finished sowing their bear seed. After frost at night, May Day dawned with wind and hail and during the night there was a heavy fall of snow which lay "to a depth on level ground of three and a half inches." The gardener immediately took the opportunity of filling the ice house at the top of the hill. The trees were all loaded with snow as in the depth of Winter and it was very odd to see the honeysuckle, "the reid Apple Blossom and the scarlet Cones of Firs all peeping through the Snow." The snow vanished overnight,

however, and on 8th May they ate their first salad cucumber and young turnips. Throughout the month the weather was changeable so that it seemed "from the middle of April to the middle of May everything seemed to go back or stand still."
It was in June in this year that Janet described a water spout in the Wilderness:

> The 2d. Sitting by the Watter in the Wilderness we seed a Piller of Watter Rise as high as the talest Tree & fall doun again, after which it Rolld along for a Considerable space in large Rolls, as if a Vast Cask had been under the Watter, & out of those Rolls, sprung up small strins of Watter, Rising pritty high, as out of the Strup of a Razer – The Noise it made was such as a Fire work of Powder makes when first sett off, but much louder – The Day was clear, fine sune shine & not a Breath of Wind.

By 10th June it was like winter again with rain, snow and hail. Three days later the ice house which had been filled in January was opened and it was "quite full of Ice – had Strawberries for our ice Cream." In July temperatures built up to the "hottest day One remembers" and thunder storms accompanied by heavy rain ensued. Two men and two horses were killed by lightning some miles from Aberdeen on the Banchory road. It was excessively hot until the end of the month. A visit to Gordon Castle on the 19th revealed that their plums were ripe, their early apricots over and a second kind ready! In spite of the hot weather it was discovered that the snow in the ice house, which had been filled on 3rd May, was "much in the same State as when putt in," and it froze their ice cream very well. The thunder storms continued through the month and rainy weather persisted until 1st August when a night of frost did some damage to the peas. The rainy weather lasted into the second week when it cleared and the harvest began. Hot, dry weather allowed the work to proceed smoothly. By the end of the month the pears and apples were all ripe and falling off the trees. Some slight showers at the beginning of September did not even hinder the shearing which was finished on the 15th. Two days later the harvest was finished and the stacks thatched. Fine dry and pleasant weather at the beginning of October, accompanied by strong winds, made the ground, after the heavy rain at the end of September, too hard to be ploughed. All these unusual conditions had a bad effect on the fruit which did not keep: "the Nonesuch and keeping Apples all rotten and spoilt. This Autumn we had many Trees as full of Blossom as in Spring, their Fruit sett and on 14th. this Month Novr. we pulled some Apples as large as a small Golden Pippin - before the Snow came the Strawberries were in full Bloom." The winter began early with snow from the middle of November and very hard frosts, so hard in fact to "allow Them to walk over the River Don on the Ice." Blizzards followed in December and the whole month was stormy. 1780 began with a brisk thaw but ensuing clear days brought sharp frosts once more. The mercury may well have plunged out of sight again as many things in the house were frozen, including "a large Jar of double distill'd Peppermint Water which was in the Garret, but not near a Window." During this spell Janet noted that horses and carts were able to cross the Don on the ice for several weeks. A cold and miserable spring followed with the "gab o' May" wrecking havoc as usual and work on the fields progressed slowly. Three nights of frost in early June caused "ice on the Pools and Beech and Ash Trees were withered like Snuff and many Things visibly Destroyed."

In the middle of this catastrophe Janet and George went over to Pannanich Lodge on Deeside near Ballater for a week's stay. Had the cold and dismal weather affected George's health, I wonder? He had suffered from a cough before and shortness of breath. They returned home on 28th July and the weather changed for the better and August was warm and dry which enabled the work in the harvest fields to start by the 20th of the month. Conditions remained good and the harvest was completed by the end of September and was much better than expected. The yield from the garden had been extremely good and the gardener had sold a lot of produce. George's last harvest must have pleased him. Nothing tells us what happened during the last month of his life. Nothing tells us how he died. Nothing tells us the cause. Janet just stopped her diary, only returning to it in May of the following year after she had moved from Kemnay to her old home at Disblair where she lived with her sister until the latter's death, after which she went to live in Aberdeen. She visited Kemnay now and then and remained on good terms with her step-children.

George died here at Kemnay on 30th October 1780 and was buried in the Parish Church. George, whom I have got to know so well through his letters. Like a diamond with many facets, his character shines through all his descendants; indeed some of them might as well pale into insignificance. I love his sense of humour and imagination. I love his sense of fairness and justice. I love his humanity; he is so real because of his faults. And I love his legacy which I see every time I look out of a window or walk into the garden.

George's spirit is still very much alive in all that he created.

ALEXANDER

My Great-great-great-grandfather, Alexander, born on 3rd July 1735, has very thoughtfully supplied me with a brief resumé of his early days when, after completing his education at the University of Leyden like his grandfather, he embarked upon his diplomatic career. His extreme youth is tied up with his father's story but, unlike George's young days, there is no detailed record of his childhood. I give here a copy of his own words, written in beautiful copperplate.

> When Sir Andrew Mitchell was appointed Minister by the Late King in the Year 1756, to the Court of Berlin, I went abroad with Him as his Secretary, and attended Him, in that Capacity, in the several Campaigns He made with the Prussian Army, during that War, to the Hazard of my Life on different Occasions – From the Numerous Enemies The King of Prussia had to make Head against the Fatigue was very great owing to the Velocity with which that Monarch was obliged to transport Himself from one Country to another, to stem the Torrent and defeat the Designs of His Powerfull Adversaries; And above all what added to the Fatigue was the Load of Business, which, from the Nature of Things, and the Posture of Affairs, attended that Mission, as Sir Andrew Mitchell's voluminous Dispatches to His Majesty's Ministers at home and abroad almost all of which are in my own Hand Writing, for I had no Assistant, can bear Witness. At the End of the War I was, by the Advice of the Faculty, obliged to go to Pyrmont to drink the Waters and make Use of the Bath there for the Recovery of my Health, being very much reduced and Weakened by the Fatigue I had undergone. On Sir Andrew Mitchell's Recall from the Court of Berlin in the Year 1765, I was charged with His Majesty's affairs at that Court, in which Station I continued until His Return to Berlin 1766.
>
> Upon his Death in 1771 I was again honoured with that Character, in which I continued till Mr. Harris' Arrival at Berlin in the Month of February 1772, when, having received Orders to return Home, I left that Court and arrived the same Year in the Month of April in London, with my Health greatly impaired, not having Recovered the Effects of the Prussian

Campaigns. On my Arrival I waited on Lord North and the Earl of Suffolk, His Majesty's Ministers, and being, from my State of Health, rendered incapable of accepting of any Employment in the Line I was in, I sollicited a Pension of Four Hundred Pounds Sterling as a Reward for sixteen Years severe Service to which I esteemed myself the more entitled as Sir Andrew Mitchell in a Paper relating to Me, wrote in His own Hand and subscribed by Him in His last Moments, of which I am in Possession, concludes with the following words "And, as He, Alex Burnet, had the Honour to serve His Majesty with Zeal and Affection I take this Opportunity of Recommending Him to some Mark of His Majesty's Affection and Favour." The Equity of the Claim was admitted, but I was told that my Father was promised a Pension for Services performed to Government by Him and His Father, there would be an Impropriety in granting one at the same Time to the Son.

Accordingly in the Month of October, 1772, My Father obtained a Pension of £200 per Annum. and I remained without any Reward for my Services until November, 1776, when a Pension of £200 was offered which I accepted of in part till my Father's Death, having always understood from General Morris, who laid my Claim before and enforced it with a Minister, That when that Event happened, which I prayed God might long award, I should receive his Pension which, in addition to my own, made £400 the Sum I sollicited for my Services, Which, after having spent sixteen Years, the prime of my Life, in so hazardous and laborious a Mission and in which my Health greatly suffered, will not, I hope, be deemed by His Majesty's Ministers an unreasonable Request. I therefore humbly beg Leave to recommend My self to Them for this Mark of His Majesty's most gracious Favour and Approbation of my Services.

Sir Andrew Mitchell's "Paper" mentioned above is a very legal document, duly stamped – Vier Groschen – and witnessed by a Councillor and Notary to the King of Prussia, says a little more than Alexander was prepared to tell His Britannic Majesty's ministers, and who could blame him? "I promise to pay to Alexr. Burnet younger of Kemnay the Sum of Three Thousand Pounds Sterling for his faithful

Services performed by him during the space of fifteen years in full of all demands as witness my hand at Berlin the tenth day of December, 1770, and as he had the honour to serve His Majesty with Zeal and Affection I take the opportunity of recommending him to some mark of His Majesty's affection and favour.

Andr. Mitchell."

Where Alexander has confined sixteen years of his life to a couple of pages, the events he experienced and the people he met with during those years cannot be glossed over in as many words.

II

When Alexander arrived in Berlin in 1756 with Andrew Mitchell the scene was already set for war. Storm clouds in the shape not only of Maria Theresa of Austria and Louis XV of France but also Russia and Sweden, whose Queen was Frederick the Great's own sister, were threatening little Prussia. Maria Theresa had never forgiven Frederick for taking Silesia and had not hesitated in allying herself with France and when it was rumoured that Augustus III of Saxony was also joining forces with the enemy, Frederick made up his mind to take the offensive.

Andrew Mitchell made an instant good impression upon Frederick when he presented himself at court in Berlin. No other British Minister had been so well liked and he became one of the King's greatest friends. It may be that the Scots from this particular corner had qualities which appealed to Frederick the Great. General the Hon James Keith who had fought in the Russian army and led them to victory against the Turks, had become disenchanted with the uncertainties of serving Russia and escaped to Berlin where he offered his services to Frederick who was happy to welcome such a superb soldier. James Keith belonged to the Keith family of Keith Hall not far from Kemnay and were well known friends of the Burnets. He was also younger brother to Lord Keith, hereditary Earl Marischal of Scotland who was living in poverty following his escape from Scotland. He had been an ardent supporter of the Old Pretender and had taken part in the 1715 Rising. Exasperated by the confusions of that ill-fated campaign, he had escaped in 1719. His lands were confiscated by George I and he was condemned to death. His title of Earl Marischal could not be taken from him however, and he was always referred to as 'Lord M'. Although he always remained faithful to James VII, he would not allow himself to be called a Jacobite: he could not abide them and had no time for Charles Edward Stuart. James Keith begged leave of Frederick to bring his elder brother to Berlin to the court of Prussia. Frederick granted this request and came to have the warmest affection for Lord M who became his intimate friend until his death in 1778. Lord M was able to return to his native land after George II pardoned him in 1769 and at one time he returned to Keith Hall but did not remain there for very long and had no opinion of life in Aberdeenshire!

Andrew Mitchell had advised the Prussian King to write to Maria Theresa asking if the gathering of troops on the borders meant war as it would indicate and the reply he received was non-committal and evasive. At the end of August 1756, Frederick sent an ultimatum to Augustus III insisting on his remaining neutral, and marched to Dresden. Frederick's bombardment of Dresden is lamented in a letter written later to Alexander by James Boswell. The Battle of Lobositz in October gave Frederick a temporary hold on Saxony but he had lost his element of surprise and further operations were postponed until the Spring. Sorties made in April against the Austrians were successful and in May he marched on Prague. There ensued a very hard and bloody battle and Frederick lost one of his oldest and most trusted generals, Schwerin, whose death he mourned greatly. The victory cost him dear. Andrew Mitchell was appalled at the carnage of the battle fields and Alexander wrote of the 'horreurs' in his nightly dispatches. What an initiation for the young man!

At Kolin in June, Frederick's armies suffered a crushing defeat and misfortunes abounded on all sides. He was prostrated by the news of the death of his mother, Sophie Dorothea. A Russian army pouring into East Prussia defeated his only ally, the Duke of Cumberland commanding an Anglo-Hanoverian force. In the weeks that followed Frederick marched his armies in the manner described by Alexander and many of his men died from exhaustion. Disaster followed disaster and still it seemed that there was no hope of success. In November, however, the battle of Rossbach was a victory and at Leithen in December the Prussian monarch was again victorious. Frederick and his escort put up at Breslau for the winter. In June the next year Frederick's nearest brother and heir, Augustus William, died from a brain tumour. The brothers had never been overfond of each other, Frederick having always loved his sister, Wilhelmine, more than anyone, but nevertheless he was very downcast. Augustus

William's son, Frederick William, became Prince of Prussia. Events went against Frederick after this and he lost a convoy of supply wagons and all the men defending it. The Russian General was advancing towards the Oder and his troops were committing appalling atrocities. Frederick attacked the Russians at Zorndorf where there was a particularly gruesome battle which lasted days. The Prussian army was exhausted and demoralised and had the Russians attacked again they would have carried off a victory but their lack of supplies prevented further offensives. There were 11,000 Prussian dead and 20,000 Russian and it was here on this battlefield that Alexander found the little silver cup that he kept as a souvenir. He had it engraved "Taken up by A.B.Esq., on the field of Zorndorff the day of the battle, 28th. August, 1758." Things looked black indeed and in October at Hochkirch the Austrian troops fell on the Prussian camp and slaughtered them in their tents. Frederick lost five generals and also James Keith and his brother-in-law, Francis of Brunswick. On the very same day his beloved sister died, the most crushing blow fate could have dealt him. The battle of Kunersdorf in August 1759 was one of the worst defeats the Prussians suffered. Their losses were horrific. There was now nothing to stop the allies occupying Berlin. Frederick sent a message to the Queen to take his archives and go to Potsdam or Brandenburg. Frederick and his decimated battalions placed themselves at Furstenwalde between Berlin and the enemy forces. But apparently the allies were falling out amongst themselves and did nothing to follow up their victory. The Russians went home for the winter and the Austrian general shut himself up in Dresden. Frederick and his entourage spent the winter at Freiburg and he busied himself with trying to reform his army. Nobody had any hopes for the coming year. Frederick tried to retake Dresden and subjected the town to a fearsome bombardment to no avail. The situation was dire and Andrew Mitchell and Alexander burnt their papers. However, Frederick's commander at Breslau besieged by the Austrians refused to surrender and had the satisfaction of seeing the besieging army withdraw. In the middle of August, a drunken Irishman with a grudge against the Austrians deserted to Frederick's camp and told him that the Austrian general was planning to attack the camp that night. Frederick silently withdrew his troops leaving some peasants to keep the camp fires burning. The enemy attacked at daybreak and found the camp empty. The Prussians fell on their flank and took many prisoners. In October of that year the Russians were at the gates of Berlin. After holding out for five days the brave city was forced to capitulate. Every one was surprised that the Russians behaved themselves in a civilised manner. The Austrian army apparently did not. Charlottenburg was sacked and many valuables stolen but luckily the Potsdam palaces were safe. In November Frederick was victorious over the Austrian forces at Torgau and the King and his escort, Mitchell and Burnet included, spent a pleasant winter at Leipzig. But then George II died and with him all the good will towards Frederick. Andrew Mitchell sent worried dispatches to Lord Bute. Everyone expected Berlin to fall. Fate now took a hand and Elizabeth, the Empress of Russia, died. Her nephew and heir, the mad Peter III, worshipped the King of Prussia. He ordered his troops to put themselves under his command and all the Russian conquests were to be returned. This seemed too wonderful to last and it was because Peter was strangled by order of his wife, a German princess who used to play with the younger Prussian princes and princesses! The following year she had Ivan VI murdered and from then ruled supreme until her death. She was, of course, Catherine the Great. Fortunately for Frederick, she found letters from him to Peter, telling him he should treat her better so, although she withdrew her army, she did not resume the war against him and ordered her forces to return home.

Austria was now left alone as France had already capitulated and signed the Treaty with Britain at Fontainebleau in November 1762. Austria, Prussia and Saxony signed peace terms at Hubertusburg in February 1763. Frederick himself never recovered his health after this war which is not to be wondered at and it is not surprising that both Alexander Burnet and Andrew Mitchell felt in need of a rest cure too.

This, then, is the picture against which one should set Alexander's brief account of his initial sojourn in Prussia. All the different states which made up the larger being the backdrop for so many of his letters and from which his friends wrote to him. Alexander too kept little notebooks which give the distances between the different states and he also had a most interesting book with beautifully coloured illustrations of the uniforms of the different regiments in Frederick's army. I imagine he must have acquired it after the war although it would have been very useful in distinguishing the various troops during the hostilities.

III

The Berlin Years

Back in Berlin after his rehabilitating spell at Pyrmont, Alexander made up for the hardships endured accompanying the Prussian monarch and settled gladly into diplomatic circles in Berlin where he made many friends. Sir Andrew Mitchell had already hinted that he was somewhat interested in food – a trait that has been passed down I fear – and it must be borne in mind that he was only twenty-seven and could be forgiven for sowing a wild oat or two! Besides the little silver cup he picked up at Zorndorf, he also acquired a self-portrait of Frederick the Great's father, Frederick William. This monarch had suffered an hereditary disease which drove him mad with intolerable suffering. It is now known as porphyria and its symptoms are some of the most horrible to bear. Frederick William was a strange man anyway but whilst suffering from these agonies, he became quite violent and uncontrollable. He also used to paint portraits of himself during attacks and entitled them "in tormentis". Judging by the one we have, he certainly appears to be suffering. As has been said, he was an extraordinary man and the result was that both Frederick and his sister, Wilhelmine, had the weirdest of childhoods and were treated with unnatural cruelty. All these early experiences must have influenced Frederick's character, which could at times be quite incomprehensible. He married, to please his father, the Princess Elizabeth of Brunswick-Wolfenbuttel. Frederick William became very fond of his daughter-in-law and gave her the palace of Schönhausen in Berlin. Great was his disappointment when no child and heir was born. Frederick William had bought his son the property at Rheinsberg and there was also the Charlottenburg Palace, a garden residence near Berlin that had been built for Sophie Charlotte, sister of George I, who had married the King of Prussia and was Frederick the Great's grandmother. Going back to Thomas Burnet's time, the reader will remember that Sophie Charlotte wrote a letter to him saying how glad she was that he had been freed from imprisonment in the Bastille. She was a charming person and a great patron of the arts and friend of Leibnitz.

In 1740, Frederick William died in fearful torment. Frederick himself had already had his first attack of the same disease and thereafter never enjoyed perfect health again. After his father's death he virtually separated from his wife. Occasionally they lived under the same roof and he always took her with him when he went to Rheinsberg but in 1744 he gave the place to his brother, Henry. The Queen never saw Sans Souci which was Frederick's special residence at Potsdam although I have been told that she did secretly visit it. She received all the honour due to her at the palace in Berlin or at Schönhausen where she spent the summer. It will be noted in many of Alexander's letters that he mentions that the King was "still at Potsdam" and he showed his preference for male company.

Alexander was fond of beautiful things and his favourite snuffbox was probably acquired at this time. It is a fine French silver-gilt one and enamelled in brilliant colours of blue and green, it can be seen in his portrait at his elbow. One of his idiosyncrasies was a fondness for "west coats". There are any number of receipts for these garments, including one which reads "To the West Coat ...12 louis d'or" which I firmly believe refers to his very best state occasion waist coat, a most gorgeously embroidered affair, encrusted with gold trimmings. It has always reminded me of that picture in "The Tailor of Gloucester of the beautiful coat with the tiny message, "No More Twist", pinned to the unfinished button-hole! You can still find some snuff in the pockets.

In August 1764, Andrew Mitchell left Berlin for Spa: "Mr. Mitchell, having obtained His Majesty's gracious Permission to drink the Waters at Spa for the Recovery of his Health, and to go from thence into England, set out from this Place for Spa the 19th of this Month", wrote Alexander. "He was ordered to leave me here to carry on the Correspondence between the Two Courts during his Absence." Alexander, who always kept copies of letters written, at this particular stage began writing them all in a book, or rather six books. As they have therefore remained flat and unfolded, they are in excellent condition. These books begin with the first letter on 21st August 1764 to the Earl of Sandwich:

> My Lord, I have the Honour to transmit to your Lordship the inclosed Letter from Mr. Mitchell who set out from this Place last Sunday in the Afternoon for Spa by the Way of Capel and Francfort upon the Main...

and ends with the last letter written at the end of his tour of office on 3rd March 1772 to Lord Cathcart in St Petersburg, and so span the entire time he was a Chargé d'Affaires. Together with the bundles of letters that he received, it is possible to build a very real picture of political life in Britain and Germany during those years immediately after the Seven Years War, and is fascinating reading.

Alexander wrote daily to Andrew Mitchell while the latter was at Spa apprising him of every matter, both private and political. A colourful and important figure at this particular time was Lord Keith and Alexander wrote that the Lord Marischal had lately arrived in Berlin and that he had waited upon him and acquainted him of the commission Andrew Mitchell had charged him with. Lord M "accepted of the offer you had made him of your Equipage but with regard to the house he now has a lodging of his own in Berlin... and as for the Cook he told me he had no use for him. Mrs. Froment added 'he loves a cook maid better.'" On 28th August he wrote

> Two days ago Mr. Boswell returned from Brunswick, he expressed great Surprise and Concern at not finding you here. He told me that he had received a Letter from his Father and that he stood much in need of your Advice with Regard to the Measures he was now to take, that his Father had given him Leave to make a Jaunt into France, but that he was uncertain whether he might not go and Pay a Visit to the several small Courts in Germany, then take a Tour through Switzerland, France and so Home; I asked him if his Father did not rather seem desirous of his returning to Scotland as soon as possible – He answered he did above all Things, and preferable to travelling any more, upon which I said it was my Advice that he ought instantly and cheerfully to comply with His Father's Desire. This he said he was resolved to do, but that he much wanted your Assistance and Advice. I desired him to write to you and I would forward his letter, he replyed he would think of it --- I then asked him if his Father had not sent him inclosed a Letter for you, he said he had and putting his Hand in his Pocket he drew out the inclosed Letter desiring me to forward it by the first Post. -- According to the Directions you gave me I have perused the Letter and talked with the Young Man in the Stile you suggested, and I am very glad to be able to assure you that in the Present Moment he seems firmly resolved to comply in every Thing with His Father's Intentions, but how long he

may continue in this Mind it is impossible to say for I can observe that the continued series of Amusement and Dissipation he enjoyed during the thirteen Days he stayed in Brunswick together with the kind Reception he met with from that Family, has given him such a Taste for travelling and Dissipation that he talks of nothing but of making the Tour of all Europe and then settling to Business. I invited him to dine with me this Day on purpose to talk more fully to him, and I have represented to him in as strong a Light as I could the necessity there was for his complying with his Father's Desire and the fatal consequences it might be to him if he acted otherwise. He entirely agreed with me: and he said he would write to you upon the Subject of his future Plan, that from your Goodness and Kindness to him he was the more encouraged to do so with freedom and that he would always pay the greatest Deference to whatever Advice you would be pleased to give him, accordingly he has sent me the inclosed Letter. Notwithstanding however, all these Assurances of Obedience etc. I can easily perceive it will be very difficult to get him to return home unless You was to allure him to come to Spa with the idea of seeing Bruxelles with you, and so carry him over to England. I have not given the most distant hint of this Insinuation to him and I ask Pardon for mentioning it to you, which I should not have done had it not been for a desire of saving this worthy and deserving young Man for it is the only means that occurrs to me...

Boswell frequently "dined Burnet" and drove in the park with him. Alexander took him to visit the Lord Marischal at Potsdam with whom they "had the honour of eating an olio". They were shown the palace at Sans Souci and the garden there and Boswell was much impressed and admired Frederick the Great's study and bedchamber. They also inspected the site of the house that monarch was building for the Earl Marischal. Alexander introduced him to many notable personalities, with the exception of the Prussian Monarch as will be understood in the following letter.

Saturday, 8 Sept. 1764
Yesterday Mr. Boswell desired me to give his Compliments to you and to forward the inclosed Letter from his Father. I have had much conversation with the young Man, his Desire for travelling increases daily, and I can observe the more his Inclination is indulged the greater Reluctance he will have to settle in the Way of Business his Father has planned out for him. He teases me to get him presented to K.P. but I find he makes such absurd Distinctions between Englishmen and Scotchmen which are increased and strengthened by what Ld. M. says to him, that I am certain something very ridiculous would happen on that Occasion. He has told me that he must be presented as a Scotchman and that if H.P.M. should ask him such trifling questions as he generally does to Strangers, He would fairly desire him to speak to him as a Scotchman and not as an English man for that Ld. M had said to him that K.P. had a greater Esteem and Value for his countrymen than for the English. You may easily judge after this if it would be prudent to have him presented. The young Gentleman is much out of humour with the good old man for not presenting him himself and says he cannot comprehend My Ld.'s Timidity in this Affair especially as he lives with the Great man on the footing of a most intimate friend; that he imagined through his means he should have seen and talked with K.P. with the greatest freedom and familiarity, otherwise he would never have accompanied him to Berlin. Boswell tells me Ld. M has just made him a present of the Life and Acts of Robert Bruce, a very ancient Book, and that before he gave it him he wrote on it with his own hand Scotus Scoto which he said was the highest Compliment could be paid him – for my Share I think the Old Man dotes in earnest – Tother Day Ld. M. asked me if your Glouster Cheeses were come, and if they were to send him one, as he said you had promised it, but Dony tells me you ordered him to distribute none without order, so I shall wait to know your Intentions.

Boswell, of course, did not obey his father's instructions as will be seen from the following letters written to Alexander.

Leipsic 14 Octr. 1764

Dear Sir

Would you not laugh if I should formally return you thanks for the many civilities which you was kind enough to show me at Berlin? I am affraid you would; and therefore I restrain a very strong inclination. Let me however thank you for your letter to Mr. Stanhope whom I found extremely obliging. He presented me at court, and I dined with him twice. His table is good and his conversation agreable. Dresden is a charming Place. I wish the King would make me his Minister there. I should keep my Post with great Pleasure. It gave me great pain to see the ruins made by the Prussian Bombardments I think the Gothic Hero might have spared such an Addition to his Glory. I past three or four days last week in this City where I saw the Fair, and made Acquaintance with some of the Professors. I have been obliged to come back again in my way to Gotha. This in my Travels is a kind of Cross, I mean a Misfortune and were a Poem to be written in the manner of the Aneade describing my Journey from Berlin to Geneva this very circumstance would take up at least thirty lines. I'll go on with you as far as you please, but there is nothing which I hate so much as to retourner sur mes pas. We have no phrase for this so good as the french one.

Pray what have you made of the Spanish Gun? I am sorry that I forgot to have it tried before I left you. I would beg that you may yet take the trouble to try it, and tell me if it is a realy good one. If I remember right, the fellow asked only 20 Thalers for it. That is rather suspicious. It is for a friend and neighbour of mine that I am seeking for a Spanish Piece. He is anxious to have one, and I would give Six or eight guineas for one that I could depend upon. You will oblige me much if you will take the trouble to manage this affair for me. What think you of so much important talk about a Gun? I shall take the liberty to mention it to My Lord Marischal who perhaps may get me a genuine one. So dont purchase till you write to me. I wish you all happiness and I am with esteem

Sir
your Very Humble Servant
James Boswell.

I could wish to know if Mr. Mitchell has written to me. I shall be at Cassel till the 27, and at Francfort the 30.

Alexander's reply to this letter is dated 20th October 1764 (MS.Yale (C 704))

Dear Sir,

This Morning I received your letter of the 14th Instant, and I was extremely glad to hear by it of your being in good health, and that you was so kindly received by the English Minister at Dresden.

The inclosed Letter from Mr. Mitchell to you I received two days ago, he was by the last Accounts I had from him in perfect health and Spirits and proposed setting out from Spa in a few Days for England.

In answer to the important Paragraph in your letter about the Spanish Gun, I must tell you that I have had it tryed and that it did not answer my Expection so I would have you think no more of it – All your friends here are well and salute you kindly – Macpherson set out two Days ago from hence for Hamburg where he proposes to take a Passage for London, his Scheme is to get Employment in a New Highland Regiment which they talk of raising, and sending to America – I regret much your Absence, I have not had an honest and hearty laugh since you left me, which by the bye let me tell you is as necessary in My Opinion for the Conservation of health as a Copiosum. I ever am Dear Sir

Your most Affectionate frind
& humble Servant
A, Burnet.

Boswell's reply to Alexander's letter was not written until after Christmas and his arrival in Geneva.

Geneva 27 Decr. 1764.

Dear Sir,

Your letter with Mr. Mitchell's inclosed came safe. I am sorry that you have laughed so little since my departure. Perhaps the Beer which was productive of a Copiosum may also excite a laudable Misibility. When the Scots Twopenny froths we say it lauchs. Does your Prussian do the same? If so it must make you laugh according to Horace's rule Si vis me flere dolendum est primum ipsi tibi. Weeping and laughing are not so different as some People think. In the mouth of a canting Presbyterian Minister it is hard to know which is which. You may remember that I was very curious about the King of Prussia's Battles, in particular about their names. Above all I was anxious to know where he fought on a Plain. Shall I tell you why. I was writing an Heroic Epistle & wanted a rhime to Slain.

And at Colline or Zorndorf's wide Plain
No trace is left of all the Heroes slain.

I inclose a letter for Mr. Mitchell which I beg you may forward. I know not his Address and as my letter is of some consequence, I did not chuse to send it upon hazard.
Pray give my kind Compliments to honest Scott and hearty Wake. I hope you are now and then three merry boys all in a row. May your Punch be strong and your mirth loud.
And so Macpherson is gone. I fancy Lauchlan will not talk much of the pleasure of Berlin. I have past my time most agreably. I am just setting out for Italy.

Adieu Dear Sir
James Boswell.

P.S. I must tell you a bon mot of Voltaire's. He asked me 'Avez vous un Envoye à Berlin actuellement? - Non Monsieur nous n'avons qu'un charge d'affaires. Ah (said he) un chargé d'affaires est guere charge' How like you this? Are you angry at him?

Alexander must have missed this entertaining character and Boswell found him "a solid, clear-headed fellow, much better than myself."

IV

In the middle of September Alexander had written to Andrew Mitchell "By the last Mail from England I received two packets of Newspapers which were both directed to me as Chargé d'Affaires, but there was no letter with them only a short note from Mr. Larpent which ended 'Mr. Larpent begs Leave to wish Mr. B. all possible happiness and Success in his new Situation.' As I have no Letter neither from Mr. Phelps nor Lord Sandwich I am at a Loss what to make of this, and as those packets were directed to me as His M. Chargé d'Affaires here it was the next Day spread about Town that it was now certain."

He goes on to report the sale of Andrew Mitchell's horses and saddle and a very odd bit of news "I have this Moment received a Letter from Grant full of Compliments and good wishes to you, his health is much better but he notifies to me the afflicting News of Orion's Death, who died of a bite by a Mad Dog, and he requests that his Children & Relations with me may be put into Mourning – he had caused Orion's Skin to be stuffed..." Orion was one of the horses perhaps?

Amongst news of troop movements and the to-ing and fro-ing of H.P.M. and other court news, an assembly of the Knights of St John and who were to be new Knights, chit-chat regarding the Princess Amelia and affairs or romances of young men in the social circle of Berlin, the following letter is amusing:

> Baron Knyphausen came to me t'other Day in great Distress he told me his old Valet de Chambre had just received a Letter from Miss West dated 10th. inst. from Hamburg acquainting him of her arrival there and of her intention of setting out for Berlin to find the Baron. He begged of me to write to Mr. Nathins (agent at Hamburg) to intreat of him to use all possible Means with Miss West to dissuade her from coming here where she would neither find Him nor any of his Domestiques, he having undertaken a Long Journey which made His return Hither very uncertain, and to prevail with her to return to London. I have written the Letter and in the meantime the Baron is returned to Rhinsberg to be out of

the way. Poor Man What a foolish Scrap he has got into with this Girl...

At the beginning of October Alexander wrote

> I am extremely impatient to hear how you do – I am however a little Comforted by a Letter which Dony has received from Anthony (Dony and Anthony were Valets to Burnet and Mitchell) wherein he acquaints him that you were all very well but extremely busy in letting down & buttoning up your Breeches, which Occupation he says proceeds from the Effects of the Waters...

On 24th November a more newsy letter answers the cheese question to some extent:

> Last Thursday I had the Honour to dine at Margrave Henry's, when I executed the Commissions with which you was pleased to charge me. His R.H. desired me to express in the strongest Terms what Pleasure it gave him to hear your Health was so perfectly recovered, and how sensible he was of your Remembrance of him. He begged you would be persuaded of his sincere Friendship for you; and he returns you many Thanks for your Cheese and the 3 Dozen of Beer – I likewise made your Compliments to the young Princesses and their Governesses. They all of them talked of you with the greatest affection and desired to be remembered to you in the kindest Manner... Yesterday I dined with Prince Dolgoruki when I made your Compliments to him, he desired me to make his in Return and to tell you that he would very soon write to you. I at the same Time took the Liberty to make your Compliments to the Chancellor and his Lady which were extremely well received. She in particular bid me tell you that she regretted much not to have found you here, at Table she drank your Health... 27 November Last Saturday Evening Sir George Macartney His M's Minister to the Court of Russia, arrived in this Place. He has been presented to the Queen and the rest of the R. Family at Berlin, K of P still in Potsdam...Sir G. proposes to continue his Journey to Petersbourg sometime Tomorrow...I have been very often with him, and have been as serviceable to him as I could. He seems to be a pretty amiable, sensible, prudent young man.

Alexander's next letter seeks advice from Andrew Mitchell. He complains that the Princess Amelia is sending him over many letters to be sent under the Secretary of State's cover "all this is only to save the Expence of franking them here at the Post Office". He wishes "you would instruct me in your next how I am to behave in the Future."!!

His last letter of the year reports that "there are no Letters yet arrived from England owing to the Wind being contrary; We have had a great Fall of Snow and the Weather seems now to be settled, and set in for frost. It freezes at present as hard as in the year 1740."

In 1765 Alexander's appointment as Chargé d'Affaires was formally confirmed and he received the following note from Sir George Macartney: "It is with great pleasure that I learn his Majesty's determinations in your favor, & beg you'll accept my most sincere Congratulations. I esteem myself extremely happy in thus opening a Correspondence with you..." A very amiable young man! At the same time Andrew Mitchell received his knighthood and returned to Berlin in March 1766. As mentioned in George's story, Sir Andrew was a tired and disillusioned man at this time and not in the best of health and he relied on Alexander more and more. In his capacity of Chargé d'Affaires, the latter was kept well informed not only of the eventualities in different parts of Germany but also of what was taking place in the other European courts. There is a whole bundle of letters from Lord Stormont, the minister in Vienna, dating from 1765 to 1773 and the correspondence so happily opened by George Macartney in St Petersburg was continued eventually by his successor, Lord Cathcart, with whom Alexander also became very friendly. Trevor Corry was the consul in Danzig and some of his letters make very entertaining reading.

Here is one dated 30th April 1766:

> Dear Burnet, I am much obliged for all the News you have been pleased to Communicate, wish I had it in my Power to amuse you in the same way, but there is little stirring here worth notice, tho' it is pleasing that we have no further accounts of the Marienwerden Dutys being laid on again, so that matter will now probably remain quiet till the Diet meets in Poland. We have likewise had very fine weather here during the month past.

23 April 1766... sorry to aquaint you, that about 14 Days ago the Brigantine John & Jane belonging to Hull Joseph Brown Master bound to this Place, was Stranded on the Pomeranian Coast at a place called Rouve in the Amt of Schmolsin, on hearing which our Factory here (who were principally concerned with the Cargo) despatched Mr. James Balfour thither to assist the Captn. in getting the Ship off again, & very luckily the Cargo was got off all safe on Shore & the Ship a float & into deeper waters, where she now lyes in a Condition to take on her Cargo again." The only trouble being that the Amt Man at Schmolsin, requiring documents to show what part of the cargo was British property and what belonged to "Danzigers", was holding the cargo on the offchance. Apparently the previous year he had managed to collect vast dues from the cargo of another unfortunate ship that went aground and was hoping to repeat the performance. A stiffer resistance was put up on the second occasion!

Personal matters also crept into correspondence and a letter in July of the same year has a very different complexion.

St. Petersburg July 1766

Dear Sir, Will you give me leave to trouble you with a particular Commission & I beg that you would be so good as to enquire whether there is any good house at Berlin either of a clergyman or other discreet person where a young gentleman of fifteen might be properly placed in pension for a Year or two, where he might perfect himself in the Latin, French and German languages & learn the exercises and other polite accomplishments. The gentleman in question is a relation of mine, has past five years at Eton School, & is of a very mild and modest disposition. You will oblige me very much in informing me what you judge the expences attending this course of education will amount to per Annum. I must make a thousand apoologies for taking this Liberty with you...

Besides the letters from his colleagues throughout Europe, Alexander received mail from his superiors in London and from home, which included numerous ones from his agent and bankers. In the 1760's his agent in London was a Hugh Atkins who wrote frequently to inform him on a variety of subjects not least of which was the recurring purchases of Lottery Tickets – a chip off the old block obviously! These tickets appear to have cost £14. 1/8 and his accounts show that he was lucky on several occasions. Another letter from Mr Atkins dated London 6th July 1770 reads, "Yr. Box of China is gone to Kemnay but this weak and I took the Liberty of writing a few lines to your Father by Post wt. the Receipt for it. I hope it will come safe, it was unpacked at our Customs house but I put it up again with the utmost Care..." And well he may have done but not much of the china survives; in fact the only piece that I can truthfully say that Alexander purchased from the Berlin Porcelain Factory is a very pretty little pot pourri... Johann Ernst Gotzkowsky's factory was sold to Frederick the Great in 1763 and became known as the Royal Factory, and this little ornament dates from that time. I feel sure that a tactful purchase now and again would be essential for a Chargé d'Affaires.

There is a very odd letter from his sister Nellie at Kemnay:

> K. January the 24
> My Dearest Brother, ...Nellie wonders in her very bad spelling why her brother has not replied to her letter of "2 months ago" in which she confided some affair of the heart... as I would not chuse that any here know but your Self But I fully trust to your good intention towards me, and if in your power would resque me, and how soon in your power I bege of you, my Dearest Sandy, only relieve me so fare as to say you got the Letter...distil the Secrets of my heart into yours and hope you will not mention any thing to the person I am chiefly affraid of knowing what I wrot to you off as it would leave very bad Effects if he thought I had mentioned such a thing without consulting him. I am sorry I have nothing more entertaining to give you bit scarce heave seen a face since I wrote you. Invers son, Mr. Fraser has falen on to a noble Fortune by the Death of his uncle George Widney who was a most worthy Character and died worth forty thousand pound.
>
> Love and tender affection, Dr. Brother your Helen Burnet.

It would appear there was something she did not want her father to know!

The February of 1771 brought a flood of condolences about the death of Sir Andrew Mitchell. The Lord Marischal wrote from Potsdam in his usual forthright manner; "2 Feby, 1771...I am told the Dr. (as is often the case) mistook his ailing, took it to be in the bowells which was in the breast, I can well imagine what you suffer from so long a connection of friendship..."

There are letters from M. Coessener in Bonn, Lord Stormont in Vienna who also offered Alexander "help now or in the future"; L. de Viene in Munich, Hugh Atkins in London, Sir John Gooderick in Stockholm, Sir Joseph Yorke in the Hague, l'Abbe Hastiani in Potsdam. From London Lord Harrington lamented the loss of "the oldest and best friend I had in the world". From London too came a letter which illustrates Sir Andrew's kindness and generosity.

> It is impossible to express the grief at the account of the Death of our most worthy Friend Sir Andrew Mitchell. I sincerely condole with you on this melancholy occasion. As I never heard of his being sick, the suddenty of his Death affected the more strongly. I can easily conceive your feelings by my own, indeed whoever had the happiness of his acquaintance must always regret him, but we who had the opportunity of knowing the Value of the Man and the goodness of His Heart must feel his loss in a particular manner. I hope however, My Dear Friend, this unforeseen unlucky accident will not break off our Correspondence, as I shall always look upon it as one of the chief advantages of my going to Berlin, the pleasure and Happiness of your Friendship, and which I shall always be glad to cultivate to the utmost of my power. In a few days I shall return to Plymouth to join the Regt. having been ordered here a Recruiting, but the late pacifick measures have put a stop to that going on. I am with great haste and Regard My Dear Burnet,
>
> Most sincerely yours
>
> James Lyon.

Sir Andrew had advanced him £1165 to purchase his commission.

From the date of Sir Andrew's death Alexander's allowance from Government was increased to £2 per day. As he had been shouldering the responsibility of the appointment for quite some time because of Sir Andrew's ill health. Alexander's lifestyle would not have changed very much if at all but in the January of 1771 he wrote to Lord Sandwich requesting some leave. I quote from his draft letter dated Berlin 12th January 1771.

> ...must desire the favr. of yr. Ldp. to be pleased to move His Maj. to grant me Leave of Absence to travel for some Months as soon as the Season will permit, or to repair to such Mineral Waters as the Physicians will prescribe, they having already declared to me that they think the same absolutely necessary for the Reestablishment of my Health which has been much out of order ever since the month of Decr. last. In my present situation I need not add that a speedy answer from Yr. Ldp. will lay me under the greatest Obligations and that I have the Honour to be with the greatest Respect...

Lord Cathcart, His Majesty's Minister Plenipotentiary at the Court of St Petersburg, wrote confidentially to Alexander discussing the situation of War and Peace, such as it was later that same year, 1771. His letters are all numbered and some are in code but fortunately Alexander has written in the decoding. Alexander always wrote on the back of each letter who and where it was from with the date, and then, underneath, the date received by him and the date he answered it and by what means he despatched his reply.

After Sir Andrew's death, the British Government had to consider how they would replace him. They chose Mr Robert Gunning who was HM's envoy at Copenhagen. Alexander wrote from Berlin, 2nd March 1771:

> Sir, Last Wednesday I was favored with a letter from the Earl of Halifax informing me that His Majesty had been pleased to remove Mr Gunning from the Court of Denmark to supply the place of the late Sir Andrew Mitchell with the character of Envoy Extraordinary to the Court of Berlin.

He goes on to offer his assistance and congratulations.

Alexander continued to live in the house Sir Andrew had rented in Berlin as there was still six months of the lease to run. He describes it as being one of the finest, most spacious and convenient for a foreign visitor in Berlin. An agreement had been made with the landlady, a Madame la Generale de Blanckenace, to lease it for "a Thousand Rix dollars, in gold, a year." Alexander wrote at great length to Mr Gunning giving him details of the accommodation and equipment and doing his best to persuade him to take it over. The greatest part of the furniture belonged to the landlady but the hangings and several pieces had belonged to the late Sir Andrew. There were also

> ...seven excellent serviceable black coloured Coach horses belonging to the late Sir Andrew. Be so kind to inform me if you will have occasion for them, they are betwixt seven and eight years old, and to the best of my knowledge cost him 100 Rix dollars apiece. The late Sir Andrew's Cook desires me to offer his services to you, in case you should want one. I can safely recommend him for his Honesty, Sobriety and other good qualities as to his capacity to cook, he is allowed by the nicest Judges here, to be the best in this place, and perhaps one of the Ablest of his Profession, as well as for plain dressing in the English way, as for the high French cookery. He is a native of Flanders. If you should not choose to transport hither your Kitchen utensils, those of late Sir A. are very numerous and in good condition being almost quite new, and shall not be disposed of until I know your Intention...The Cellar too is well stocked with wines, and if the heirs of the late Sir A. should order them to be sold, you shall have the Preference for any or part of them as you shall like to have.
>
> PS. Mons. de Lancy who arrived here about 10 days ago, has had an Audience lately of the King of Prussia to deliver his Letters of Credence. I yet hear nothing concerning the departure of Mons. d'Arnheim for Copenhagen. This place offers little or no news worth writing at present. His P.M. still continues at Potsdam, and I hear has got gout in his hand which obliges him to keep his Apartment.

Our Alexander was nothing if not practical! But one suspects that Mr Gunning was a little put out at his lack of promotion from the remarks made in his letter to Alexander which he wrote after receiving

Alexander's lengthy descriptions of the situation in Berlin. He wished to know the cost of everything

> ...the Wages of Cook, Maitre d'Hotel, livery servants etc. What the Rate of wood, Hay, Corn etc., upon what footing most of the Ministers from the principal foreign courts live. By the Account I have here, Berlin seems to be much more expensive residence than even this...My intention is (as it is my Duty indeed) to support the dignity of the Post I am honoured with in becoming manner, but as I suppose my opportunities are only to be those of an Envoy Extraordinary, I cannot upon them live as I should on those of a Minister Plenty., and it is upon the footing of the former that I must regulate my family with respect to servants, Equipage, table etc, Till Mr Keith informs me whether he will take my Wines & Kitchen Utensils here, I can not determine on those of Sir A.

Mr Gunning had also requested that his appointment be postponed on health grounds as he wished to return to England and repair to Bath to take the Waters. In the meantime he had replied to one of Alexander's epistles as the latter wrote back.

> I immediately acquainted Late Sir A's Cook with the prospect therin made to him, of which he readily accepted. As for the Maitre de Hotel recommended to you by Countess Kanke, I have many years ago heard so much of his Character that I declined writing to you in his Favour, upon his applying to me for that purpose, on the first News of your Nomination to this Court. He being a man that I cannot in Conscience Recommend. With Regard to your Wines and other Effects etc., there will be no Difficulty according to what I have been able to learn, as to their entry here, next Spring, free of Duty and Imports etc. provided you inform the Prussian Secretary of State that you have ordered your Provision of Wines and necessary Baggage to be sent to you next Spring and desire him to procure a pass from the King his master for the free transit and free entry of the said Effects here...

Mr Gunning obviously thought the rent for Sir Andrew's house, however fine it was, more than he could afford and Alexander writes:

> I have made an offer to the Landlady here to engage it for you at the rate of 800 Dollars provided she purchased for the use of the Lodger the small yet necessary pieces of Furniture that belonged to the late Sir A. to which she answered she could not think of letting her house under 1000 dollars to be paid in Gold, and that her Circumstances did not permit her to buy Furniture. I represented to her in strongest terms I was capable of, the impossibility of getting so high a rent for a House, which, if she suffered the Effects to be carried away was absolutely Empty etc. etc. she could not think of lowering her terms. Houses fit for the Reception of Foreign Ministers are very rare...The late Sir Andrew's State Coach cost upwards of 900 Dollars, it has been very little used and really is as good as new. He paid too dear for it...betwixt us it was a piece of Roguery in those that bespoke it. I have had it examined by the ablest and honestest Workman in Town and he frankly told me he would make a new one of the same kind, with the same Varnish and in every respect equally as good for 700 Dollars. I therefore offer it to you for 350 dollars being half the price and I am sure when you see it you will think it well worth that money...Sir A. paid 30 Fredericks d'or to his Cook.

Alexander, in the end, got accommodation for Mr Gunning in a good inn, and no doubt thought he could sort out his permanent lodging when he arrived in Berlin. He appears to have caused a considerable amount of bother! He had of course all the other affairs of the Embassy to attend to as well. A letter from Trevor Corry in Danzig thanks Alexander for the "assistance You have given Mr. Seefeldt's Brother and Friend towards the recovery of their legacy in your City." There was an agent in Hamburg who received and shipped all manner of things for the Embassy and the staff:

> Hamburg 29 Oct.1771.
>
> Oisters with a small Cagg (?) containing 200 loose gently pickled and a fresh Cod if to be had - it will always give me pleasure to have it in my power to be of the least Service to you Sir, and I begg You will freely count on me without making the very least Apology."

Besides goodies for the Embassy, Alexander had many commissions from the Lord Marischal. A letter from the latter from Potsdam on 8th October 1771 mentions,

> I have a letter from Mr. Boswell in high spirits from Paoli's visit to him at Auchinleck castle..." and a PS "Please try and send me one pound of best sealing wax." Another communication dated 15 Oct. sends compliments to Count and Countess Herrenia: "I flatter myself they will stay a few days also here. I manage my tomates y pimintones dulces with intention that they shall eat part of them...Look out for a lodging for me without bugs if possible...The English hate the Scots more than we do them, even a Scots tune offends their ear...You know Lord Galloway, after more than 40 years patience, is separated from his Lady; he gives for his reason, That he desires to dye in peace, he is gone with one of his daughters to the south of France. Ever yours M.

I believe he must have been quite an amusing old boy.

Mr Gunning's repeated postponements of his arrival in Berlin must have exasperated his masters at Westminster and a certain James Harris was sent to Berlin in his place. The same Mr Harris who had been at Madrid at the time of the Spanish bombardment of the Falkland Islands, and who had successfully negotiated that settlement with the King of Spain.

> London. January 3rd. 1772
> My dear Burnet, I have literaly but a moment to tell you that I have this morning kist His Majesty's hand on being nominated Envoy Extraordinary to Berlin in the room of Gunning remov'd to Petersburg, I shall delay my departure as little as possible, & shall therefore be very troublesome to you on my arrival; I must beforehand then bespeak your forgiveness, and I rely on that Friendship you have so often shewn me, and on which I set so high a value...James Harris.

> London. January 17. 1772
> My dear Burnet, Would I had it or now have it in my power to write to you as I wish. I leave England Monday next the 20th. and intend going by Calais and the Hague where I

shall stay 3 or 4 days and afterwards continue my route to Berlin as expediently as possible. I must beg you dear Sir to secure the same house Mr. Gunning had taken and concerning which he has been so good as to write to you likewise any provision of wood, hay etc. that he might have laid in - as also the stock of Claret which he tells me he has taken from Sir Andrew's cellar.

Brousselles. Feby 1 1772
The bad weather prevented my passing by the Hague & putting my equipages in order and taking other preparatory steps necessary on the eve of so long a journey in so bad a season has detained me here for these past four or five days, I however now in spite of those and other unfavourable appearances propose leaving Brusselles to-morrow early, and losing no time in the road before I arrive at my destination. I have taken here the Porter that formerly lived with Sir Andrew, and who has a very estimable Certificate from you. I long to be with you & so you will then find me very troublesome I will avoid being so now by sending you a long letter. James Harris

Hanover. Feby 13th. 1772
The vile roads and bad weather prevented my receiving your obliging Letter of the 31st. Janry sooner than yesterday evening; my Patience has cruelly suffered by this Tediousness & the Loss of that has more fatigued me than the want of sleep & meals. I rely greatly, my dear Sir, on your Friendship, & repay it with the sincerest sentiments. I am glad to find Mr. Gunning's House is not dispos'd of, I was in some alarm about it. If the Scot you mention still holds his resolution of not going with that Gentleman to Petersburg, I shall certainly be glad to take him. I intend leaving this place tomorrow -I shall stay at Brunswig two days, of course set out from thence Monday the 17th. instant & by the Grace of God & able horses be at Berlin the Thursday following, or at latest Friday morning - adieu my dear Burnet, I am impatient to assure you viva voce how truly and sincerely I am Your affectionate Friend & faithful servant

JH.

He must have arrived on schedule as there is not another communication from Brunswig!

A letter from his friend Cathcart:

> St. Petersbourg, April 1771...It is impossible not to interest oneself in the situation of the Friend of a Friend one esteemed so much, I therefore make no excuse for expressing a desire to know your destination after Mr. Gunning's arrival; it is a strange thing to say but it is too true that nothing is more necessary for the State than that men the most properly qualified that can be found should be employ'd in foreign Commissions, and yet the choice generally is guided by favour or by accident. I shall be extremely glad to hear that Justice is likely to be done to your Service...
>
> Lord Cathcart

Cathcart's wife, Jane, died in the November of that same year leaving him with three sons and four daughters to care for at which time Alexander proves to have been extremely kind and helpful. Cathcart asked to be recalled and so Mr. Gunning, being more or less at the ready, was sent to St. Petersburg instead of Berlin.

That Alexander had made numerous friends during his long sojourn in the Prussian capital is more than proved by the many affectionate letters and expressions of regret he received prior to his departure from Berlin. James Boswell, although he had no intention of following Alexander's advice, had thought him a thoroughly good fellow!

> Mittau. Novr. 1st. 1771
>
> Nothing, beleave me, could give me greater Satisfaction & Pleasure, than hearing of Your being well & in good Spirits, which I think You was when You wrote me last. But pray, why will You leave Berlin? All the fine beautys? these enchanting faces, which captivated our hearts! I thought You never wou'd, even for the finest Lasses of the land of Cakes. But novelty pleases! & I must on [own] to be of the same Opinion – for my Part I sincerely shou'd have wish'd You for ever established in Berlin. I certainly wou'd hear more

often of You, than perhaps I shall when You are once at home – I suppose you have heard by this Time of the horrid and dreadful Attempt to assassinate the King of Poland, whom nothing else by Providence, th' almighty Protector of Sovereigns, has saved from destruction. Th' inclosed acct. of this event was given out by Authority. I hope that Pulawsky a second D'ammier, who bribed the fellows to assassinate the King, will be catch'd somewhere, & deliver'd up to receive sentence…Adieu, my dear Friend, Pray write me a long letter before You leave Berlin, & let me know when You think of departing that I may once more give You my adieux.

Baron Klopman.

James Harris arrived in Berlin on the 21st February 1772. Alexander's last letter to the Earl of Suffolk confirms this.

My Lord,

I have now the Honour of informing Your Lordship that Yesterday about Noon Mr. Harris, His Majesty's Envoy Extraordinary to this Court arrived here and delivered to me Your Lordship's Letter of the 19th. of January. In Obedience to the Orders it contains I have given up the Cyphers etc., therein specified to Mr. Harris, and the other Cyphers in My Possession, I shall, according to Your Lordship's Directions, carry along with me, and deliver to Your Lordship on my Arrival in London which I expect will be some Time in April as I hope to be able to set out from hence about the latter End of next Month.

This Place offers no News of any kind worth transmitting to Your Lordship. Yesterday afternoon Count Rwilecki, Minister from the Republick of Poland to the Court, arrived here from Warsaw. When he will have an Audience of the King of Prussia to deliver his Letters of Credence is uncertain as that Monarch still continues to be confined to his Apartments at Potsdam by the Indisposition mentioned in my last to Your Lordship.

I have etc., A. B.

The very last letter in Alexander's Letter Book was written to Lord Cathcart at St Petersburg on 3rd March 1772:

> ...I was honoured by Post with your much esteemed Favour of the 20/31 January together with its several Inclosures for all which I return my hearty Thanks to yre. Excy. The distinguished Mark of Friendship you have honoured me with in giving me a Copy of the printed Paper[9] addressed to Lady Cathcart's Friends does more particularly demand my gratefull and sincere acknowledgements. It is indeed a valuable Present – On perusing that Paper I could not help shedding Tears whilst I admired the Virtue, Piety, Magnanimity and superior Fortitude of Mind of that truly great and good Character. – It is the best Lesson to learn how to die I believe, ever was given – For my Part I never read any Thing with which I was more moved or more edified.
>
> Mr. Harris, His Majesty's Envoy Extraordinary to this Court arrived here on 21st. of last Month, and on the 26th. he had an Audience at Potsdam of the King of Prussia, when he delivered his Letters of Credence and was most graciously received by His Prussian Majesty. As the arrival of Mr. Harris renders my Staying here unncessary I am busy in preparing for my Return Home, and expect to be ready to set out from hence some Time this Month, as therefore I may not probably have Occasion to write again to Yr. Excy. before my Departure – I beg leave to return my very sincere Thanks for Yr. Excy's Correspondence, and to express the high Sence I shall ever retain of the many eminent Marks of Friend ship and Confidence You have, my Lord, been pleased to distinguish me with in the Course of it. May I request the Continuance of Yr. Excy's Countenance and Protection of which I am very Ambitious, and offering my warmest wishes for Yr. Excys. safe Return to England and for Your future Happiness and Welfare I have the Honour to be etc
> Alex Burnet.

9 *The printed Paper mentioned is the most harrowing account of Lady Cathcart's last days, her last words and so on.*

A hurried letter of farewell from his friend Captain Scott at Potsdam written:

2 April 1772

My dear Burnet,...If I should not have the Pleasure of hearing from you before your travil in England; I shall conclude this with my most sincere wishes for your happiness and prosperous araivel in England and will for ever Remain my dear Sandy

your very sincere loving friend

James Scott.

Poor Jamey will be very unhappy at parting with you fairwell

Dear Burnet : dear friend

believe me till death your friend.

And so, having paid his final respects to His Prussian Majesty who was pleased to present him with a heavy gilt snuffbox, Alexander left Berlin a very much more mature and experienced man and a much richer one, not in tangible wealth but beyond measure in many affectionate friends.

V

The Years at Home

Alexander travelled back to Britain by way of France and arrived in April 1772. During the whole time of his sojourn in Germany he had never returned home for any form of leave. In spite of a regular correspondence with his father, he felt he was almost a complete stranger to his family, not having seen any of them for just on seventeen years. On his arrival in London, he waited on Lord North and the Earl of Suffolk, delivered up the various ciphers and documents he had brought with him from Berlin and made known his claim for some form of pension. We know that his father had tried his best to secure a Parliamentary seat for him but to no avail and no doubt he enjoyed a period of rest and relaxation after his long tour of duty. It was necessary before travelling north to visit his bankers and agent, John Larpent, in Jermyn Street who had written regularly to keep him up to date with his affairs. Some time after his return, he decided to have his portrait painted and, I suppose in some ways it was an obvious choice for him to have made, he commissioned Angelica Kaufmann. She was at this time at the height of her fame in London having painted a portrait of her great friend Sir Joshua Reynolds and become the first woman RA. She later married the Italian artist, Antonio Zucchi, and settled in Rome.

Angelica Kaufmann's receipt for the portrait:

> Rcd. March the 4 1773
> From Mr. Burnet the Sum of forty
> Guineas being the full payment
> for a half length by me Angelica.

It shows a kindly faced man of 30 years sitting at his writing table, the quill and ink nearby and his favourite snuffbox, the silver gilt enamelled blue and green French one that I treasure, at his elbow. He looks down on us from his vantage point over the dining-room mantlepiece and I hope he enjoys the parties and musical evenings we have there. I am sure he does!

What a contrast the transition from the busy life of a Chargé

Portrait of Alexander Burnet
by Angelica Kaufmann, 1773

d'Affaires to that of a country laird's son! It must have been quite strange and difficult for him to re-adjust. He spent the first years mostly in London, trying to get his pension adjusted and just paying visits to the family in Aberdeenshire.

The year 1777 seems to have been the year for settling down and, not having had an establishment of his own in this country before, he had a considerable number of purchases to make before this was possible. This year produces a vast number of receipts for practically everything you can think of and a few more besides! Luckily for Alexander, Seaton House was still in the family and it was here that he made his home. For one who was fond of his food, the stocking of his kitchen with all the necessary equipment was of prime importance and there is a lengthy order for all the usual pots, pans and implements from three different kinds of candlesticks, a "Neat Jappan'd Tea Board at £1.17/-," sugar nippers, a Beef fork and Steak Tongs to the latest of mod cons – "1 three wheel Multiplying Jack with weight Line etc. Compleat at £6. 6/-". Unfortunately we do not still have it and it remains a mystery! Beds and bedding were, of course, essential purchases as were curtains and other hangings. He spent quite an amount on cutlery and had every piece (60 of them) engraved with crest and motto: it all came to more than £34. Needless to say, none of that has survived. One of his more important acquisitions has, I am glad to say: "Three Knife Vauses and stands" which he bought in 1777. The stands have vanished but the three knife urns, Adam ones, still grace a sideboard. He had brought some china from Germany but new dishes were bought and an amazing number of fenders and grates. Presumably he had to buy one for every room. He did not buy just household things either and there is a big tailor's bill with several different coloured and embroidered "westcoats". Another purchase was a pair of spring Garters with buttons etc., complete £1.16/-. I fancy our Alexander liked to cut quite a figure. He was also very keen on fishing and shooting. He regularly purchased materials for making his fishing tackle and he had his guns attended to on his return from Germany:

> To cleaning a brass German Bullet Gun 2s:0d
> New hunter pins
> To altering one Lock from going off at half Cock 9d.

Very necessary.

After he had taken up his abode at Seaton, Alexander, like the good secretary that he was, kept a daily journal. Some of it is missing, I am sad to say, but there is enough left to show the kind of life he created for himself and the friends he made. He also gives the exact wind direction and the weather each day and I am sure he must have got on very well with his father's second wife, Janet, who, we already know, kept her diary of the weather in great detail. The earliest date in Alexander's Journal that I have is "September, 1778 when on the 27th. the Kemnay Chaise came at 9 o Clock morning set off with Miss Dyce to Kemnay at Dinner. 28th. The Ground very wet no shooting, the Hills white with snow in the morning. 29th. Walked out after Breakfast with Dog & Gun towards Cluny by Craigearn. Killed 2 Partridge. 30th. Constant Rain went out with John to stalk Dier saw nothing." He would stay a few days and then return home. Early in October he left Seaton at "7 o Clock morning got to Kemnay to Breakfast went a shooting after and killed 2 Partridge." The following day after break fast and accompanied by his two sisters, Nelly and Betty, he went to Crathes where they were "kindly received by Kgt. & Lady." They spent the night there and returned next day to Kemnay in time for dinner which was the late mid day meal, not supper. The next day it was so wet he did not go back to Seaton but played "Shuttle Cock with Mr. Mearns." He had a small farm at Seaton and, by the length of the seed list, quite a large garden. He would inspect his crops and garden and walked considerable distances, sometimes as far as Grandholm and often into Town with whichever one of his sisters was staying with him at the time.

On September 28th the following year "Kemnay etc left me after Breakfast and returned home, walked to the Sea Side in the evening went & supped at Mr. Leslies." This is the first mention of the Leslies. John Leslie was Professor of Greek at Aberdeen University. Alexander mentions going to church or not going to church but perhaps walking with Sister Betty to the North Links instead. On 2nd December he walked to Aberdeen and "Bought a Tea Boiler of Mr. Ewen pd. 45 Sh. for it." The next day Mrs Leslie and family drank Tea with him and spent the evening!

Alexander kept note of the letters he wrote and I am glad to say that he wrote at least twice a month to dear old Dr Lamont. He spent Christmas with the family at Kemnay, leaving Seaton about the 23rd December with Betty "after Ten o Clock and arriving there to Dinner."

On Christmas Day there was quite a party and Inverallochy and Miss Fraser (Castle Fraser), Mrs Grant and Professor Dunbar "to Dinner and all Night." On New Year's Eve he went with "Kemnay (his father) in Mr. Duff's Chaise for a Tryal, blew a Hurricane at NW. in evening." He and Sister Mary returned to Seaton on the 3rd January and on the 9th of the month "Many Ladies called in & prevented me getting out, at home all evening". Towards the end of January he packed his trunk and did other necessary things in preparation of setting out the following day at "half an Hour after Four o Clock in the morning" for Huntly Lodge where he was to pay a visit to General Morris and his Lady. The time was spent stalking in the deer park and company for dinner. His journey home seems to have been accomplished in pretty good time as he left Huntly at 6 o Clock morning and arrived at Seaton House before 2 o Clock after noon! At the beginning of February he set out once more for a few days at Kemnay and on the Sunday he "Went to Church being in the General Taste" ! The following day he was struck with "Rhumatism in my Heel" but nevertheless felt able to ride out with his father after Breakfast. The rheumatism got much worse, however, and he was not able to walk for several days and then "it went off in the Evening like a Charm so that I walked with great Ease" and he returned to Seaton with Mary next day to find the gardener had sown peas and beans. He was not able to walk much "for the remains of my Rhumatism" so he mended his fishing tackle. Every now and then there is mention of going to Inverurie and holding elections, burgh elections I suppose. He ends the journal for 1779 with a summary of the year's farming:

> 1779. Harvest this year was finished and housed almost every where in the County of Aberdeen by 20th. of September and Kemnay had in His Corn Yard a large Rick of Clover Hay being a second Crop which He never had in any former Year since He began to farm. Got besides 1 Grilse and a Salmon 8 Trout.

Christmas and the New Year were spent at Kemnay again and on the 2nd January, which must have been a Sunday, it was "Bright Sun Shine. Wind West North West. Did not go to Church as Company at Kemnay." Next day he and Mary set out for Seaton once more and a few days later they walked after Breakfast to the New Pier. He and sister Mary went to the Queen's Assembly in the New Town and they took very long walks in spite of bad weather. It appears it had to be very severe before he was deterred from taking his exercise. There is mention of the Leslies dining again. Miss Leslie was later to become his wife. On 29th January he "Walked before Dinner & called on Miss Leslie who is ill of the Tooth Ach." On the 1st February, which was a typical February day "Gray Day frost in the Night Cold raw Air. Mr. Wales at his Breakfast. paid for K of P's & Sir Andr M-----ll's pictures." Mr Wales was a well known and extremely talented 'copier' and had copied the two portraits - much in the same way as today we would have photographs taken. In fact the one of Sir Andrew Mitchell is so good it has been taken for a Ramsay!

The following day he "Got a little Cold & soar Throat" which got a little worse as two days later he had a "Great Cold not able to go to Mrs. Paton's evening. The next day however Miss Annie Farquharson came to her Dinner and stay'd all Night. Miss Leslie and her father dined once or twice during the month and there was an Assembly in the Auld Town. It was a nasty cold month. However, "The Spring Flowers were putting fourth and the Hawthorn was budding last year in the Course of this Month, and many People in the Neighbourhood of Aberdeen etc. had sown Oats. But this year during the whole of the Month of February it was very severe Winter Weather especially far into the Country nor was there the least appearance of the Approach of Spring – few Salmon were got at the Creves or below Bridge – I did not throw a Line into the River owing to the Severity of the Weather – I was busy all this Month preparing my Fishing Tackle —— On the 29 of this Month The Thrushes and other Birds began to sing."

On the 2nd March Alexander spent the evening at the Leslies and as he walked home afterwards he noted that the "Sky was blood red." Some very high winds followed this sighting of the Northern Lights. Every month he spent a week or so at Kemnay, rode out in the Chaise with Papa and sometimes went to Dinner at Castle Fraser. In the April of this year he started playing golf with Major Mitchell and there are several entries to that effect. In September of 1780 much of Alexander's time was spent at Inverurie consulting, dining or visiting with the Duke of Gordon. Lord Kintore and Bailie Robertson at Keithhall are also on the list of visits and on the 12th of the month a Council was held "& fixed for Friday for chusing a Delegate. 13. Walked up and down Inverury observing their Motions. 14. dined at Inverury & baffled all their Attempts. 15. Came wt. the Provost in ye.

Morg. held the Council when in spite of Gnl. Grant & his Party I was Chose Delegate. 16. Rode to Keithhall dined at Kintore with D. of Gordon & L^{d}. Kintore in y^{e}. Council Room. 18. Went early w^{t}. the Provost & held the Annual Election when He & his Friends were returned & the opposite party turned out."

Alexander spent much of this month at Kemnay with his father "rode out an Airing w^{t}. Ky. in y. Chaise" and they twice went and dined at Castle Fraser as old "Inverallochy quite alone." and spent the night there. Another election on October 2nd saw Alexander as delegate (in the role of returning officer, I imagine) attending the poll at Kintore where General Morris was re-elected. He and sister Mary dined at Cluny before returning to Seaton. He did not remain long away from Kemnay and his entry for the 16th October is "Ky extremely ill." That is the last entry until the middle of November so once more the story of George Burnet's death is a blank. There is just a letter from Lord Adam Gordon who wrote "to condole with you on the loss of your Father which however could not have been an unexpected Event in the precarious State of Health He, poor Man, had for some Time been in..." His letter ends "...You will surely be looking about you soon; and I desire you may acquaint me of it – when you have determined it – because I am a Party much concerned in your happiness. she should have a pickle siller – and be good humoured and young..." Adam Gordon obviously thought a laird should not be single! He was the son of the third Duke of Gordon, was MP for the Mearns and later C-in-C of the Army in Scotland. He was a close friend of both George and Alexander Burnet and his many letters are full of humour, good friendship and gossip.

Alexander's Journal ends half way through December after the death of his father and one of the last entries is "Christie Leslie dined w^{t}. me." Christie enters Alexander's history at the end of the following year as his wife – but that is another chapter.

VI

Alexander the Laird

Adam Gordon was not content with writing one letter upon the subject of marriage and a second one of 10th March 1781 reads "…I know You will forgive my mentioning a delicate Subject which interests Your-self more than it does any other Individual but the Fair One – who shall captivate your Affection – but I must add - that thinking it will add to your Comfort, the sooner you are at Liberty to give me that notice – the better shal I be pleased – pray lett her have good humour, & good sense! ingredients for happiness – not to be found on every tree – Mille Rose sans Epine! and at all Events – forgive my Impertinence!"

Amongst the personal banter there is a wealth of political tittle tattle, no doubt very welcome to Alexander who must really have sometimes felt quite cut off from the diplomatic scene which had been so large a part of his life. Alexander made a journey south in the summer of '81 and received a scolding from Lord Adam for not calling upon them but all is forgiven in his letter of 31st December:

> I am to thank you my Dear Sir, for Your obliging Letter of the 12th. Inst. & very cordially to congratulate you and Mrs Burnet in the name of all here – on Your late Change of State – which we sincerely wish may be attended with every possible Felicity to you both. It will always be a great Satisfaction to us, to see You & Yours, at Stella [Hall] – or at any other place we may chance to be at – and not less – to have it in our power, to wait on You at Home – for I assure you – there is no friend, I esteem more than your self – and think it is mutual – and therefore more like to continue – I wonder Ben Gordon has not been to call on You – & I have told him so – He is a good Man – and one of your nearest neighbours – I hear Lord Kintore means to sett about repairing and adding to his House of Keith Hall in Spring – which is a sensible determination, and will, I hope prove so, both to Him self, and his family – apropos – I never saw a more promising young man in my Life, than Lord Inverurie…We are much concerned at the accounts you send us of poor

> Miss Annie [his aunt] the mildness of this winter (if with you as it has been here with us) should be for Her...

A letter from Murdoch Middleton, a keen gardening friend of his father, from Hoxton.

> 12 Dec. 1781.
> ...Coming home last night after a little excursion I found a letter from My Good Friend Mr. John Ewen, which among other things, informed me of your having tyed the Gordian Knot, never to be untyed till cut by -------- I most sincerely congratulate you on the Happy Occasion and wish your days may be long & happy together, and withall, blessed with a numerous and virtuous Progeny, and may Health, Happiness, Peace, Prosperity and Plenty crown your Days. I beg to know in particular how Miss Anny is in respect to Health, how Miss Burnet and Miss Betsy are and at the same time tell me how old my Late good Friend was that I may have it put upon the stone which is now about and wants only his age.
>
> I will not forget the seeds for the shrubbery.

Alexander's brother-in-law wrote from Boath "...may you and your aimiable Consort enjoy every Conjugal Felicity." Alexander and Christian moved to Kemnay and George's widow, Janet, went back to Disblair to her sister, Miss Dyce. Alexander's sisters appear to have visited around quite a lot but otherwise they seem to have lived at Kemnay. His Aunt Annie spent a lot of her time in London where the climate was more suited to her state of health.

Alexander was determined to prove himself as good a laird and as efficient a farmer as he had been a Chargé d'Affaires and he continued to care for the estate and increase and improve the gardens in the way his father would most definitely have approved. Letters from Murdoch Middleton at Hoxton continued to instruct him as to what he should do and he proved invaluable in providing a vast amount of plants.

> January 20th. 1782 Hoxton Dear Sir, I have packed up for you , which I hope you will receive safe, a parcel of seeds, trees, shrubs and a very few others. The principal are

evergreen oaks - acorns which, when they come to hand, should be put in a box with mould to preserve them from drying out too much till the Spring comes in for sowing. The turkey oaks must be used the same way. Cedar of Lebanon 2 cones of different sorts.

Cayan pepper, ice plant, snapdragons and alkekengis [?] are the two first for the hotbed, the others for the common ground. All the rest must be sown in the common ground in beds. Many of them will not come up this Spring so that the ground must not be stirred, only kept clear of weeds. I forgot to tell you that the Myrtle Berries are to be put in a pot in the hotbed. There are no wych elm to be got in the nurseries, and in my journey to Bath I enquired by the way in several Nurseries, and none to be got.

Mr. Middleton presented a marble plaque as a memorial to George Burnet; this is the stone he mentions in his first letter:

Hoxton, March 30th. 1782

Dear Sir, Yours of December 23rd. received, and should have returned a suitable Answer long ago, had not an unlucky Accident prevented me, namely, after the inscription was finished the stone was broke in the shop, so that I ordered another, which he accordingly did. I put it aboard the Fortune of Aberdeen William Brown Master. It is in a Box, directed to you, and writ upon "GLASS", in order to make them more careful. Mr. Robert Gibbon, the owner of the vessel, promised it should be took particular care of. It is well done, and I hope it will come safe to hand. And as it was my proposal, I look upon myself liable to the expence, and which I think due to the memory of an Honoured Friend.

I could wish it put up in or near the place I pitched upon. There is a long stone lies upon Sir Archibald Grant's land. I wish you could get it by way of a support. Kemnay carried me to see it. I shall describe the place as well as I can remember. After you pass the Brig of Ton, you come to a small farm town on the left hand, on a rising ground, about a hundred yards, from the road; there we rode up and enquired of the first we met, who was a young woman. She readily carried us two or three hundred yards, or perhaps more, into a field on the right of the road, almost covered with broom. There the stone lay. It had formerly stood upright and has an inscription, but not legible - at least not to us. If you can procure this stone and cut it off square at the top, the other [stone] may be fixed upon it by a piece of iron inserted into both. However, this method I submit to your better judgement. Please to let Mr. Ewen take notice when the Fortune arrives and take care of the box. As the Box is but light, I would not trust it in a cart but on a horse, lest the marble be broke, your roads being sometimes rough, and your carters not over and above careful. I hope ere this you have received by Mr. Ewen a parcel of shrub and tree seeds with the best directions I could give for the management of them, with some flower seeds. Mr. Gammack presents his compliments. He has put aboard the same ship [the Fortune], directed to you, 10 wych elms that he met with by the mere chance, they being all left off in the nurseries. Also two large roots of the bella donna lily and two cyclamen (sows bread). The sow bread will do in the flower garden; I think the bella donna will not; and therefore wish you to set a very large pot or old cask and fill it with good earth and plant one of them in it, which may be sheltered in the winter. The other you may try in the ground in a sheltered situation if you please...Murdoch Middleton.

The Monument
to George Burnet.
Pencil drawing by
S.L.Burnett

Heaven only knows whether they ever discovered the stone which they were to filch from Sir Archibald. I should have thought it quite a chore! The marble itself was an oval shape and it was set into a large stone which had been cut to sit on top of a very big stone. Whether it came from Monymusk or not, I have not been able to find out but I would fancy not. It stood about five feet high and the topmost stone which had the plaque inset sat squarely on the top of it, I think without the iron bars! Surmounting the entire memorial was a plaster urn and the whole was erected in the Wilderness in a small ring of seven beeches, some of them almost touching. The inscription read: "Erected to the memory of George Burnet who planned, planted and brought to perfection this grove." followed by the date of his birth and death. It was a lovely place and I remember it well.

The hurricane of 1953 blew all the trees down and the monument itself vanished. I was not in the country at the time but my Nanny tried her best to find it. Unfortunately the firm of tree fellers or whatever they were that my mother employed to tidy up the estate, did not make a good job of it at all and were not interested in the recovery of the monument. In 1964, working from memory alone as the Wilderness bore no resemblance to the place where I had played as a child and which I knew like the back of my hand, I found a place which looked as if there had been seven trees standing from the mounds of roots and holes in the ground. I got down into one of the biggest holes and poked around and felt a very large and hard object which could only be a stone. Feeling amongst all the dead leaves and bits of wood and soil, I recognised the shape of the big stone of the monument. It took several men and a caterpillar tractor to lift it out of its grave. Some pieces are missing and Mr Middleton would be very vexed because his marble plaque was broken in two and the one bit missing. One day I must have it replaced for the third time!

Mr Middleton wrote again in June of the same year:

> I am pleased you find so great advantage in what was done before you, I beg you to consider what has been said of one of your Neighbours - He has no right to cut down a Tree because he never planted any. Now as you begin to cut down, I need not tell you, you are bound to plant, to supply your Posterity, who, I hope, a long time hence, will enjoy

what you plant now. My Dear S^{r} the bit of Marble deserves not any thanks, It only obliges myself who thought such a small tribute due to the memory of one who so well deserved it, and am bound rather to thank you for putting it up.

He observes with interest the work going on at Kemnay which includes the "tilling of the new Byre"

> ...You ask my Advice and approbation in what you have already done in the Grove. I doubt not you have done right. My advice can only be of use in what you may do hereafter. In that, you are to observe to plant thick, a mixture of Firs, Pines & forest, or deciduous trees, two or three evergreens (Firs & Pines) to one deciduous, the greens will shelter and draw up the other to stems, and the greens to be cut down as the others require room, at the same time fence them well from Cattle, and remember it require a certain degree of Obstinacy to command success. And remember Sully's Rule to do one thing first, Never let too many things at a time encumber you. And if a Country Life delights you, as I hope it will with so agreeable a Companion, you will have a constant fund of Pleasure in seeing everything succeed, and thryve under your Care, and you will always have something to amuse you.

Lord Adam Gordon wrote in much the same vein but more briefly! He wrote to say that as yet there was no move regarding Alexander's pension:

> We must have Patience. You are as happy, if not more so, than you was ever at any time of your Life - If Circumstances answer, I know nothing more desirable than living at Home with a Wife one loves and esteems - and culltivating in the garden. If it is arriving at an earlier Period of Life at what all men look forward to with anxiety and wish to possess at the Close of busier Scenes - and what the wisest men have prized most...

Life did have its ups and downs and in the Spring of 1782 Alexander's sister Annie died. According to a letter from Alexander's friend Dr

Wright, condoling the loss "of an aimiable sister", she had been suffering from a lingering illness and had been in considerable pain. She died in England. The news of the calamity of that spring was contained in a letter from Alexander's London agent, Alex Thom:

> ...the Ship Robert & John Captain Chivers Master is Taken by the Shellelea Privateer of Dunkirk, this is very vexing. I hope your dec. Miss Burnet's Trunks was not very valuable. A piece of Silk for Miss Dyce is also gone. Two Trunks, Two wire fenders and two Paper Parcells.

Hard work is the best antidote for sadness and Alexander flung himself into his plans for improving the Wilderness still more. On the west side of the house a little lake had been made and there was a small island in it which was reached by a bridge. A letter from Mr Middleton in October of 1782 tells us more about it:

> ...I am glad you have finished your Offices you will have time to attend to something in my way, and shall say as much as occurs to me at present, if I give no instruction, let me amuse you. I approve of your re-building the Bridge, as it was not very safe to pass on before, as to the colour, that must depend upon your fancy, but whatever colour shows best at a Distance in the Shade of the Plantation should be chosen. I doubt not your Hermitage will answer your end entirely, I have seen the front of a Hermitage cased with Fir Slabs with the Bark on, have a very pretty effect. The Door and Windows, gothic, which I perceive you have done, and must be very pretty if your Island be large enough. I shall be glad to have a Sketch of it, altho' I fancy I see it already in your Description. Your having removed the West Gate was right, and was talked of when I was at Kemnay, and a narrow Plantation on the right hand by continuing the Line will hide the Cottages effectually, but at the same time I beg that your Plantation may not be allowed to grow up so as to hinder the Sun from visiting the Cottages in the Winter. Remember Diogenes and Alexander...your Observation of the Cones of the Silver Fir growing erect is really what I have not observed. Many things occur daily to our Senses that pass unperceived because we see them every Day. But

I will take the first Opportunity to take notice of it.

But I have considered your next Summer operations. It is impossible for me to be so often in sight of the top of Benachie from your hall Door and not regret that the Avenue was not made exactly to take it in. It is a kind of eye-sore to see it bearing too much to the right of the Line of the Avenue. When that was set out there must have been some very Strong Reason for Kemnay neglecting so fine an Object, I suppose the offices that are now pulled down confined Him upon that Side. Now, my dear Sir, it appears to me upon Reflection, tho' I did not think of it when we talked of it before, that, if you continue the Avenue towards the River thro' the Moss, you will add greatly to that blemish, which is the only one that I observed in all your Father's Designs. And which I think you will not approve of when executed. Was you to carry it on it must be in a streight Line and of the same breadth, by the Rule of Option it ought to be wider, But that is never observed, by any that I know. By no means a Curve added to a streight Line. But I hope that what I have said will be reason sufficient to save the Top of Benachie from being a Deformity instead of a Beauty...

I beg my Sincerest & best Comp. to good Mrs. Burnet, Miss M & Miss Burnet and am Dear Sir your most obed. hbl. Svt. Murdoch Middleton.

In the same month a letter came from a man who had trained as a gardener at Kemnay under George Burnet. He was Francis Masson, who had gone on to become one of the most famous and successful plant hunters of the century.

London October 6th. 1782

Sir, I had the honor of receiving your much esteemed letter yesterday. It gave me infinit satisfaction, and I have long had a wish to correspond with your family, but during the period of twenty years since I left Kemnay I have been continually wandering, and not without a considerable share of adversity. During the last ten years I have been constantly abroad employed by His Majesty in collecting; in which I have been so fortunat to give entire satisfaction. But indeed the last part of my peregrinations was attended with many disagreeable circumstances occasioned by the War.

I have been an enthusiastic lover of Plants since I received the first rudiments of science in your Worthy Father's Gardens, whose loss I sincerely regret. My first Voyage was to the Cape of Good Hope, where I remained three Years; and explored the country to the distance of about Nine hundred Miles from the Cape; where I discovered an incredible number of Animals and Plants entirely unknown to former Natural Historians: the great number of beautiful plants which I sent Home has so enriched his Majesty's Botanic Garden so as to become the envy of all others of that denomination in Europe. My last Voyage of Six Years was to the West Indies; where I was very successful until I was interrupted by the War which prevented me from Visiting the French & Spanish Settlements. On my passage to the West Indies I visited the celebrated Madeira, Azorian & Canary Islands. Among which I spent a considerable time and made a Journey to the top of the famous Peak of Teneriff. This is a short Detail of my travels; but I have not the pleasure of congratulating myself on any fixed residence in future. My Brother is mistaken in saying that I was established in his Majesties Gardens. Their principal Gardeners are never changed but continue from Father to Son and there is nothing in the subordinate line that is worth accepting. But am happy in having it in my power to send you any Trees Plants or Flowers wither Hardy or Exotic, as I am in Friendship with all the curious men about London; and I shall in a Few days make a Collection of some Good things which I think may best suit your Soil & Climate; and what others you may think on I beg you will give me instructions. I wish you to have a Greenhouse, as it would be in my power to furnish it with Plants & nothing is more Ornamental, besides it would be very useful in nursing many things which when young are tender and often lost when sent abroad too small, but with a small indulgence untill they come to a proper size & texture would resist the severity of your climat.

As I am quite Iddle I intend going over to Portugal to spend the spring, where I am in hope of collecting many curious things; having a kind invitation from a Gentleman in Lisbon.

Any letters which you may please to favour me with may be directed to Mr. Wm. Aiton at Kew who will forward them to me. I congratulate you on the happy State into which you have entered and sincerely pray for your long life and prosperity that you both may long be an ornament to your country. May I beg my best wishes to all your Sisters.

I have the honour to be
with the greatest respect....Fr. Masson.

We think that Alexander must have built a greenhouse as some years later he bought from a London seedsman ¼ ounce of Love Apple seed. I am sure Mr Middleton would have approved this acquisition!

Another purchase which Alexander was anxious to make was that of a chaise. It appears that such things were not to be had in Aberdeen and he had asked General William Gordon, Fyvie, who may well have been an authority on such things, to make enquiries in London where he was going. A letter arrived from the General telling him that a chaise in London would cost him anything from 60 to 70 guineas and he thought he would do better to look in Edinburgh where they could be had for as little as 24 or 30 guineas.

I was so pleased to find some letters from Dr Lamont amongst Alexander's correspondence. He was an old man by this time but it is interesting to realise that he was a link through all the family from Thomas' time to that of Alexander's children. This letter written on New Year's Day 1783, shows the years had left their mark.

Green Street, Leicester fields.

My dear sir, I had the favour your kind and obliging letter for which I return you many thanks. I would have answered your first letter if I had been in a condition to write I was so bad at that time with the gout and other infirmitys that I desired your Aunt to acquaint you with it but whether she did or not I don't know. I am extremely sorry to hear the distress of the country it is a most affecting scene. I am now recovered of a severe fit of the gout, I am become so indolent that I hate stirring or moving anywhere. I wish you all the compliment of the Season and many happy years may you enjoy. Your Sister Miss Betty is going to Bath, She had been seeing her Aunt she told me of it, your Aunt is just the same idle thing going from house and seeing every idle thing. Pray give my best respect to your Lady.

I am Dear Sir

your most affectionate friend. Geo Lamont.

Poor old man. One could have hoped that Anne would have been a help and blessing to him in his lonely old age. Sister Betty was suffering from some stomach disorder and her constitution was generally delicate. Here is another letter from the doctor written two months later:

> My dear sir, I had the favour of your kind letter and I am glad to hear you are well. I have not heard from Sister Betty since she went to Bath, I hope she'l find benefit by drinking the waters, and for your aunt she is a most troublesome being, and goes about after the same manner she did at Aberdeen but to do her justice she has told you truth about Mrs. Whitaker's present of twenty pounds as a genteel present for a ring and your aunt had the same which she did not desire by her beheaver to Mr. Gardiner, in a most insolent manner I have not seen her much since. We have a very great fall of snow as I am writing it has continued for some hours. I shall tell Mr. Gardiner about what you wrot me and you may depend upon receveing it when he has settled every thing. Give my best respects to your Lady and all the family and I am
>
> your most affectionate friend Geo. Lamont.

Remembering George's very stern and condemning letter to his sister which I found difficult to understand at the time of reading, I find Dr Lamont's letters show that she was indeed an odd and troublesome creature.

The spring of 1783 saw the birth of the first child, a little boy who was named George after his grandfather. Letters of congratulations poured in. Lord Adam Gordon wrote:

> Accept my sincere Congratulations, and Best thanks for your letter of the 18th. May and its contents & believe me, an Event, that interests you so nearly must be very satisfactory to all your friends here. May the Lady recover well – & the Young Man thryve – as I wish him to do!

Dr Lamont of course was one of the first to be informed about the exciting addition to the family and he sent his good wishes in a letter dated the "31st. May, 1783...

> My dear Sir, I had the pleasure of your kind letter and it gave me the greatest pleasure you can imagine upon the happy event of the safety of our Lady and the fine boy. I congratulate you and your Lady on this happy event and long may both [of] you enjoy this and all other happiness in this life. Mrs. Burnet is not like the modern Ladys in this age that thinks it trouble to nurse their own Children, it shows her good sense and humanity in the highest degree. I have heared nothing of Betty some time but I imagine she is at Bath yet, your Aunt is just the same. I have seen Mr. Gardiner only once since you wrot me before. He was in such haste that I could not speak to him. Pray give my respects to your Lady and all the family and believe me to be your sincere friend,
>
> Geo. Lamont.

Mrs Professor Dunbar, whoever she was, wrote a most gushing note:

> I cannot excuse myself a single Post from acknowledging the satisfaction of yours & offering my warmest congratulations on the joyous tidings...I hope the <u>little object</u> who promises to be the Heir of your Fortune & of your Honour will inherit a large proportion of Mother's virtues..."
> Another letter, this time from Mr Alexander Leslie in Aberdeen who was a close friend, says how glad he is at the news that Mrs Burnet was continuing "in a good way of recovery, and was intending to appear in the Dining Room on Thursday, I am always afraid of them when too stout, as they are apt to think themselves stronger than they realy are, and so little Cold does harm. But Mrs Leslie [Christian's mama] knows better than any of us, and I know will be cautious in every

> respect. It will be fortunate for the young Gentleman if he gets his Mother's Milk, and along with it her Disposition. My sincerest best wishes attend you all...Alex. Leslie.
>
> PS I hope to see you at Kemnay about the time of the Hay Harvest, health serving.

Sadly all these good wishes and kind thoughts were to no avail as the poor little boy did not live much more than one year. Infant mortality was very high in the seventeenth and eighteenth centuries and smallpox was the chief cause. In the eighteenth century it was by far the worst epidemic killer: Professor T C Smout states that "so common and frequent were its visitations" and like measles, mumps and whooping cough, it was so overwhelmingly a disease of young children, that for them it was more often than not fatal. Quoting an anonymous source in his history, Professor Smout writes that "half the deaths in society were of children under ten years old and the proportion of child mortalities caused by smallpox must have been nearer 20%"

Mary Burnet had contracted the disease in the epidemic of 1781 but, as she had been thirty-four years old then, had been able to overcome it. Dr Wright, a family friend, again supplies the information in a letter of October 1788. "Tell Mis Mary that I have seen your Sister. I think the Sisters much alike setting aside the Honble. Scars in the face from 1781..." As the outbreaks were so frequent it is a reasonable supposition, considering the lack of contradictory information, to presume that it was this vile disease that killed little George.

At the end of the same year, 1784, a little daughter was born on 19th December and she would have consoled them in their loss but, as anyone who has lost a child will know, one cannot replace another. The baby was baptised Helen. Two years later another son was born and named John after his mother's father and the first of that name in the Kemnay family. Having lost one child, Alexander and Christian were not unnaturally concerned about the welfare of the other children whenever the neighbourhood was threatened by another epidemic. Their old friend, Dr Wright, had by this time returned from a spell of office in Jamaica and had settled in Edinburgh. Alexander kept in constant touch and it is from the doctor's replies that we learn about the story. Here is a letter from him dated Edinburgh, World-end-Close

27th June 1787, which reads: "I am still on Mrs. Burnet's side of the question & am of opinion the cough in both children is no other than the Wooping Cough, there are degrees of violence in all diseases happily they have but little disturbance and render medecine unnecessary. The measles you observe are still in your neighbourhood." He goes on to recommend inoculation against the small-pox and also gives a prescription for red eye-lids should the measles strike. Two months later he wrote again: "Now respecting my young Friends as I suspect the Small Pox to have disappeared in your neighbourhood, the Wooping Cough so lately got the better of; that the Boy is getting Teeth fast, and above all the situation of my dear Mrs. B; [Mrs B was expecting another baby] I think the inoculation may be postponed till a more favourable period. But if the disorder rages near you, there will be no choice and I see my Friend has enough of Fortitude. After a few months elapse and necessary precautions used against the Infection being brought by people visiting Kemnay the Inoculation may be made in the Spring nor need you be apprehensive of failure even under the management of men of moderate abilities and plain understanding. As I have been more conversant with Small Pox than the generality of my Profession. I regret exceedingly the distance that separates us..." The inoculation that Dr Wright speaks of was the first step in the attempt to conquer smallpox and was tried first in 1733. Inoculation consisted of giving the patient a small dose of the pox – a shallow cut was made with a knife and the serum inserted. The subject was thus allowed to have a mild attack under controlled conditions. The child of course was a carrier whilst undergoing this treatment so had to be isolated and kept in bed in a warm room – sometimes difficult to maintain in poor houses. The custom of inoculating children in the more remote areas of Scotland was widespread; in the Orkneys and Shetlands particularly it was common practice but in the Lowlands it was condemned as being a criminal act and interfering with Divine Providence. In the Clyde valley too there had been no progress at all and in the town of Dundee when an epidemic was raging deaths of children under five rose by 250%. It was not until 1796 when Dr Jenner in England devised the means of immunisation by vaccination – giving an attack of the harmless cowpox – that this was immediately taken up by the Scottish doctors. Given all these facts, it is quite easy to understand the Burnets' concern and Dr Wright's advice was most certainly followed.

A second daughter, Elizabeth, was safely born in the spring of 1788 and a third the following year, who was called Christian. A fourth and last daughter was born in 1791 and she was baptised Lamont after the good old Dr Lamont who had died in November 1789. How pleased the old man would have been to know she was named after him.

The Lamont Bequests

I have no record of the exact date of George Lamont's birth but as he had entered the story of the Burnets sixty-three years previously and was possibly in his early twenties then, he could well have been quite a bit more than eighty when he died. Although he was old and suffering the usual ailments connected with age, he had been in fairly good health and his death must have come quite unexpectedly. A letter from the Rector at Tunbridge Wells tells us what happened.

> Tunbridge Wells. Nov. 8th. 1789. Sir,
>
> I am sorry to inform you of the death of Dr. Lamont: he had not been very well for some days but not apparently in immediate danger: this morning however whilst preparing to come down as usual he was taken worse and died almost immediately. His servant not knowing to whom it would be necessary to write, induced me in the presence of two other Gentlemen to look for information in his will, by which we find that you are his sole Executor. I have taken charge of his will and likewise the key of a box wherein his papers and money were deposited. I shall be glad if a line by the return of post that we may know how to proceed. If possible the funeral will be deferred till I hear from you: but if circumstances will not admit of that delay, as the servant gives me to understand that the Doctor had always expressed his wish to be buried in the parish wherein he died, I shall take the Liberty of seeing that he is decently interred. As by the Will you are Executor & Heir I shall not give up the Will and the Key but to Yourself or Your Order.
>
> I am etc...The Reverend Martin Benson, Tunbridge Wells, Kent.

Dr Lamont had made his will on the 20th September 1787 and named Alexander as the sole executor. Before the will itself there was another document stating that John Lamont of Lamont in Argyle was debtor to Dr Lamont for the sum of £500 sterling (6,000 pounds in Scots money) since 1769. Following this statement and the naming of executor came the bequests. His property in Scotland he bequeathed to John Lamont of Lamont. His entire property situated in that part of Great Britain called England he left to Alexander Burnet. This included the "Tennements, Lodging Houses, yards, gardens, orchards, Coach Houses, Stables, Out Houses and other Buildings together with several fields or parcels of Meadow Land. The Great House and furniture. All my Medical Books and other Books and Pictures." To each of the five sisters he left £50 and to Miss Anne Burnet £50. To Martha Cripps, his servant, he left £20 and "all my wearing apparel of every kind as well as Linnen as woollen" and he also left her an annuity of £20.

In his capacity as executor, Alexander recovered the bond from John Lamont of Lamont as the "Bond was lying in the Testator's Repositories in England". Then, really out of the blue appeared other close relations! John Lamont of Lamont was but a distant relative but a certain Agnes Lamont, wife of one James Thornton, a shoemaker, claimed that the £500 should have been left to her as she was the only living close relative of the late doctor and therefore his next of kin. The subject of the Bond had been in Scotland, her advocate claimed, and therefore Alexander had no claim on it. Alexander claimed that, as has been said, the Bond itself was in England and not Scotland and that she had no right to it. A law suit followed in the middle of which two more relations appeared; oddly enough they were a brother and sister of the said Agnes Lamont, Walter and Janet Lamont! During his lifetime, the doctor had endeavoured to discover if he had any living relations but had met with no response. The courts eventually found that Alexander was heir only to the English property and that the Lamonts were due the £500. There is a letter from Agnes' husband – she was blind – saying that her father's father and Dr Lamont had been brothers. Whether Agnes had to share it with her brother and sister, history does not relate. It seems very odd that she did not know they were alive! All this of course took months to resolve and no doubt all the lawyers concerned did well out of it. It was 1791 before the matter was all settled. Alexander was ordered to pay £418.9/- to Agnes Lamont. In the meantime Martha Cripps, the doctor's old servant, lived in one of the Tunbridge Wells smaller houses and acted as caretaker for the other properties, She was of course very well known to Alexander, having looked after the doctor for years. She seems to have been quite a character.

Tunbridge Wells March 16. Sir, I am very glad to find by your Leter you seem so well satisfied with all I have done for you (I have done the best to my nowledge & as for myself) I went to town 13 of Janry, came back 23. I left only poor Tom whom is very good does all that is in his power in the ground & Every Else. I am as Clean about the house & the hedges all mended Sahll Roul [?] and drudge the fields next week if their should come Rain (I am washing the Beads [beds] shall be Ready for any Family this month) Sir I should be glad to now if I may let the great house when I have an ofer I hear has not been nobody a looking at it for buying as yet But I am certain it never looked as it does now same it was in the Doctors posesion as I have been a True Slave to it I have done a great deal to the Beads in Turning Them & many things which I hope you will see & many Things I have done as I did them myself they will be no Expence. Mr. Adgate was hear to day I sent for him to now when Mr. Fry wold fetch his Hay the Remainder of the old Hay, he said he wold 25 of march I told him I should be glad if he wold fetch it a way sooner for I was sure he had had it a great Bargain I think then he will pay for it. Adgate has not medled with him as yet Fry & he are great Friends & Brothers in Art he longs for your Estate so they can get it as cheep as the hay. I see through Mr. Adgate.

I should be glad of hearring from you soon I should have wrote sooner But waited to see Mr. Adgate as he sees he cannot do with me as he likes as I am sure he has Been only a disservice to me & he thinks I am to much for your Interess I told him whilst I was hear I wold do as for my self as my friends had done before for the Doctor, I see this is a Troubelsom world to live in but it is not but for a short time. I was at Mr. Sargants if they come To Tunbridge & the House is not sold they will come again in June. I saw Miss Burnet when I was in town she is younger & looks Better than I Ever saw her. The whether is hear delightfull fine I should be very Hapy Could I see you & Mrs. Burnet whom I despair of Ever seeing. I hear nothing of Mr. Lamont nor Dont Expect it. Which is from youre Sincere Servant M Cripps.

Tom johns me in duty to you & Mrs. Burnet & all in your Family.

There are several letters from Martha Cripps and one is left in no doubt that she was a proper Cockney and after the property was sold found a place "in town" to live. I hope poor Tom went with her!

The Tunbridge Wells property was sold in lots and there is a lot of correspondence dealing with it. It is not much use saying, "If only he hadn't sold it" as some other Burnet would have done and probably not so satisfactorily. All his agents assured Alexander that he had got a very good price. It realised in excess of £12,000 sterling.

George Lamont saw four generations of Burnets and has always been regarded with respect and affection by later ones. We have a fair amount of his possessions still here at Kemnay: a lot of his books and among his pictures, there is a very large half length of himself showing a pleasant faced man surrounded by books. There is a smaller portrait of him too and very imposing one of Elizabeth Brickenden's brother, Richard, who married Caroline Somerset of the Beaufort family. He is always referred to as 'Beau Brickenden' but that may be a modern epithet. He is a very gorgeously clothed gentleman and may well have earned his nickname. Documents among the family papers show that he lived above his means! As this portrait was not mentioned in Elizabeth's 'catalogue' of her husband, Thomas's, pictures, she must have had it in the house in Green Street, Leicester Fields. I am most grateful to one of his descendants for supplying the Brickenden family tree. It transpires that George Burnet had written to a Francis Brickenden, a nephew of his mother, in 1775 asking for details about his family. His letter was never replied to until after Francis Brickenden's death when it was found amongst his papers by his daughter, Eleanora. She wrote to George in 1777 explaining that her father had been ill and neglected his correspondence for some time. She sent a family tree but unfortunately without any dates! George copied it all out and sent a copy to Dr Lamont. The only thing we have to remind us that part of Tunbridge Wells once belonged to the Burnet family is a very pleasant picture of the Pantiles!

The Closing Years. His Friends

Alexander's correspondence continued to be one of the important elements of his life. Adam Gordon was a first class friend and excellent correspondent. His letters are full of amusing references to Alexander's neighbours, sometimes kindly and sometimes the reverse. Lord Kintore was the subject of many epistles and it seems he was a genial man and overfond of the bottle. Here is a letter from him written from London where he had been struck down with an attack of pleurisy. He writes with the compliments of the New Year.

> I received yours of the 29th. ult. with the Inclosures which are much in the Stile as we both you and I expected Cold from our district. I shall leave the Rest till we have a tête à tête. I am glad that Mrs. Burnet Received the Woodcock I hope your Cock got a little of it. You may tell your sister that the pocket book is very near wore out, So I expect (since she has undertaken the Office of Pocket Book Maker) a new one will be ready by the middle of March. I certainly received her Card which was like herself. As to your Gun it was sent a fortnight ago, and it surprises me you have not Received it. The man is so honest that he said it did not Require half the Repair you mentioned to me and that it is a very fine Gun. I hope myself with my Single Barrel to have a Trial for a bottle of Claret or port to best you with your double shots. May you and Mrs. Burnet and the Rest of the family at Kemnay have as many happy Returns of the Season as I wish you. I hope with our good friend Dr. Thom we shall have many happy Returns of the Season in the Garioch yet, And I have not forgot my promise to the Ladies for their Salmon dinner at the Old Castle...
>
> Ars longa vita brevis. I am My dear Sir Toujours fidelle
>
> Kintore.

Adam Gordon said in one of his letters that you could always tell whether Kintore had written before or after dinner!

Murdoch Middleton did not think a birth in the family was any excuse for easing up on the work of the estate.

Wandsworth Common. April 8 1783.
Dear Sir

About the 20th. Inst. I sent you by the desire of your Sister Miss Betty, 3 Samples of Potatoes in a small Keg. She only desired Samples, tho' I think the Potatoes about Aberdeen equal in point of goodness, whether as early I know not without trial. The smallest sort is the earliest here, but is not at all prolific. Fit only for Ladies that love the first taste. The long sort is not the most advantageous. The other sort mark'd Champion is reckoned earlier than the last, and the most prolific of any. Your own experience will tell you more of Potatoes than I can. To which I refer you. Ten days ago I sent a large Hamper for you, to the care of Mr. Alex[r] Thom, who had previously promised to take care of it containing 24 sorts of Shrubs & some trees, some of the Plants are very scarce and valuable, but such as all grow here in the natural ground. Mr. Thom was to put them aboard and send you the ship Receipt, which I hope he has done, and that by this come to hand, they will have. They are small, and must be put in a Nursery, and carefully kept moist & shaded with Mats supported by Hoops, to protect them from the scorching heat of the sun, but they may be exposed to the rain and dews, but not to Frost. I hope you will take such care of them as they may not miscarry. If they do, it will be difficult to replace some of them, & so, I wish them success.

I well remember you told me that as soon as Harvest was over you would put up the bit of Marble I sent you. If it is I shall be glad to hear it. If it is not, I shall imagine you design something more elegant, and more worthy of the Person for whom I intended mine. I hope you and your good Lady and the other Ladies are well and which I shall be exceeding glad to hear, when you have a quarter of an Hour to spare, to all whom I beg my best Compliments. I bless God I am in perfect good Health, and not quite Idle. A Life I hate. I hope the Country begins to look a little pleasing, and that Ploughing and Sowing goes on. I could wish you Gentlemen of landed property thr'out the Kingdom may take the case of the Farmers & Crofters into consideration, many spirited Young Men will emigrate, and who can blame them? When I was in the Country, I am sorry to say, that oppression reigned triumphant with only a few exceptions. And I am positive you must have taken notice of it. The Gentlemen in that case do not study their own interests. By a Reasonable Rent & long leases a Farmer may be able to improve the Estate, but never by short tacks & high rents. This truth represented by you to others may have some effect.

I am Dear Sir...etc. Murdoch Middleton.

The Hamper Mr Middleton speaks of contained 200 plants in 24 species which included twenty Red Virginian Cedars and four Cedars of Lebanon, several different varieties of Spruce, a Magnolia, walnuts, thorns and hydrangeas, azaleas, moss roses and clethras and a great many others with long botanical names.

Adam Gordon echoes Mr Middleton's sentiments regarding the bad state of the country after the Peace with America.

It still promises to rain and if it does all will be safe – and the Grain & Hay out of danger, a very great object, considering how the last Crop turned out. The Risk of having sowed bad seed seems now the greatest Risk. If the landlords have been attentive and assisting to their poorer tenants and neighbours I hope the Country will be able to weather the consequences of last year's bad cropp...that an emigration will not be the immediate consequence of it. You would see poor Sir John Ramsay's Death in the Papers – & of his Successor Mr. Alex. Burnet's appointment – as soon I presume, as you expected to find it – in the Gazette. I hope he will enjoy it longer than any of the two last have done – and do the Business of it with propriety. He is in luck – & I was happy to be able to get it for Him. Sir Alexander Ramsay – and his other friends seem pleased – and he certainly from his numerous connexions, in the Mearns, had a prior and stronger claim to be their Sherriff than any other advocate I know. Lord North was the Official Person to whom application was to be made – & I made it Officially – & He did it in the handsomest Manner – for which I have thanked Him...I hear Lord Kintore is gott home to Keith Hall...you very justly observe – There is not a better hearted Man exists

– I wish the Son may have all his Virtues - & that the Dominie was in the Lake of Geneva,...Major General Ben Gordon is by this time sett down probably for Life at Balbithan – and I dare say will call on You soon. I am sorry to see by your accounts of honest Inver [Inverallochy at Castle Fraser]. He scarce can hold it long – His Son is sensible – But will never make a good Neighbour – as he most probably will neither marry nor reside in Scotland – Miss is always crossing the Bay of Biscay – and seems to have a greater passion for Lisbon than for her father & all her Kinn...

Besides his work at Kemnay on the estate and administering the farms, Alexander was also occupied as Sheriff in the Mearns and with his work as the delegate or agent for the borough of Inverurie. In December of 1784 a daughter was born on the 19th of the month and baptised Helen.

Major Mitchell who used to play golf with him in the days when he lived at Seaton, had moved to London but wrote very regularly. Here is a letter from him written in June 1787.

I am much rejoiced to hear of your success in the River & often wish myself with you to partake of your country amusements. I hope you enjoy them with your wonted Relish & that I shall find you as keen a Sportsman as I left you...No news here, public attention wholly taken up with the present alarming troubles in Holland which have disappointed me of my intended jaunt there, and will be a great loss to my Brother by depriving him of his Pupils I had procured for him with whom he was to have had very handsome Allowances. We are considerably alarmed here on account of the present situation in Holland: Our Stocks have fallen considerably and a report prevails that a Prussian Army has marched to the assistance of the Prince of Orange. We are anxious for Dutch Mail and matters seem to have arrived at that Crisis that something decisive may be expected to take Place soon. I pray God we may be able to keep clear of the Broil...I send you a few Fish hooks but I don't think them excellent & imagine you can furnish yourself with Flies better adapted for Don Water. Mr. Forbes of Seaton dined with me a few Days ago & made me glad by telling me there was like to be a good Salmon Fishing this Year, in which I hope you will partake...If Mrs. Burnet will let me know the Quantaty and Quality of Raisins she wants and when, I will desire my Friend Garden to send them. By a letter from Doctor Gerard I am informed of your being chose their Rector, which is the most sensible person they have adopted for years...affect. Respects...Mitchell.

Adam Gordon added his congratulations on Alexander's being made Rector of the University and wrote also that he did not wish to be re-elected to Parliament. Two years later the following letter from Principal Chalmers proves that the choice of Rector was indeed a good one:

> Kings College, 4th. May, 1789 Dear Sir, I write this in name and by appointment of the Members of Kings College to inform you that they have unanimously elected You Rector of the University for this Year, requesting at the same time Your acceptance of the said office. We have enjoyed so much quiet & tranquility under your administration hitherto that we have good reason to wish for the Continuance of it. and to pray that You may be long spared to be a promoter of Peace on Earth & Good Will towards Men.
>
> Mr. More now of Scotstown a young man of the very best of Characters is elected Assessor in place of his father and the other Assessors are continued.
>
> The Gentlemen of the University desire to present their Compliments & best wishes to Mrs. Burnet and Yourself and with much affection & Esteem I am Dear Sir Your most obedient & humble Servant, Jo. Chalmers.

Alexander had always endeavoured to be of assistance to his sister Jean Dunbar of Boath and had done his utmost to secure places for her two sons at Edinburgh University where they studied medicine. His friend Dr Wright appears to have lectured there (and with his superior knowledge of such vitriolic diseases as the smallpox, who better!) and in October 1789 he wrote

> Your Nephew Dunbar got his Degree with much Credit. I showed him some attention on your account, but his Brother

> was my favourite, he was every Way the Burnet in appearance and manner" and adds the information "Miss Betty Burnet all at once formed the Resolution of going to London and seemd undetermined on what stay she should make.

Writing from Spandau that same year, Scott reckoned he had "three score of years upon my necke" which is another way of saying time was passing fast. He wrote a letter in response to the news of the death of Dr Lamont:

> Fortress Spandau. June 12 1790. My Dear Burnet, The contents of your most Agreable favour gives me the greatest pleasure. I remember very well Doctor Lammont, a jovial good hearted Man He was, I only regrate He bestowed his Estate in Argaill Shire to such an unworthy man who has put you to so much truble certainly the honest Doctor has been Ignorant of the mans Character other ways would never have thogt to Bestowing such a large Fortune to the Pregeduce of his near Relations on such a man.
>
> But however I am exceding happy as my dear Constant Friend may well belive That by this addation to Your fortune you are so much more at ease and can live in health and happiness to be a Confort to your family and all your good friends - ever while I breth
>
> Your most Affectionate Friende James Scott.

There are many letters from Martha Cripps, always keeping Alexander abreast of the developments over the sale of the Tunbridge Wells property and there is a note that Alexander had sent down some "sammon" to Martha and to Mr Benson (the Rector) who was much obliged and desires his respects. As Dr Lamont had left Martha Cripps an annuity of £20 the ever efficient Alexander had to make arangements for this to be taken care of in the event that he died before she did, and on his instructions the Purchase Money received from the said property at Tunbridge Wells was transferred to his agents in London to administer. "All the Papers relating to the same, and the sale of the Tunbridge Wells Property are to be found in the Lower Drawer of the Upper Cabinet having the Figure of Fame on the Top of it." I always thought it was Eros!

In one of his account books Alexander notes

> In the Year 1795 On seeing a Prospect that the Canal projected to be cut from Inverury on the Don to the Mouth of the Dee, the Harbour of Aberdeen, was likely to be carried into Execution an Act of Parliament having been passed in Spring 1796 for making and maintaining the said navigable I subscribed to that Undertaking the Sum of Two Hundred Pounds stg.
>
> 1796 The first Call for Money on the Subscribers to the Aberdeenshire Navigable Canal was made in the month of April this Year. By the Committee of Management in Terms of the Act of Parliament: and being Ten p. Cent of the Subscription Money, I paid Accordingly into the Hands of the Commercial Bank at Aberdeen, Treasurers for the Aberdeenshire Canal Company, on My Proportion on £200. of the first Call...£20.
>
> The final Call was on 20 December 1800.

I should have thought that £200 was quite a large investment in those days, and no doubt Alexander thought it was a sound undertaking. I am sure it was a great improvement on the very indifferent roads but I am afraid it was a short lived venture and Alexander's son, John, saw the final days of the canal. Now there are only a few places where traces of it can be seen.

Alexander also "succeeded as Heir to my Father to Obadiah Burnet's Property in the new Jersey Society amounting to Twenty Shares." The latter had been a cousin of Great Grandfather Thomas and they had corresponded. Obadiah had lived mostly in Holland and from there had gone to America and settled there. The inheritance did not amount to very much: Alexander's twenty shares yielded an income of only £9 per annum. He kept them until 1800 when they had increased slightly and sold them for £87. 6/-.

In 1797 there was a proposal to alter the house. His friend and neighbour, Miss Eliza Fraser, recommended an architect. As there are no plans it is very difficult to determine exactly what was carried out but here is an estimate for alterations from one, James Rhind:

> Estimate from James Rhind for wood wanted for your entended adition as I think will serve...about 18 trees.

> The Estimates of highting the West Wing of Kemnay house 12 foot high and caring the three Chimney heads twellve foot above the Level of the Side walls as good work as the rest below & quaring the whole Stone and furnishing hewen work and building the whole for the Summe of fifty eight pounds Str. or if the Stons is quared to me I furnish the hewenwork and build the whole for thirty one pounds Sterlin.

The name of the architect is unknown but we do know that some form of alteration was undertaken because in Alexander's son's time further work was done to make good the rather indifferent work that had been carried out in 1797.

Alexander's commitments as laird of Kemnay were executed faithfully right up to the end of his days. The farm accounts were all kept up to date and there is an annual mention of the Dr Anderson's Bequest to the poor of the parish, which Alexander administered. The actual bequest was ten pounds sterling which would have come to £120 scots, so presumably it was quite a help to the needy. In 1801 Alexander made his final will. He left provision for his wife to have an annuity of £225 sterling a year and his four daughters shared a legacy of £6,000. The document was witnessed by his grieve, James Davidson, and the gardener, Alexander Winehouse.

Alexander's last letter book, unlike the first one, contained just the date, name of addressee and sometimes the reason for writing, but it stretches from 1782 right up to the time of his death and it is all I have got to fill in the last years of his life. He quite often wrote as many as seven or eight letters a day, although not quite so many towards the end. He was very much a family man and wrote regularly to his aunt in London and to "Sister Jean Dunbar at Boath" and sister Betty of course and to his eldest sister Helen who had married Dr James Bannerman, a Professor of Medicine at the University. Quite often his letters to his aunt were sent under cover to Major Mitchell who was written to almost monthly. The Major had been practising as a Magistrate with the hope of getting a seat in Parliament when there was a vacancy. Alexander's last letter to his aunt was written on 22nd January 1797 and on 8th February following he wrote to "Dr. Morrison abt. Aunt's Funeral." His father's widow received letters frequently and we learn from the book that she moved from Disblair to Aberdeen in the Gallowgate in 1799. All his friends of course are mentioned and James Scott at Fortress Spandau was promoted to

Major General in 1799.

A Mr Forsyth appears to have been his lawyer and he wrote to him with Power of Attorney in December 1800. He also wrote to "my Son wt. Masters Fees £4.14/6" at the same time. John was at school in Edinburgh, keeping up the tradition. He wrote a lot of letters to the Principal at Kings College. The very last entry is a letter to Mr Forsyth, Upper Wimpole Street, London on 21st October 1802. He died on 30th December that year. Dare I say the last of the really great Burnets? The last of the eighteenth century lairds anyway and with his passing passed all those admirable qualities that century is so famous for. Alexander was an intensely sincere man, devoted to his family and his friends, a great lover of nature and of beautiful things. His proficiency as a secretary never diminished and the family are so grateful to him for the wealth of information he has left us. So now we must bid farewell to the century which has given us so much and go forward into the nineteenth with all its vagaries.

CHRISTIAN

After Alexander's death, the figure that took centre stage was not his son, John, but his widow, Christian. From the letters that we have written by her to her son, she emerges from the shadow of her husband and appears as a capable, sincere and humorous woman with an engaging character and plenty of energy. The children were all still quite young, Helen, the eldest, being eighteen and Lamont, the youngest, only eleven. Christian certainly had her hands full as she took a great interest in the running of the estate as well as the welfare of her young family. We know that Alexander had planned to send young John, now sixteen, to England to finish his education and it appears that he was sent to the Reverend Mr Moore's Vineyard at Richmond in Surrey. It sounds a most extraordinary address but that is where he went and remained for one year and possibly more.

Christian wrote regularly to John, giving him all the news about the family and the estate and fortunately John kept his mother's letters. They date from April 1804 when she wrote from Aberdeen at an address in Castle Street where she had taken lodgings for the winter. After saying how much the family were looking forward to his homecoming once his year at Mr Moore's was finished, she went on,

> I have fixed with a Governess – God knows how she may answer, she is well recommended has everything but music. She is a Clergyman's daughter in Roxburghshire & is to be here the end of April. I shall remain a week longer than I intended, we took our lodgings only till the 20th but Mr Douglas' Ball is the week after and I thought it would be a pity not to let Christy and Lamont get to it, so it will be the lst of May before we get home. Miss Bristow is very happy you are coming home as you will be able to talk to her about Richmond where she lived many years...

Miss Bristow was a close friend of Eliza Fraser at Castle Fraser and the two households saw much of each other. I cannot believe it was a ball as we know it that the girls were to go to as both Christie and Montie would have been too young for such an adult occasion and in another letter written towards the end of the same month Christian writes,

> Betsy and Helen were at the Assembley on Tuesday it was a very good one & Betsy's first appearance (Betsy was sixteen) – We are to dine at Charles Bannerman's on Wednesday. You cannot think how attentive Sir Alex. is to us. Sir Arcbld Grant called here today and was asking very kindly after you. I have not seen Miss Fraser since we came to town but I was expecting her in some day soon.

John's tutor in Richmond was very anxious for the boy to go to Cambridge after leaving Mr Moore's establishment. Christian, although desiring the best for her son, was also concerned about the finances entailed:

> My dearest John…I have had many conversations with your Uncles and Mr Bannerman. We all agreed that £400 a year was more than you could afford, and being obliged to remain 4 years, was a long time at your age, but upon receiving your letter with the Tutor's account of Cambridge, it appeared to us the very best place for you to spend a year or more if it should be found to your advantage. Mr Forsyth had an Idea of entering you a Gentlemen Commoner. I am assured the best people's sons in England are entered Commoners, indeed Miss Bristow told me the Mr Lytleton, who you remember to have heard of at Castle Fraser, was a Commoner at Oxford… so I hope to hear soon that you are a Commoner student…

I have not found any evidence, however, that her wish was granted and letters written by her to John later that year are addressed to Edinburgh where he lived in lodgings in Hanover Street run by a Mrs Brotherton so it is possible that he was unable to enter the English University and chose a Scottish one instead; he certainly continued some form of education. Christian wrote at the beginning of November 1805 and touched on world shattering events with the same matter of factness as she treated mundane affairs:

> Lord Kintore gave a great dinner party yesterday at Aberdeen serving Heir to his Father, he was here seeking after you, he was to have 70 people. What grand news, but what universal regret for Lord Nelson. As the carrier is waiting I must have

> done, this is dear of 8d. but I wish to tell you that I am unhappy till I hear of you after your blednose.

Christian was always rather over-anxious about her son's health. There was never any further mention of the governess so we are left to wonder whether she answered well or not! Christian was ably assisted and advised by the family advocate and the factor, Mr Bannerman and Mr Innes. Some of her letters consist solely of tenants' affairs, sometimes good and sometimes bad, and building repairs, re-slating of barns and houses, new lets and outgoing tenants and valuations. Always she asks John to reply by return to signify his approval. Occasionally he was not over diligent in answering his mother's requests and complaints were forthcoming..."it is now three weeks since I heard from you." There was also much news of the gardens and wilderness. The gardener sent numerous messages via Mrs Burnet and sometimes wrote direct to John himself. Christian wrote news of planting new trees and shrubs in the garden – "plants all in good health, are they to be transplanted? Are the carnations to be put in the Garden or in potts?" John had inherited the family love of growing things. In February 1805, while still in Aberdeen with the girls, Christian had sent on a letter to her son from Alexander Winehouse, who was the grieve, telling of the damage done "by one of the tempestuous horicans I ever remember to see, it approached very nigh as sevear as the horican in Jany. 1775." A great list of damage follows – trees broke or torn up by the roots and tiles and "schlates" off many buildings.

In April 1805 Helen, the eldest daughter, had married Dr James Bannerman, Professor of Medicine in the University of Aberdeen and second son of Sir Alexander Bannerman of Elsick, but it seems that James Bannerman had mental problems. In December of that year Christian wrote to John from Kemnay.

> Dearest John, I shall begin with what nearly interests us both, Helen has been for some weeks in very poor health. Sir Alex. came here on Thursday last and said there was a visible change for the better in James' mind and had been observed coming on for ten days by his friends. This you may believe had a good effect on Helen and the carrier tonight has brought a most agreeable letter from Sir A. and letters from Himself both to Helen and me saying every

thing you could suppose from a Man recovering from such an Infatuation.

She goes on to say that she will not let Helen write to him herself until she has seen his father, which she was going to town to do. She "thinks he should be tried for some time before she returns to him when he is perfectly himself again." Early in the New Year, however, "James now by his conduct is showing that he still possesses the best of hearts." It was soon considered that he had recovered sufficiently for Helen to return to him. What the trouble had been has to be mere conjecture. The use of the word 'Infatuation' did not, I think, signify a love affair but rather a mental illness.

Other illnesses beset the family. Betsy, the second daughter, had gone into Aberdeen to stay with her sister and James Bannerman. She was troubled with a very bad cough and had given Helen and James a "great fright" when she coughed up blood. In March 1806 Christian wrote to John, "Betsy is greatly better her cough gone and sleeping and eating well. Helen is quite well, She, the doctor and I are going over to-day to dine with John (Christian's brother-in-law) and my sister, it is his Birthday. Lady Powis got another daughter yesterday." Betsy's recovery was short lived, however, and she died later that same year, I imagine from consumption. Lamont also was unwell and had something wrong with her face.

Poor Christian had a worrying time with her children's troubles and health but in December of that year another subject arose which took her mind off immediate problems and she forwarded the following letter to John in Edinburgh:

December 2, 1806. Fintray House.

Dear Sir, A publication of the papers of the late Sir Andrew Mitchell is likely now to be brought forward, you may probably know that these papers belong to me they are at present in Ld. Glenvbervie's hands and I am in hopes that he will be the Editor: as your Grandfather was so great a friend of Sir Andrew's and your Father lived so long in his Family as his Secretary and was on the most intimate footing with him you may probably have some papers which might be of use, particularly as to the early part of his life. With sincere respect...etc. Wm. Forbes.

Christian wrote on the reverse of the letter,

> I opened the letter thinking it was an invitation to a dinner to be given by Skene at Kintore. I have often heard your Father say that all Sir Andrew's papers of consequence Sir Arthur Forbes had got, which he regretted very much as they were mostly of his own handwriting and many of them short hand which he only could thoroughly understand. He put a great value on them, and Sir Andrew had at one time left them to him, but upon Sir Andrew's coming over to England in the '63 or '64? Sir Arthur showed such a desire to have them that when he returned to Berlin He altered his Will. You will know best yourself if you can assist Sir Wm. but I should suppose what you are possessed of with regard to Sir Andrew is of a private nature, correspondence between friends...

There is no chance of misunderstanding her wishes!

The early 1807 letters concern the planting of trees and the gardens and letting of farms and an estimate for some alterations in the house which came to £65

> if you agree let me know and Wallace will immediately set to work to cut the stones in the Hill for the windows...

Finance is the main subject of her letter of 22nd April:

> My dearest John, I got your note in the paper on Monday night, (a newspaper sent up from Edinburgh) I had no intention of making you pay 9d. but I thought perhaps you would be looking for a <u>draft</u> and the truth is I had not the money – and as the Pension will be payable in a few days, I trust you will get is as soon as I would have got a draft from Aberdeen and sent it to you. Last April's Quarter pension had about <u>ten pounds</u> kept off it – Mr. McKenzie wrote me about it and said that some redress could be had however Mr Bannerman said something of its being the tax upon it but I wish you would enquire either at Mr McKenzie or the Exchequer Office, it is a pity to lose anything we can get which belongs to us...I wish you would call on Dr Wright

> before you leave Edinburgh. I wrote to him a week ago and am afraid he has not got my letter it was asking him a Question concerning the kind directions he sent me for Lamont…Any old Clothes that you have bring or send them, as we are getting a new Boy. Willie would not stay & he will repent it, only think he told me he could get 6 pounds in the half year. I offered him 4 and clothes just because you was pleased with him - he would not take it so I have got another. What cold weather Miss Fraser is getting. I expect to hear of her arrival in Edinburgh if she make no stop. We have been anxiously looking for Mr. Massie. The Masons and Sawers are all at work. This is a very backward season the oat seed not near done it is as cold as at Christmas & severe Frost every night. You never said whether your carnations were going to the garden or in potts – remember to bring all your shirts with you it is so inconvenient to be always washing…

By Christian's next letter it seems that there had been bad weather and high winds and also that she did not approve of her son's intended culling –

> We are just exactly as you left us. Sad devastation among the trees, but Oh John how could you mark so many in the beautiful Birch Avenue I was horrified yesterday when I went down…

1807 was drawing to a close and just before Christmas

> When we were all sat busy working our Stockings on Tuesday evening out behind the screen came Colin Innes [the factor] to our great astonishment. I was very much vexed he had not come when you was here, however he has let Craigearn and Dalriach to two Reids and settled the Mains pasture to Peter Mathison's satisfaction…what made me write to-day was to ask you where you laid the Inventory Book of the Houses. I could find it nowhere and he could not get the Craigearn houses settled. Perhaps Robt. Mathison may have a note.

In the new Year there was a report on the progress in the house.

> The first coat of Plaster is on, and the Nursery is really a very comfortable room...and another piece of news your namesake Countesswells played the Part of Jacques in As You Like It on Thursday last for the benefit of the Poors hospital and made a very full House". Dramatics were obviously the `in' thing just then as the following month she wrote once more – "Mr Massie is busy plastering. We have been very quiet since Nelly left us except for Massie we have not seen a soul. Henry 4th was twice acted last year. Countesswells Henry 4th. Andrew Hay Hotspur and Mr Rose Feughside did Falstaff nothing been seen like him since the days of Garrick.

The new rooms were a great source of excitement and news.

> You will be much pleased with the new rooms. I am happy you have been enjoying Edinburgh. Christy and Montie have had a very dull winter and I am going into town next week for a day or two for a little amusement to them and we have some thought of going to Keith Hall in our way.

Christy, who longed to see Edinburgh, wrote a very envious letter to her brother saying how she would have loved to visit "the darling place." John, however, was not good at writing and Mr Massie, the builder, was becoming rather impatient for an answer to his questions.

Kemnay. 6 Feby. 1808.

> Dear Sir, I am now at Kemnay and finds the first coat of Plaister is now laid upon the Walls. I wish you to inform me what kind of Cornice you intend for the large Room as in my opinion it should have an ornamental freeze and Cornice which I think may cost nearly 25 pounds, and a plain freeze and Cornice about 9 or 10 pounds. Please send me a notice soon as I cannot finish the Plaister till I hear from you. I am etc., Jas. Massie.
> PS. Will Mr Burnet please say what kind of Chimney he intends for the large room.

It is very frustrating not to know definitely which rooms were altered by Massie. The story which has been handed down, which I think it is the true one, is that Massie had been employed by Miss Fraser and she had recommended him to the Burnets. Massie built on, rather badly, new rooms on the west side of the house and these were later improved by John in 1830 when he employed the services and advice of the first city architect of Aberdeen, John Smith. It is doubtful if the Massie rooms were the low panelled dining room and parlours as they are mentioned in John Smith's letter which we come to in due course. I think the comfortable nursery was the little room on the right of the new front door, but really so many rooms have been nurseries to different generations that it is practically impossible to be certain. One regrets the decision to alter the low panelled rooms which must have been charming and so much easier to heat.

Christian remained at Kemnay for quite a while after her son's return from Edinburgh, only moving into Aberdeen after his marriage in 1814. She lived then at St. Machar's Cottage in Old Aberdeen where she by no means led an idle life. Her correspondence to the family at Kemnay remained very regular and she was always looking for the 'carrier' bringing replies from John with all the latest news and answers to her enquiries. John was not always as prompt as she would have liked and after the birth of the second grandchild in 1816 she writes –

> I am expecting soon to hear the name of the dear Baby. I hope he is always a Good Child to his Mother. Sweet Mannie, I should like to kiss him..." and later "...I am very impatient for my letter to hear how you are particularly, and how Mary and the darlings are keeping. I have sent the Boy to meet the Carrier but he is not yet returned – but he surely will bring me a letter...Meggy Evans was here she told me much of all the children but Stuart has made the greatest impression – he spoke so much to her and was so kind and "sic a bonny white creature." I am sorry that Mary is looking but poorly she would maybe be the better you would bring her In for a little change of air...

Now and again some of the children would be allowed to go and visit their grandmother in Aberdeen. Indeed on one occasion when John had gone down to see Dr Stuart, his father-in-law, who was unwell, the girls remained with their mother at Kemnay but Alexander George went to stay with Grandmama in Old Aberdeen. This we know from a letter written to Master A G Burnet at Mrs Burnet's of Kemnay, St. Machar's Cottage, by his mother:

> My dear Alexander, I hear from Papa this evening and am happy to tell you he got safely to George Sq. on Monday evening without being at all sick and found Grandpapa as well as he expected, but saw a great change upon Aunt Christian[10]. Your sisters long to see you again and I think that you will have much to tell them. I drink your bason of milk every evening with Mary and Christian instead of Tea and then we all go out and walk. The hooded Crow has taken another duckling. I hope that you always obey Grandmama and are polite to all remember the polite little children. Tell Grandmama that I got her letter and that we are all well and happy to hear from her... Give my fondest love to her and all your Aunts. Affectionate Mother, Mary Burnet.
>
> PS Perhaps G.mama or Aunts will heed to help you to read this... MB

Later on Christian felt it was time that the grandchildren had ponies so that they could learn to ride. She wrote to John telling him about the

> Cargoes of Poneys brought to Peterhead and commonly sell for 2 or 3 pounds and if you offer a pound more than they ask you will get the pick of the ship. The great thing is to know the tempers of them and be able to judge. He[11] was so good as to say to Helen that if you chose he would make His man get one for you. I wd. be afraid one of the very small ones would not carry Alexr...I have been out every good day for the last week and have enjoyed it much. I am longing for my Kemnay letter I hope to hear good of you all. Very affec. CB

10 *Mary's sister*
11 *Charles Bannerman*

On yet another occasion Christian and Helen had been looking for a carriage for John and she wrote with great detail –

> My dear John, I am very sorry to hear that you have been unwell and hope you have now improved... I set out and sent Mr Campbell to examine the carriage and give his opinion. He said it was a strong good carriage, had been very little used. Wheels etc. as good as new and he thought well worth the £200. It is perfectly clean outside and In, it is lined with blue cloth and red leather stuffings and cushions and very roomy. I wished to try it if it was easy and sent to Campbell for Horses and drove to Helens and we found it very much so and we all four came back and sat very comfortably, it has a chaise box and trunk below the dickey so I have written to Campbell to go and conclude the bargain this evening with Emslie on terms he promised me. If you would send in your Arms he would put them on over Mr Forbe's and varnish so as to make it as well as new. The Body is Yellow but perfectly clean and if Mary Chose she cd. have a cotton lining as sometimes where there are children it is convenient to have a thing that will wash...

She was ever practical!

I am sorry there is no picture of Christian. I think there is just one reference to her stature which gives the impression that she was well built and probably fairly tall but whatever her appearance, she must have had a kind face with laughter lines round her eyes and a smile on her lips more often than not. She died on St. Valentine's Day 1842, a competent, warm-hearted and very likeable woman.

JOHN

John returned home in 1810 having completed what studies he had set out to do in Edinburgh. He took up the reins at Kemnay and immersed himself in the running of the estate and gardens. During his years in the city he had become friends with the family of Dr Charles Stuart of Dunearn in Fife and in 1814 he married the doctor's third daughter, Mary. Mary's family on the Stuart side was descended from the second son of the third Earl of Moray. Her mother, Mary Erskine, was the daughter of Dr John Erskine of Carnock whose ancestor, the Earl of Mar, had been Regent of Scotland and faithful councillor of King James VI. John Erskine had married the Hon Christian MacKay, daughter of George, third Lord Reay.

Mary brought some lovely things to Kemnay – beautiful embroidery and other belongings which were all fondly cherished by her daughters and carefully marked: "My dear Mother's Marriage Stockings" and on some meticulously worked cross-stitch initials "the first work she did at Kemnay". There is a charming sampler worked by Mary in 1795 and another by her eldest sister, Christian Erskine, dated 1770. After her father's death many of the Stuart family portraits found their way to Kemnay. Unfortunately there is not one of Mary herself but there is one of her grandfather, Alexander Stuart, who fought at Culloden on the Government side and whose letters were quoted in the chapters on the life of George Burnet. There is also a delightful little Heaphy water-colour of Mary's father, Charles Stuart, who had a very kindly face. There are more portraits from her mother's side including the "Black Colonel" Erskine who looks as if he has a rather nasty smell under his nose. He accompanied William of Orange to England and was later Governor of Stirling Castle which is depicted, going up in flames, in the background of his picture. Hanging beside him are portraits of three of his four wives, the last one being yet another Mary Stuart, our Mary's great-aunt.

From the Reay side of the family there is a lovely Torond silhouette of the first Lord and Lady Reay, a beautiful conversation piece. Perhaps the most treasured of all the Stuart things is the marquetry longcase clock which Mary's father left to his eldest daughter and on her death was left to Mary who brought it to Kemnay in 1836 where it has kept excellent time ever since and given much pleasure with its pretty chimes.

The young couple settled down at Kemnay and lost no time in filling the house with children. The first child was born in 1815, a daughter, who was baptised Mary Erskine. A son and heir followed a year later, Alexander George, and in 1818 a second daughter, Christian Leslie, named after her grandmother. Thereafter the children arrived at two yearly intervals – Charles John, George, Stuart Moubray, Henry Martyn and Erskine William. Quite a brood! John wrote to his sister-in-law, Betsy Stuart, on Christmas morning 1828: "...your sister is remarkably well and the infant well. A stout fellow and able to manage a great deal of suck and she has much to give him." This was Erskine William, born 16th December.

II

Apart from his family and the estate, John's other great interests lay in more spiritual matters. The Temperance Society and the Tract Society of Aberdeen both claimed his attention. Tracts arrived very regularly – delivered at four pence three farthings. A letter dated 24th December 1825 from Wm Brown in Inverurie asks advice on getting up a petition about the Slave Trade and there are numerous communications from the Bible Society. John made arrangements for visiting preachers to the Chapel, now long since disappeared but believed to have been somewhere near Craigearn. There are many letters like this one from Edinburgh written on the "3rd. of the 2nd. month, 1836:

> Respected Friend John Burnet,
>
> Knowing Thou are interested in the Temperance reformation, I send thee herewith six of each of 1 and 2 penny Temperance Magazines...

And another dated Aberdeen 22nd July, 1830:

> Sir, I take the liberty – requesting you to Patronise the Aberdeen Temperance Society which has been formed, so far the Society has gone in an unorganised state – it has prospered but the friends of the measure are decided by opinion that while firmness and perseverance in the members are necessary they cannot go on without a Gentleman of Influence to Patronise them.

If John Burnet was as full of good works as his house was of religious tracts, he must have been a worthy man. There are still mountains of pious and extremely dull literature and I am sure a great deal has been thrown away in the past. He may well have practised what he read even if he did not preach; all I know is that it is very hard going! Did he become influenced by religious teachings at the Reverend Mr Moore's Vineyard at Richmond or did he join in some evangelical movements during his years in Edinburgh? The nineteenth century was certainly the era of pietistic beliefs and practices. Letters written by his father-in-law to the children show this solemn and depressing approach to life which, looking at the kindly face in the pictures of him, comes as a surprise. Here is one written to his nine year old grandson in 1825:

> Windlestralee, Oct. 11th, 1825
>
> My dear Alexander,
>
> I have written a long letter to your Sister Mary and this disables me from answering you at equal length. Your letter is tolerably written but not so well as hers. It is ill directed. I am glad to hear that all at the Nursery is well. Say to Christian that the next letter shall be to her – but Alas! we know not what a day may bring forth – perhaps I who write and you to whom this is addressed may be among the dead before that is executed – Do you think, my Dear Boy, what shall be our state after death? We are made to live for ever. We die on Account of the Sin of our first parents – but when we die, we only exchange one manner of life for Another and we must give an Account to the Judge who is acquainted with every thought, word and action, for all that is done in the body! – happiness or misery awaits us – the gift of God is eternal life thro' Christ Jesus but the wages of sin is eternal death! Should not this be seriously thought of? [and a great deal more in the same vein]...The weather is still very warm but misty. The Crop is very safe, five or six weeks ago and its quality very good. My dear Alexander,
>
> your very affec. Grand father,
> Cha. Stuart.

Fortunately not all the child's letters were in the same vein. One from his mother, written to him after he had been sent down to study in Edinburgh, has quite different instructions:

> My dearest Alex^{r}
>
> I send you three Shirts, 2 Night Shirts a Nightcap – 2 Pockethandkerchiefs, the Silk Handkerchief Aunt Betsy gave you which would do well with the stiffener – 4 Pairs Socks – 2 Flannel Waistcoats (Put on the New One and the New Shirt on Sunday) 2 Prs. Flannel Drawers – your india rubber and pencil. Never forget to put on the breast flannel all day, and the New piece all night up to your throat – you may wear the new flannel Waistcoat a fortnight the first time – and your drawers a fortnight – never go out in Edin^{r} without either your boots or gaiters – do not omit to brush your teeth, I send you a piece of soap – never wash Y^{r} hands without taking off your coat and putting your wristbands well up. I will get you Nightcaps like your Fathers, if you will try on the one I send doubled up as it is, and pull it well down about your Ears, and tell me how it fits you. – may God himself be your friend and guide – rem^{r} me to Mr Milne – do <u>speak your heart to him</u> he will understand and feel with and for you –
>
> Your ever aff^{tc} Mother,
> Mary Burnet.

Do I detect a fusspot?

Alexander was later joined by his brothers Charles and George and in 1840 he wrote to bring his father up to date with their studies and health:

> Dear Papa,
>
> Charles has been complaining of his stomach etc. and George is quite well. We have started classes upon <u>Clock and watch escapements</u> lately which is a subject that interests me extremely. We have commenced Meteorology. The Gt. and

general examination of the three maths classes on 29th. of this month in order for the Nomination of Candidates for the prizes which I think is very absurd. It will last the whole day from morning to night. Kelland thinks that George is quite sure of a prize. His name is 2nd. on the List.

George was always the most clever of the boys and Alexander was jealous of him. A letter from Papa shows John Burnet to have been a kindly man and obviously a devoted parent:

1 April, 1841 Victoria Hotel, Euston Sq^r London.

My dear Alexander,

While sitting resting in my Hotel here after some fatigueing exercise in the noisy streets of London, I have got pen and ink to write a few lines to my dear boys at 48 Frederick Street – from whom I have heard very little for some time.

The conclusion of your Winter Studies is drawing in and the business I believe something thickens towards the close. If an assiduous devotedness to the necessary duties of the class has been in any measure the cause of your silence I shall the less regret that for a time I have so seldom had the satisfaction of receiving a letter from You. I came from Leamington to London the day before yesterday and having taken up my abode in the immediate vicinity of Your old residence [Judd Place][12] I have before my eyes almost every time I go out of doors what forcibly recalls my dear Alex^r to my remembrance. Write me and tell me what You are doing and what You are thinking.

I have of late been much concerned and busied about getting some suitable arrangements made in reference to your three youngest brothers [Stuart, Henry and Erskine]. I suppose You know that Mr. Young is leaving them about this time [Mr. Young was the Tutor]. I have not yet got anything fully settled. I was in London – and spent a week here – about a fortnight ago and not getting my business

12 *Alexander must have been at school in London before going to Edinburgh.*

finished I had to come back again. I left Your Mother and all the rest pretty well except Mary and Christine. They had both been ill and confined for some days in bed, but were both better before I left. I had a letter from Your Mother this morning. I hope Henry is upon the whole considerably stouter though he has been rather unwell again lately. Not having heard how Your Money stands I cannot exactly know what balance You are likely to have in hand but I would wish You out of the money You may have in hand to give ten shillings to Charles – the same to George & to take fifteen shillings to Yourself. Tell C and G I long to hear from them.
I write this in haste

Your affec[te] Father J. Burnet.

P S I hoped to have written to You some weeks ago but my former Journey to London with other matters prevented.
Love to C and G.

The arrangements John was having to make for the three younger boys and which were the cause of so much concern and worry resulted in their being sent to Twinham Green as the pupils of a Mr Frederick Tappenden. Stuart and Henry were the first to be sent off and Erskine followed shortly afterwards. Here is a letter from the worthy Mr Tappenden:

My dear Sir,

I shall have much pleasure in receiving your two Sons any day after Thursday and I trust that their residence with me will prove of very great advantage to them as well as of comfort and pleasure to ourselves. Their real welfare will be constantly studied, and at the same time that we stimulate them to prosecute their classical and mathematical studies with assiduity, we will endeavour to lead them to the constant perusal and study of that sacred and all important book – the Bible.

Mrs. T. unites with me in kind remembrances and
Believe me...

Another letter from Mr T written later on makes me feel very sorry for poor Stuart:

> My dear Sir,
>
> Mrs. Burnet has expressed a wish that Stuart should write under my Superintendence – he has made several attempts but has failed in each from want of neatness. I have said to him that no letter with a single blot in it can leave my School if it be submitted to my examination. Unfortunately for him his blots are very numerous – & lest he should not be able to write by this day's post, I have thought it advisable to say that they are all quite well and fitting into the regularity of school & its disciplines by degrees. Erskine manages very well & is attentive to the injunctions given – but very different it is with Stuart, he is either very inattentive or has a very treacherous memory. He would also like to have long arguments with his masters and myself which I have been obliged to stop. I do not think his thoughts & observations are quite so freely uttered as they were – still he seems never to consider whether they will occasion pain or excite resentment. His great fault seems to be want of consideration. I hope the constant reproof given by myself & even the little annoyances which he at times must necessarily feel in consequence of his remarks and want of neatness will soon have some perceptible influence upon him. His manners at table are much against him…

He did improve! and Mrs T was most sympathetic when he had a bad eye. There is a note made by John – "Kemnay, 1842, Sept. to Mr. T. credit sent for £180:10s for my sons. – Stuart's eye better… J.B." The next thing Henry was ill and "had great difficulty in removing the constipation of his bowels – it has required strong doses of the common black draught to do this." Mrs T was living up to her husband's original promise that the boys' "real welfare" was constantly studied. The boys travelled down to Twinham Green by boat. There is no mention of any arrangements being made for the two girls although I came across an advertisement among John's papers from another establishment south of the border:

MRS SHERWOOD

Now residing in the neighbourhood of Worcester
Wishes to undertake the Education of a Few
YOUNG LADIES

Her Terms are 80 gns. a Year when the Young Ladies go home for the holidays, and 100 gns. when they remain with her the whole year, including every Thing which can be taught in the Family without the Assistance of Masters, namely:
Plain Needlwork, English, French, Astronomy, Geography, History, Grammar, Writing & Ciphering – And the Learned Languages if required.

No extra charge except for Medical Attendants and Washing.

There is no evidence that Mary and Christina went there and of course it was not considered really necessary to educate girls properly at that time. Henry did eventually become "stouter" and he lived to be fifty-five. It was Erskine, the youngest, who died when he was just twenty which was the year after his father's death. Stuart, who had a mind of his own and liked an argument, remained a bachelor like the other brothers – only Alexander and George ever married. He farmed one of the Estate Farms, Cairnton, and in later years he lived at Balbithan near Kintore in Aberdeenshire where my father and my aunt remembered him. He wrote verses which did not have a lot to commend them but which show a nice sense of humour and he was greatly loved by his nephews and niece. I do not know if his original manuscripts had blots but two of his poems are printed at the end of this book for you to read. Stuart had always been a likeable person and according to his grandmother's letter beloved by Meggy Evans and was "kind and sic a bonnie white creature."

George, the third son, was the one of the family who made a name for himself and great success of his career. He was admitted to the Scottish Bar in 1845. According to James Allardyce (Spalding Club "Family of Burnet of Leys") George had always had a taste for historical research and after he joined the Bar, he became associated with many men who either became historians or did much to further the study of records and of family histories which encouraged his inclinations in this direction. In 1863 he was appointed Lyon Depute, practically the head of the heraldic executive in Scotland, and when the Lord Lyon died three years later he was appointed Lyon King of Arms. He administered this office wisely and well for nearly a quarter of a century. He was a shy and studious man, a patient scholar and an expert in his field. In 1870 he married at Dresden his cousin, Alison, daughter of John Alexander Stuart of Dunearn. They had one son, John George, and one daughter, Alice Christina. George died on 23rd January 1890.

The second son, Charles, outlived all his brothers and sisters and reached the ripe old age of eighty-seven. He was also well remembered by my father and lived for a time with his brother at Balbithan. Mary, who was the eldest of the family, died the same year as her brother George, in her seventy-sixth year and Christina, according to my great aunt, was never very strong and was required to rest a lot. A very large sofa was made especially for her to recline on as she was quite tall. The sofa can seat five with ease and is extremely comfortable to lie on. Great great aunt Christina died when she was only forty-eight and is always remembered on account of her sofa! Poor Aunt Christina, that is very unfair as she should also be remembered for her poetry which is far better than her brother Stuarts, though of a more serious vein. Besides being a victim of ill-health she also had to live in a house dominated by a most unlovely brother and although she would have had both the companionship of her Mother and elder sister, Mary, her poems reveal a longing for some sort of fulfillment. They were published for private circulation after her death under the title of "Songs of a Caged Bird". Some of the poems Mary considered "too sacredly private" for other eyes and so they were omitted. I have never come across any of Christina's manuscripts, perhaps Mary destroyed them.

John Burnet did much to improve and develop the estate, planting many more trees and modernising farms and buildings. He is particularly remembered for the extensive alterations he made to the house - very significant to us as they affect our daily life. In 1820 he built the ram: "For building a pump Well at Offices of Kemnay...£6. 4/-." This must have been a great advance on fetching water from the well. All these innovations no doubt increased the rates payable on the house! In passing it is interesting to note the receipts for taxes "payed To the Collectors of Cess for Aberdeenshire":

		£ s d
Duty on 35 windows 1 yea		23:14:06
"	a House valued at £20	3:07:06
"	2 Male Servants	6:04:00
"	2 Work Horses	1:15:00
"	2 Dogs	1:08:00
"	Armorial Bearings	1:04:00
		1:03
		£37:14:03

Wheeled carriages, carriages and saddle horses were liable for tax but at this particular time John had not yet acquired his smart yellow carriage, neither did he wear hair powder which was also taxed. Window tax had been introduced in 1696. In 1782 the tax was graduated – 1/- per window up to ten windows and rising steeply thereafter. In 1792 the tax on less than seven windows was abolished but five years later it was trebled to help pay for the war with France. The highest amount ever due on windows was in 1808 but 1832 saw it reduced to a lower level and window tax was withdrawn completely in 1851. Do note that the dog tax was almost twice the amount in the nineteenth century than it was when abolished in this.

Back in 1813 John had invested in a "Showr Bath all compleat £5.15/- paintint ditto in & out 11/-." According to Great Aunt Francie the bathroom was the little vaulted room at the foot of the new front stairs, now the gun room. There is still a stout hook in the ceiling where the bucket hung over the rather coffin-like box which stood on end and the top was tin punched with holes. I remember the remains of this contraption when I was a child; perhaps John's original one was not quite so Heath Robinson! It must have been quite an arduous chore carrying the water indoors and hoisting the bucket up on the hook so it is not surprising that in 1830 John decided to undertake considerable modernisation of the house, including laying the water on properly. He was also anxious to improve the "improvements" carried out by Massie at the beginning of the century. For his architect he chose John Smith, son of an Aberdeen builder, William Smith, known in the trade as "Sink'em", who was responsible for some very fine work. His son, John, became, with Archibald Simpson, one of the earliest regular architects in Aberdeen. John Smith's work in the Tudor style gave him his nickname of "Tudor Johnny" and he later became the first City Architect of Aberdeen. In 1830 though, none of this had happened and John Smith had yet to make a name for himself. Here is his letter to John Burnet detailing his plans for the updating of the bathrooms and kitchen premises:

Aberdeen, 17th June, 1830

Dear Sir,

Herewith send you plans of part of three floors of the House of Kemnay shewing the proposed alterations and additional stair and water closets etc.

The building for the WCs will require to be carried the whole height of the side wall of the house and roofed flat, otherwise the appearance of it would be very bad – but will have a pretty good effect in the manner intended by forming a small square tower at the east and a little above the middle wall.

I have shewn a sketch [in red line] for a new kitchen etc., with servants' rooms over the same connected with the circular staircase, which I think would be better situated for the Dining room than the present one, and which is likewise very small, low and dark, but of this you will best judge.

I shall make out the rest of the necessary drawings how soon you let me know which you will adopt and whether the other arrangements meet with your approbation.

I am, dear Sir, your very respectfully,
John Smith.

The Back Door & John Smith's Tower left, 1830.
Pencil drawing by S.L.Burnett

I regret to say that none of John Smith's plans have come to light, which is very lamentable. The new kitchen did not materialise and it certainly would have made fetching and carrying easier for the servants but what would have lightened the work load for the cook, table-maid and butler did not really influence the shape of things for someone who probably never set foot in the kitchen. On the other hand John may have had the sense to want to retain a kitchen which had a west facing window and through which the sun pours as it does at this very moment as I sit at my typewriter. It is still not convenient for the big dining-room upstairs but it is the one corner of the house which is used above all others and the place where everyone homes in. It is always warm and cosy. It is dark and except when the sun is shining, one nearly always has the light on. Like all the ground floor, except the new part, it is vaulted which is attractive and everybody loves it. The other room which John Smith fancied for a kitchen is equally dark, if not darker, but maybe he had plans for new windows. It was what was known as the womens' room.

The new dining-room and library replaced the low, small, if dark, rooms and although the dining-room is one of excellent proportions, one hankers after the low panelled parlours of the 17th and 18th centuries. The library is one of John Smith's most attractive and pleasant rooms still with its original wallpaper and lined with well-filled bookcases – a fitting abode for old Thomas Burnet's volumes. The "new circular staircase" was built and led up to the servants' bedrooms and the square tower which housed the three WCs, one on each floor, has always been known as the water tower. The spiral staircase rises higher than the square part and the water tanks are still housed at the highest point. It is quite a height and I can remember when the water, which came as far as the womens' room, had then to be pumped all the way up by a hand pump which took an immense amount of time and muscle. Now, of course, electricity does the hard work. John also had to undertake the piping of the water from the well in the Wilderness mentioned in Janet Dyce's diary, from whence it comes by gravitation to the ram house. Where the pipe has to cross the ditch in the woods it is quite unlagged and merely has a wooden bung in a hole in the side which pops out if the pipe is frozen. This works perfectly. So much for modern technology! One feature, which I am sure never entered the head of either John, is that the new large dining-room has excellent acoustics and is perfect for the chamber concerts we hold from time to time. I am sure Christian would approve.

1830 also saw the beginning of the quarrying of stone on the hill at Paradise. Formerly any stone required for building had been brought down from the quarries up on the Leschangie hill to the south of the house but John discovered that the stone at Paradise to the east was of better quality, whiter and harder. Three years later John had a fine porch built for the new front door for which he used stone from the new quarry and he must have had extremely competent masons as the granite is beautifully cut.

The wide Left handed spiral stair – the old front entrance.
Pencil drawing by S.L.Burnett.

John was a good laird and an excellent manager of the estate and no doubt a nice and kindly man even if he did not show the brilliant qualities of character possessed by his father and grandfather. We cannot all be swans. He died in 1847, just sixty–one years old. Only his sister, Elizabeth, predeceased him, having died as a very young girl of eighteen. His other sisters lived on into much riper old age. Mary, his wife, remained at Kemnay as Alexander George was still unmarried when his father died. She was greatly loved by all and lived until 1872; the date is scratched in a pane of glass in my bedroom window. It is curious that in the nineteenth century it is the women of the family who emerge as the greater characters.

ALEXANDER GEORGE

My Great Grandfather, AGB, was not a nice man. I have always disliked him from what my Great Aunt Francie has told me about him. She was his youngest offspring. She was sure that he never knew her name as he never referred to her as anything else but "Child". "The things he liked best," she said, " were his food and writing to the papers." He had a small dog which he quite liked and he used to ring the outside bell at the back door if the animal was missing at his mealtimes and the dog would come running back from the village for its dinner. He showed more affection for the dog than he ever did for his daughter. Roman Catholicism was his prime hate and he wrote lengthy condemnations, so extreme and malicious it is a wonder that he was never taken to court. Some of the essays or sermons that he wrote were just the rantings of a sanctimonious bigot and probably he was never taken seriously. In secular affairs too he was tyrannical and contentious and from the muniments here one finds numerous accounts of interdicts and court cases against the tenants or the local merchants, the latter usually for selling excisable liquor. On one occasion in March, 1886, public feeling against him ran so high over an alleged case of eviction of a crofter, that six hundred people attended a meeting in Kemnay. The Daily Free Press ran column after column on the affair which culminated in the headlines "Extraordinary Demonstration in Kemnay – Mr A G Burnett Burned in Effigy". Despite all this, I still felt that I did not have a valid reason for disliking him so much so it was a great relief to come across the following letters from his mother written in 1859. If a mother could write in such strong terms to her son, there had to be a very good reason.

25th. Jan, 1859 — 21 Ainslie Place.

Mr dear Alexr.

I hope that your other suspicions as to George are as my letter[13] to you. That he was a favourite of Aunt Helens from an infant we all know and that she left him £100 is true and also that she left Stuart £50 is as true, and also £20 to Mary and Christina which they never got. Poor Stuart's was all lost

13 *Her first letters are missing.*

> by a bad debt, a man to whom he sold wheat to that amount and who absconded and he never got a quarter of it. George was asked and accepted the office of being cautioner and of course his position was different from the others – and I remember hearing him say that on this acct. and because you seemed so ill affected towards him, blaming him for much that he never had anything to do with – that on these accounts it was better to be independent, but not one of them ever wished their portions paid up till Mr. Ogilvy wrote to say they were to have the interest decreased to, I think, 3 or 3½% – and but for that it would have been on Kemnay still. You chose to come when you knew he was here. It is a very great trial to me to see brothers on such a footing and really injured me. – but I knew it was likely from the response I have had – but should it occur again – I would see it my duty to tell you not to come here when he was here – his nature is blunt and honest – and certainly when he was not speaking at all, you kept warning him, which few young men would tolerate. Think little of trifles and they will cease to trouble you – I am ever your
>
> affte, Mother.

In another letter she goes on to say:

> ...be persuaded that you have all God sees meet and be contented. I feel sure I asked nothing and I consider what I got was not more than was right – or that your father intended. I hate dispeace but until you can look more directly to God and cease from [animosity] – these sad unlovely traits and suspicions will be always rising up and rankling in your bosom. I believe I was very careful of your Father's property and enabled him to improve it both with his own money and mine, and it was not natural after all my services (unworthy in some respects as they were) that I should sit down a widow with much less than, as my Father's daughter, I would have had. I assist Stuart [it] is both a duty and a pleasure, and to support others has become an impervious [imperative?] necessity. It is a most painful thing to write about anything of affairs to you – and I will say or hear no

more "religion is first pure then peaceable, gentle and easy to be entreated" full of mercy and good traits – let us keep this in mind and bid away from our hearts unkind thoughts of others. I love you all and little thought ever to see you so willing to believe evil. Love to you and the children,

Ever your affte. Mother.

The explanation of this unpleasantness is that John Burnett had died without making a Will which meant that the clauses of his marriage contract were brought into effect. This stated that an annuity of £250 was to go to his widow plus a lump sum of £500 in lieu of household furniture, mourning and aliment. For some reason John had seen fit to make an entail of the estate and this displeased his heir, AGB, who tried to get himself included in the division of the moveable assets which were due to go to the younger children. He took the matter to court only to be refused satisfaction there as was to be expected. He took this very badly and when Aunt Helen cut him out of her will he became even more aggrieved and proceeded to fall out with everyone else and behave in a thoroughly unchristian manner.

Of all his brothers, it seems that it was George, who had made such a name for himself, that AGB disliked most and was jealous of. I am sure that the chapter about the Burnetts of Kemnay in the Spalding Club Family of Leys would have been written by George, and the fact that nothing at all is mentioned about "the present laird" in itself speaks volumes. I have always wondered why George Burnett never consulted any of the Kemnay papers when he undertook to write this family history but, of course, it is now obvious that he was never welcome here to study them.

Two years after his father's death, Alexander G married on 4th September Letitia Amelia, daughter of William Kendall of Bourton, Gloucestershire. They had two sons and two daughters. My Great Aunt Letitia was born in 1850 and my Grandfather, John Alexander, in 1852. William Kendall Burnett, my Great Uncle, was born in 1854 and the following year Great Aunt Amelia was born on 22nd April and her poor mother died eight days later. After only six years of marriage and left with four small children, the eldest only five years old, AGB was perhaps to be pitied but like so many Victorian parents who regarded their offspring as mere incumbrances, he never showed

JOHN, 5TH of KEMNAY
b. 1786 d. 1847
m. 1814, Mary d. of Dr. Charles Stuart of Dunearn, Fife

Mary Erskine
b. 1815 d.1890

ALEXANDER GEORGE
6TH. of KEMNAY
b. 1816 d. 1908
m.1.1849 Letitia Amelia d. of
William Kendall of Bourton, Gloucestershire

Christina Leslie
b. 1818 d. 1866

Charles John
b. 1820 d. 1907

George
b. 1822 d. 1890
Lion King of Arma
m. 1870 Alison d. of
John Alexander Stuart of Dunearn

Stuart Moubray
b. 1824 d. 1893

Henry Martyn
b. 1826 d. 1881

Erskine William
b. 1828 d. 1848

Children of Alexander George by m.1:

Letitia
b. 1850 d. 1936

JOHN ALEXANDER
7TH. of KEMNAY
b. 1852 d. 1935
m. 1877
Charlotte Susan d. of
Arthur Forbes Gordon
of Rayne
Croix de Guerre, 1914–18

William Kendall
LLD.,
b. 1884 d. 1912

Amelia
b. 1855 d. 1941

m.2 1877 Anna Maria d. of Ebenezer Pledge

m.3 1893 Emily Julia d. of Joseph Burch of
Toddenham Hall, Suffolk

Ebenezer
Erskine
b. 1877 d. 1951
was called Erskine

Alexander
Douglas
Gilbert
b.1879 d. 1962
(was called Gilbert)
Croix de Guerre, 1914–18

Henry
Martyn
b. 1881 d. 1915

Octavious
Winslow
b & d
1882

Stuart
b & d
1883

Frances
Mary
Stuart
b. 1884 d. 1976

Children of John Alexander:

Arthur Moubray
8TH. of KEMNAY
b. 1878 d. 1948
m. 1921, Muriel d. of Colonel Henry S.
Andrew Speed & widow of Seymour Langham

Lettie Muriel
b. 1880 d. 1966

Charles Stuart
b. 1882 d. 1945
Air Chief Marshal

Thomas Leslie
b. 1885 d. 1940

Robert Lindsay
b. 1887 d. 1959
Admiral

Irene Dorothy May
b. 1893 d. 1982

them any affection and it is the children who receive one's sympathy. Servants were employed to care for them and keep them out of sight and sound. Unfortunately there are no more letters from Mary, their Grandmother, or any of the aunts to fill in the gap of five years until 1860 when AGB decided to advertise the mansion house, shootings and fishings to let, put an agent in charge of affairs at Kemnay and take himself off to the Continent. Where he lodged the children I have not been able to find out; perhaps with their Grandmother or with some relations on their mother's side.

To finance his travels and his children's welfare, AGB had in 1859 announced that he was

> now prepared to feu off for Villas eligible sites on that portion of the estate known as Paradise or on the Mains of Kemnay both of which are conveniently placed for the Alford Kintore Turnpike road.

and also

> Mr Burnett of Kemnay has resolved to lay off for Feuing and Building purposes about 10 acres of Ground in the vicinity of the Station of Kemnay. The situation is both convenient and attractive. Besides the facilities of communication which the Railway now affords the ground is in the near neighbourhood of the Parish School, Post Office etc. It commands a pleasant view of the river Don and of the surrounding scenery, and its amenity is further enhanced by its proximity to Kemnay House Policies and Moorland. It is intended that the area in question shall be laid off in different Sections. Section I is suitable for small Villas. Section II is arranged that two feus which front the Kemnay Station would afford suitable sites for Houses for the Railway Servants, and the remainder of this Section presents a good site for the accommodation which is wanting in the district of a small hiring establishment and Lodging house. Sections III and IV would be suitable for Village Trades men, such as Baker, Butcher etc., and Section V is intended for Labourers Houses etc., to which neat gardens will be attached, and the whole Feuars are to have the advantage of a Village Green especially reserved for their accommodation.

The advertisement for "Furnished Residence in Aberdeenshire to be let...The Mansion House, Offices and Policies of Kemnay with Shootings and River Fishings" is lengthy and detailed. The "Rent for Six Months will be £135, payable on removal; and for Twelve Months, £220 – payable one half at Martinmas, 1862 and the other at Whitsunday, 1863. A yearly tenant will be preferred."

The agent in charge of the house does not appear to have been very diligent. The first offer to rent it came from Lady Leith of Fairfield for the sum of £170 a year. She went to view the property and found it in a dreadful state. A letter from the solicitor to AGB apprises him of his agent's neglect. On inspecting the place, Lady Leith "had found the House in an accordingly dirty state the Cats appearing to be allowed to do what they liked in it on Beds, floors etc...the water pipes want to be put in proper order as at present the water is all over the floors and none coming either to the Washing House or the Pump at the Stables and moreover, Lady Leith would require the Gardener to pump it." She also required all the broken windows to be repaired before she took up residence. Not an unreasonable request. It was in the agreement that the tenants of the house would be able to purchase produce from both the garden and the Home Farm and estate accounts show that this was indeed done. An Army Colonel rented the place after Lady Leith gave it up. In the meantime AGB on his travels was not idle and took up his pen very regularly to inform the world what he thought of "France and the French" published in 1868 and "France since the War" which followed four years later. He journeyed on to Italy but his treatise on his "Italian Experiences" was not published until 1878 by which time he had returned to Britain and matrimony.

The life of a celibate held no charms for AGB and in 1877 he remarried. This time his wife was Anna Maria Pledge, daughter of the Reverend Ebenezer Pledge of Peabury Chapel, Kent. Children arrived rather too promptly. Ebenezer Erskine in 1877 and Alexander Douglas Gilbert in 1879. Another Henry Martyn was born in 1881, Octavious Winslow born and died 1882, Stuart Alexander born and died 1883 and in May 1884 Frances Mary Stuart made her appearance and lived but never to remember her mother who died when she was fourteen months old. AGB, who styled himself The Reverend, preached a sermon in Kemnay Chapel, "Christianity – an antidote to weeping" on the occasion of his wife's death. It needed a woman of remarkable stamina and vigour to endure many years of marriage to

AGB and this poor Anna Maria did not possess and once again there was a young family left motherless. This time, however, there were daughters of an age to be useful. In fact his eldest son had married the very same year as AGB's second marriage. Letitia, who was thirty-five, had left Kemnay and gone to live in England but Amelia, now thirty, was keeping house at Kemnay and tended to regard herself as chatelaine, even before her step-mother died. One could be forgiven for supposing that, never having known a mother's love herself, she might have felt compassion for the younger children but this was not the case at all and they were brought up with a rod of iron. She was not the maternal type and should never have had the care of children entrusted to her; she was far too like her father. She preferred the boys to Frances whom she dressed like herself, always either in navy blue or grey. Colours were frivolous and undesirable. Years afterwards Aunt Francie could still remember a visit from another small girl who arrived in a beautiful red velvet cloak. She longed to have one like it and dreamt of red velvet for years. She was in her eighties when she told me this.

AGB may have been a bit of a tyrant in his home but his beadle was not intimidated. He had had a chapel built at Kemnay where he could preach for hours on end. On one occasion he went on so long the light had faded and it had become quite dark. The beadle got out his matches and endeavoured to brighten up the proceedings by lighting the candles. He struck matches on the soles of his shoes, his seat, the floor, but nothing sparked. "Strike the match box, John" shouted the laird. "Aye, sir," replied John, "but the box hasna a scratter."

In 1893 AGB thought it was time he married again and so for a third time he took unto himself a wife. Emily Julia, daughter of Joseph Burch of Toddenham Hall in Suffolk, became the object of his salacious desires. Emily must have been made of sterner stuff, or else age had diminished his fervour – after all he was seventy-seven by this time – and she managed to survive; in fact they both died in the January of 1908. Fortunately for Francie, Emily was a kind, caring woman and showed her little step-daughter the only love she could remember receiving. She told me that nobody else had ever taken her onto their knee and cuddled her before and she was very, very sad when she died.

And so, at the age of ninety-two AGB, we presume, met his Maker. It is indicative of his character, wrapped up as he was in self-importance and religious fanaticism, that he could live through an agricultural depression without its making any impression upon him. It was surely obvious to all country dwellers that the old methods of estate management – or estate non-management – could not continue and yet he made no effort to train his eldest son for the position he would eventually assume. He had no thought for the future and the last three generations have had to suffer for his shortsightedness. Oh yes, he has a lot to answer for. Possibly the only thing he could be proud of is that two of his sons were awarded the Croix de Guerre in the First World War.

THE GREAT AUNTS

From 1885 to 1893 Aunt Amelia ruled the roost at Kemnay in so far as her father would permit; certainly the management of the house and upbringing of her father's second family were her responsibility and here Miss Amelia's word was law. It must have been very difficult for AGB's third wife, when he brought her to Kemnay, to find the daughter of the first marriage mistress of the house. Miss Amelia was very good to the tenants and I knew some who would not hear a bad word about her but it was quite another story for the junior members of her family. It is possible that she resented her father's second marriage and therefore had little feeling for the children of it. She was particularly strict with Aunt Francie. Whenever Amelia considered that she had been naughty, she was shut up in Morrison's Room at the top of the house. This room had once been occupied by a factor of that name who was said to have committed suicide there, giving rise to the tale of its being haunted. Poor Francie would cower, petrified with terror, until Amelia let her out. She was not allowed to attend any school – Amelia taught her all she considered necessary. Francie had a natural gift for art and it is a shame it was not encouraged. Her collection of water colours of wild flowers is very attractive.

After the deaths of old AGB and Emily Julia in 1908, Aunt Amelia became engaged to the Reverend James Stark DD. This should have been the opportunity for Francie to escape. Her other half-sister, Letitia, begged her to go and live with her at Cossington. For some unknown reason, Amelia wished to keep Francie with her – I suppose she was useful – and threatened to cancel her betrothal and marriage if Francie left her. Francie, of course, did as Amelia wanted. The three of them went to live at the Braes of Bennachie, a very pleasant house which they rented from the owners of the Place of Tillyfour. Later on they moved to a house which had been built by the estate in Kemnay village which they named 'Windlestrallee' after the house their Great Grandfather Stuart had lived in near Edinburgh. A pretty name. Amelia and James Stark were married in December 1908. The occasion was marked, somewhat irreverently, by my Uncle Robin in verse:

Her aching heart was beating fast
As through the beeches quickly passed
A man who now for many years
Had loved this maiden, it appears,
'Twas Starky.

His heart, I ween, did also beat
As he approached with hurrying feet,
And saw at casement open wide
The face of his affianced bride
Amelia.

Into her chamber quickly flew
A chair towards the window drew
And said, "My loved one, marry me
And so be Mrs Stark DD,
Amelia."
She, blushing, sat upon his knee,
And murmured so "For fiftythree
Long years, a Burnett I have been
At last I'll reign in Aberdeen
A Starky."

And so, as Charlie in the play,
A negro aunt I have to-day
From far Brazil where nuts do grow;
A sorrier and a heavier blow
Will come, when up the aisle there rushes
My maiden aunt, a mass of blushes,
And takes as husband unto her
A non-conformist Minister
Named Starky.

It would have been strange indeed if AGB's children had not developed some peculiar quirks of character with the unnatural childhood they had had. Amelia became more like her father than any of the others but her eldest brother's children were not intimidated by her as some of the others were. Thank the Lord for providing my side of the family with a sense of humour! Amelia was always nice to my sister and myself; I think she was quite fond of my father and mother but she was rather a dragon to the grandchildren of her second brother, Erskine. His youngest daughter, who had married John Souter, used to visit her aunts at Windlestrallee quite regularly and brought her children with her. The youngest, Felicity, was much the same age as me and I liked her very much and looked forward to her visits. I remember once she had fallen and broken her arm which was, needless to say in plaster and a sling. Both of these I thought fearfully romantic and I was green with envy! Felicity has told me since that Aunt Amelia used to be very strict with them and impressed upon them that when they walked in the Wilderness or up the avenues they were to make quite sure that they were never to be seen by my parents. They had to remain invisible and not be a nuisance. I spent a weekend with the Aunts once and quite enjoyed myself. Aunt Francie did all the cooking. They had a Cairn terrier which Aunt Amelia used to take for walks. Actually the terrier took her for a walk and the commonest view of Aunt Amelia was of her being dragged along on the end of a lead at a fairly smart pace and usually at a forty-five degree angle.

As Amelia grew older, she treated Francie even more unkindly. When she was ill the last time, she could not even bear to look at her sister and she had a screen placed round her bed to hide Francie from her as she moved about the room attending to her every requirement. "I hate you, Francie, you're a fool" were the last words she spoke to her. Poor Aunt Francie could never stand up for herself and later on she was tricked into parting with her own home. After that fiasco she came to live in the Home Farm house here and I think it was perhaps the happiest time of her life. She could walk in the woods and watch her beloved avenues unfold into delicate green after winter and into brilliant golds and reds after summer. She had a wonderful person to look after her, for a change, and my aunt got her a red cardigan and a pretty blouse with pink and blue flowers! But always there was at the back of her mind the remnants of her old existence. During a General Election I had gone to ask her if she would like me to take her down to the polling station. "Oh, no, dear, I don't think so. You see I could never have voted against my father's wishes, and I don't want to vote against you, so I think I will just forget all about it." Poor Aunt Francie. I used to pick her brains and memory about the past and the family and the house; she enjoyed talking about everything and anything to do with Kemnay and I am grateful to her for a lot of information and an insight into her life in the nineteenth century.

Aunt Francie's photograph of Nanny, Jean and myself in the avenue.

MY GRANDFATHER

My Grandfather, John Alexander Burnett, was born in 1852 and his early days with his brother and two sisters are lost in the haze of AGB's European travels. Just three years old when his mother died, we can only hope that he and the other children had kind nannies and nursemaids to look after them. We know that their father had no interest in them or their future. Old George Burnett's opinion that a young man should follow a career or trade was certainly not held by his great grandson. Kendall, the second boy, studied law and eventually made quite a name for himself in the legal profession although his handling of certain Kemnay Estate matters does not reveal a vast degree of proficiency. Grandad, however, studied rather haphazardly at Oxford and Edinburgh Universities and was not allowed to enter the Army which was his ambition nor was he encouraged to prepare himself to handle the mechanics of an agricultural estate. He studied medicine, which was his second choice, but never qualified as he threw it up to join an expedition up the Amazon! He was a brilliant sportsman. The house is full of cups and trophies that he won for various feats of speed or jumping. They are most useful for flower arrangements! He was a very keen and able cricketer and kept wicket for Surrey at one time. Later in life he took up curling and became extremely competent and captained the Scottish team for the, then, record number of consecutive wins at Wengen. In a completely different sphere, his pencil drawings are delightful. None of this prepared him for his destined role of laird. He was hopeless with money, partly, I suppose, because he had no means of earning any, and also because he had to wait until he was fifty-six before he inherited Kemnay, by which time he had borrowed rather too heavily on his expectations. Of all the irresponsible parents that this family has produced, AGB was probably the worst - far too busy thumping his particular tub to worry about the future of his children. He no doubt held the view that an eldest son was hardly worth educating for a profession as he would inherit the estate and be a country gentleman and there was no need to learn anything about that. Nobody knew, of course, that old AGB would live on into his nineties but you would have thought it might have occurred to somebody that a married man with a family required some form of income.

The same year as his father's second marriage, Grandad married the daughter of Arthur Forbes Gordon of Rayne, Charlotte Susan. There is a portrait of her as a young girl by Joseph Farquharson showing her red hair tied with a blue ribbon. Several of her children and grandchildren look very like her.

Grandad had met and made friends with Richard D'Oyley Carte and been offered the post of "medic" to the opera company and, with his qualified medical knowledge, accepted. My Father, the eldest child, was born in 1878 and his sister, Lettie, in 1880. In 1882, when they prepared to accompany the D'Oyley Carte on its American tour, my grandmother was expecting a third child. Lettie was left with her Grandmother Forbes and Arthur accompanied his parents. Grandad settled his wife and son at Devil's Lake, Dakota and went off with the company on its tour of American cities. My grandmother was all alone with the little boy when the baby was born. This was Charles Stuart, ever afterwards to be known as "Doodie" by his family - from Yankee Doodle. It must have been a worrying time for her and money seems to have been a problem as Grandad raised a loan with a financial company in Dakota. History does not relate what he was paid by way of a retainer by the opera company. They never forgot him, however, and to the end of his life he was presented with complimentary tickets whenever the company visited Aberdeen. It was with Grandad that my sister, Jean, and I saw our first Gilbert and Sullivan opera, "Iolanthe". Unfortunately for us two smaller children (the boys were all right), Grandad's tickets were always for the front row of the orchestra stalls, which we both found too close to get a good view. At "Iolanthe", Jean sat on Grandad's coat, rolled up, to make her higher but she was not heavy enough and the seat folded up on her, coat and all! Incidentally, my Mother's cousin, Percy Anderson, was also connected with the D'Oyley Carte - as a designer. With this link on both sides of the family, it is not much wonder that we were brought up on Gilbert and Sullivan.

The year 1892 saw my grandparents living at Braehead at the Old Bridge of Don by Aberdeen. My father told me he was once caught walking along the parapet of this bridge, showing off no doubt, and received a telling off for his daring. By this time the family had grown by two more sons, Tom having been born on the following American tour. My Aunt Dorothy was born in 1893 - the year of AGB's third marriage. A larger bond on the estate he had not yet inherited was negotiated for £6,000. Grandad did not have a financial clue in his head and the situation did not improve. Eventually my grandparents separated. After his father died, Grandad lived at Kemnay all by himself. My grandmother made the eldest children keep in touch with their father and he saw them from time to time. He has always been blamed for everything by most members of the family and accused of not caring about his children. This is simply not true. After he died, my father found all the letters that he had written to his father carefully preserved – surely not the act of an uncaring parent. I never ever heard my father say a horrid word about Grandad. I think these letters probably speak for themselves. Unfortunately only three are extant; my sister found them when my mother was turning out papers after my father died. Sad to say, all the other letters had been consigned to the flames. These three are all written in 1887.

> My dear Dady I hope you are quite well. Mumy has got a new Baby I hope you will like it, I have not seen it yet Mumy said he has blue eyes. Doodie sends you a great many kisses & lovey. Lettie sends the same. I am your loving son Arthur Moubray Burnett Granny sends her love & so glad that Mumy well.

> My dear Dady I am writing to you to wish you many happy returns of your Birthday. The baby Robert never cries except when he is hungry. I send you ten loves & a lot of kises. Merry sends her best love to you as does Letty and Doodie. We went out a drive on the 2nd. of August. I am your loving son Arthur M. Burnett.
>
> Kinmundy House, Skene, Aberdeenshire.

> My dear Dady,
>
> I hope you are quite well. When are you coming back? Letty has a sore throat. Doody sends his love, and Letty sends her love too. I send you a great many kisses and loves. I go to school in the morning by the Bus and come in the evening. we have reading, and spelling and grammar. Latin, dictation, arithmetic, geography.
>
> I am your loving son
>
> Arthur M. Burnett.
>
> Granny sends her love.

Admittedly these letters were written before the marriage really broke up but it is touching to think that he treasured them all those years. That he had many faults I do not deny but I do think he should be given credit for the good qualities that he possessed. It is very easy to judge and condemn and I think it has been proved that it takes more than one person to create a situation. I do know that Grandad was blamed for things he did not do and in one instance by the guilty party. Sometimes the truth takes a long time to manifest itself. There were two Raeburn portraits here at Kemnay that had come with others belonging to the Stuart family. They were of the Honourable Christian MacKay and her husband, John Stuart of Carnock. They disappeared. Grandad was blamed for "popping" them when he was short of money. In 1965 I received a letter from the National Portrait Gallery in Edinburgh asking me if I could shed any light on the whereabouts of these pictures which had last been listed by them as being the property of Miss Amelia Burnett. The old devil had sold them herself and allowed her brother to take the blame and unfortunately the Raeburns were not the only things she removed from the house. My cousin, Bunty, who had a vivid imagination, made up a wonderful story to explain her actions.

When the war broke out in 1914, my Grandfather tried to enlist in the British Army but was turned down because of his age. He then went across to France and tried to enlist there but 'soixante-deux' is sixty-two in any language and he was again refused. Determined to serve in some way, he enlisted with the French Ambulance Corps and drove an ambulance in the front lines until he was gassed. He was awarded the Croix-de-Guerre.

My Grandmother died when I was quite small and I cannot remember her at all. Aunt Francie used to say that she was an angel and my father's youngest sister, Dorothy, was just like her. Aunt Dorothy, much as I loved her, was no angel (she had far too great a sense of humour and fun for an angel) and I very much doubt if human ones exist – they would be awful to live with anyway! Although I had been brought up to Aberdeenshire to see my Grandmother when I was quite small, the first time I remember coming to Kemnay was just before my seventh birthday. It was in the autumn and I can still visualise it all quite clearly. My Grandfather lived here all alone except for his dog, Barney, and an old crone of a housekeeper called Elizabeth. She was an extraordinary creature and took a great delight in frightening people, jumping out at them from behind doors.

There was, there still is, a white plaster bust of a woman in the attic which Elizabeth used to put into one of our beds in the hopes that we would think it was a ghost. I can remember our breakfasts in the old dining room, the long table laid for many more places than usual – porridge, soft brown sugar (sand we called it) and milk in a glass jug which had a crinkled surface, like ice. I can smell those breakfasts still. Old Elizabeth had a herd of turkeys which roamed all over the place and we had never seen so many rabbits in our lives: there were millions of them, black, white and brown rabbits. Barney was obviously not a good rabbiter. I had my seventh birthday while on this visit and Elizabeth made me run round the kitchen table seven times. Of course we knew Grandad quite well as he used to visit us sometimes at Enmore in Somerset where my brothers and I lived with our Granny, while my parents and sister were in Calcutta. At this time Grandad sported a large, white beard and I was convinced that he was therefore much older than other children's grandfathers who had no beards. It was essential to have the oldest grandfather. One day, in London, he was mistaken for George Bernard Shaw and immediately went into a barber's and had his beard shaved off. I was very upset. On one visit to London, Grandad had taken my youngest brother, Michael, on his first visit to the Oval. Michael was mad on cricket from a very early age. He says he can still remember the almost reverent respect with which Grandad was treated. It had been rather a long day for a little boy and he went to sleep on Grandad's knee. Michael hero-worshipped him after that.

The year after our holiday at Kemnay, my mother, Jean and Nanny returned from India for good and we all moved up to Kemnay permanently. My father had not yet retired from his business as a jute broker and came home on leave periodically. Grandad still used the Laird's bedroom with the Library as his sitting room. It was there that we used to visit him and have great games. He always called my sister 'James' because she ought to have been a boy! We had a house under the library table. It had a thick velour cloth, a rusty red, which came right down to the floor and was very private. He was very sweet to us three youngest ones and we were devoted to him. He was particularly interested in conifers and planted quite a lot of specimen trees in the Wilderness. He taught us how to germinate the seeds by putting them in tins in wet cotton wool - that was before the days of plastic. He suffered from asthma, either as a result of the gassing during the war or aggravated by it and he used to spend the winters in Switzerland where the drier air suited his chest better and he could enjoy the curling. Gradually his chest worsened and he died in London in 1935. His eldest daughter, Lettie, a nun in the Sacred Heart Order, was with him and he became a Roman Catholic on his deathbed. Great was the consternation here at Kemnay when the news arrived because he had been a great figure in the Freemasons and everything had been arranged for a fancy Masonic funeral. Hectic cancellations of all the pomp and ceremony that had been laid on ensued and Grandad ended up with a far holier burial. I dare say he was amused. Jean and I were not allowed to go to the funeral – too young again, I expect – but we watched out of the drawing room window as the funeral party set off for church. "Look at them putting on their funeral faces", we said. We three were sad. Perhaps we were the only ones who knew what he was really like. I hope we made his last years happier – we certainly gave him the love that had been denied him for so much of his life.

GRANNY

It is essential to include my grandmother here particularly to give a background for my Mother. She was a very special granny and the only one I knew, my father's mother having died when I was a year old. A great romantic, she told us many stories about her early life the start of which must have been very difficult. Born on 26th February 1872 at Mercar in India, she was the eldest child of Alfred Anderson and Fanny Isabella. Alfred Anderson was serving as a captain in the 8th. Regiment of the Madras Native Infantry. A sister, Georgiana Fanny, was born a year later but died when she was quite young. A brother, Edward, followed some years after. Granny adored him but he was always a delicate child and needed constant care. Her mother died when she was in her very early teens and both children were then sent to a boys boarding school. Granny really to look after Edward. Children of Indian army fathers did not have much home life. They were very unhappy at this school where the other boys teased Granny unmercifully and the people who ran it were not very nice. Edward never gained strength and he died at the school. It was a ghastly time for Granny. Her father then re-married to Selena Constance Parkinson, usually called Lena. They took Granny back to India with them and her life took a turn for the better. I think she and Lena liked each other and Granny certainly never lead us to believe otherwise. Selena was very artistic, her pencil and paints went with her everywhere and she definitely had great talent. She was very good looking with long golden hair. This I remember only too well as long years afterwards when, as small children we stayed with Granny in Somerset, Liss Mummy, as Selena was then called because she lived at Liss and 'Step-great-grandmother' is rather a mouthful, used to come and stay now and again, and she wore as headgear a man's peaked cap under which her golden plait was wound round her grey hair! But I digress – In India Granny met her future husband. This was a story, she loved to tell and we loved to hear. He was a Major in the Royal Engineers, Henry Speed Andrew Speed, and twenty years older than she was. One particular afternoon they had been playing tennis, Granny was wearing a little gold ring like a lover's knot set with an opal which had fallen out while the game was in progress. A search revealed nothing and Henry said that he would have the stone replaced. When he brought it back to her, set this time with a turquoise instead of an opal, he asked her if she would allow him to give her another one. They were married on the 3rd. June, 1893 at Bangalore with Alfred Anderson and Lena as witnesses. My grandfather was forty and Granny was twenty and ecstatically happy. She was a very handsome young woman and carried herself beautifully.

Henry Andrews Speed had been born in Gibraltar in 1852, the son of James Speed Andrews, a grocer and native of Gibraltar. His wife, Louisa Fostero, also of Gibraltar, was of Italian descent. When Henry was sent to school in England he was more fluent in Italian and Spanish than he was in English. At some date the surname was changed and Speed added to the Andrew becoming Andrew Speed. My Mother, Muriel, was born in 1894 in Daquhai, and a son, John, was born in 1900 in Coonor by which time Henry was a Lieutenant Colonel and Granny's father a Major General. Henry was an exceptional officer and liked and admired by all. Mother adored him. He wrote her the most charming letters with little drawings in the margins and Muriel all written in kisses!

The death of their son, Jack, while still just a young man, was a devastating blow to both parents. One of grandfather's brother officers has written that he never really got over this tragedy. For Granny it must have been like history repeating itself. I do wish I had known my grandfather but he died of Hodgkins Disease on the 22nd October, 1922, just after I was born. During the first World War my mother, who was then married to Seymour Langham and living in Calcutta, wrote to her mother that she had to confess that she had taken up smoking cigarettes. Her letter crossed one from Granny confessing that she had started smoking and blaming the zeppelin raids!

Granny was in many ways responsible for shaping our characters. Us four older children stayed with her while my mother and father were still in Calcutta. Morning prayers after breakfast every morning when all the household assembled in the drawing room. Granny played a hymn on the piano and the singing would be very hearty, she was a great churchgoer, sometimes going twice on a Sunday. She also instilled in us the necessity of writing thank-you letters, money presents by return of post, and many of those politenesses which are so important and so often forgotten. She had a gift for reading aloud – better than anyone I have ever known and she must have enjoyed it for she read to us nearly every day. She re-married in 1928, a retired Colonel RA, Frederick Temple Cole, and after he died she sold her home at Enmore and came to live at Kemnay. She was a wonderful person and we all loved her dearly.

My Mother had been sent to school in Somerset but had returned to India where she had married Seymour Langham, a great friend of my father, just before the 1914 War. My eldest brother Geoffrey, was born in 1914, the second son, Philip, in 1916 and the youngest, Michael, had been born in Somerset in 1919 at Granny's house. Their father died two weeks later and never saw his little boy. Granny must have been a great help to her daughter then and took a large part in Michael's upbringing. I think he was always her favourite.

Granny died here at Kemnay on the second New Year of the last war. We missed her dreadfully.

LETTY MURIEL BURNETT, 1880–1966

I feel it is desirable to insert a short account of my Aunt Letty's life by way of explanation to the frequent references to her in my Father's letters, apart from which it was a life more than worthy of inclusion in this family story.

Aunt Letty, my Father's junior by two years, was left behind with her maternal Grandmother when her parents went to America with the D'Oyly Carte, taking my Father with them. Aunt Letty wrote quite a long memoir of her childhood and early life, the original of which is in possession of the Society of the Sacred Heart who have most kindly furnished me with a copy together with an edited version of the short 'life' written of her by one of her nuns. Letty wrote that she adored her Grandmother, who, with a devoted Nanny, filled her Mother's place during the first ten years of her life. 'No child could have been happier – but I'm afraid that I was spoilt!' She remembered only two visits from her parents during the first eight years, each time made exciting by the appearance of a new brother. Her Mother returned from America when she was ten and she spent a riotous holiday trying to do everything the brothers did, after which her Mother decided she could manage boys but not girls and she was sent back to her Grandmother in Edinburgh. She then had a German governess whom she hated and who taught her nothing until she discovered the poor woman was devoted to cats after which she reversed her opinion! In 1890 'I was in Princes Street with my nurse. At the far end was a gypsy with budgerigars who offered to tell fortunes. On the tray were a number of tiny coloured envelopes, and the bird, when taken from the cage, would pick out one with its beak. My nurse let me ask for one. I read what was inside but would not let my nurse see, but, as I dropped the envelope, she picked it up and read "You will enter a Convent". The only thing I knew about Convents was from Sir Walter Scott's book *The Monastery* where, I think, a nun is walled up! It can't have been a pleasant thought for a ten year old! But the sequel is the strange part. Ten years later, when I was just twenty, walking with the same old nurse, we met a gypsy woman who offered to tell my fortune. She took my hand in hers and said "I see Convent written across." I told her that I had never been in one. "Nevertheless, I see Convent written across" was all she would say'.

When her Grandmother died, Letty returned to her family and after the birth of her sister, Dorothy, the family migrated to England where, at the age of fourteen, she went to a boarding school at Eastbourne. She did not like it at all, and it was only the thought that her brothers would say it was cowardly that kept her from running away; later she spent eighteen months in Switzerland, which she loved. In 1899 the family returned to Old Aberdeen, and in the following Spring the second incident with the gypsy occurred. On rejoining her Mother she met and made friends with a Roman Catholic family in Aberdeen, the Hays of Seaton, and it was Miss Hay who took her to the Convent of the Sacred Heart at Queen's Cross and introduced her to Reverend Mother Walpole who was to become her great friend and councillor. There were many questions in her mind and she at last plucked up courage to speak to her Mother about her wish to become a Catholic. Her Mother was most distressed and begged her to do nothing for a year; not to visit the Convent or see her Roman Catholic friends. The day the year was up Letty presented herself at the Convent and asked to be instructed. She was received in December, 1903. The years that followed were not easy but she travelled and visited friends on the Continent, always keeping in touch with Mother Walpole. At last she realised herself that she had a vocation but mentioning it to her family raised an instant storm and one elderly relative told her that the matter with her was that she had not enough to do! Faced with this accusation, Letty wrote to an old governess who was then in Russia asking if she could find her a post teaching English there. This the governess managed to do, and in March, 1909, Letty set off as governess to a family called Paltoff who lived at Tsarskoe-Selo near St. Petersburg. The letters she wrote home to her Mother during this year are most interesting.

> Dearest Mum, I arrived here yesterday, Miss Wilson kindly escorted me, a short half-hour from St. Petersburg, this little town, about as large as Stonehaven, very good air and no collera (I'm sure that's wrong spelt!) This is a large house and I have a nice room, always without carpets – which is their way in these parts, such an uncomfortable idea, don't you think?'
>
> 'Easter Monday. The great Day is over! It began on Saturday night at 11.30 when the whole Russian world goes off to Church. I had an invitation to go with Madame Paltoff who

went to the Palace Church, evening dress white and high for the women, full dress uniform for the men...The Palace is gold and blue, a magnificent place – every two steps a lackey in scarlet and gold – we were shown from one anteroom into another, all in dead silence – till we got to the Church – I should never known it was a Church, just a room on first sight – very high and lit entirely by candles – most wonderful colour, panels of sapphire blue and raised gold, not at all gaudy or 'tinsellie' as is generally the effect of much gold. But wonderfully beautiful, a frescoed ceiling – and at the far end three golden doors, one great large one in the centre... At a few minutes to midnight, the golden doors opened and out came a procession of six footmen carrying an Icon, a cross, two banners and two lanterns followed by the priests, the choir and joined by a large number of the congregation all holding lighted candles. We were all given these candles on coming in to Church. This procession made a tour of the Palace "In search of Christ" and returned singing "Christ is risen".'

'...We saw a review of the Life Guards on Saturday, and to-day a review of the Cossacks. I did not think much of the first regiment and thought their cheers for the Emperor were lacking in fervour! But the Cossacks were very fine – three different regiments – the Red, the Blue and the Yellow, entirely got up, uniforms, lances and saddles, in one of these colours, they make a very brilliant sight (I think I liked the Blue best) they are mounted on rather small horses with long manes and tails, and go like the wind! These reviews take place in the huge square before the palace, and the public are not allowed in; it was at one of these two years ago, a soldier threw a bomb at the Emperor.'

'...Madame Paltoff is really very nice, of course I don't see much of her and of General Paltoff hardly ever a sight. He seldom comes home till the small hours. He has some very good state appointment but what it is I can't quite find out!...Last Sunday I went into St.P. and made for the inside of St Isaac – the pillars, I shouldn't like to guess how high, of lapis lazuli and a beautiful green stone called malachite, were perfectly beautiful – I could have stood and looked at them for ages... We have been here in Tverskaia Goulbernia

> about a fortnight… about twelve Verst from a small railway station halfway to Moscow; miles and miles and hundred of miles of uncultivated ground, rich in forests of pine and birch – wild flowers of every kind, no roads to call roads, houses big and small made of wood. They never build in stone. Most of the houses were burnt down by the peasants about three years ago when the country was in such a state; the peasants are nearly always drunk whenever they have a few pence. Do you know it is not fifty years ago they were slaves, it seems extraordinary. The feeling of this huge wild land is strange, unlike anything I have ever seen before…

The time for entering the Society of the Sacred Heart came nearer and nearer and still she had not told her family of her plans. Then she became ill and the date went past before she recovered her health. She went to Roehampton and a new date of entry was fixed for June, 1911. In her memoirs, Letty gives no hint of what passed between herself and her Mother when the latter was told of her intentions, perhaps she wished to forget what was said, but she does say that no noviceship could have been happier than that of 1911 to 1913. 'How privileged I was to have for Novice Mistress Mother D'Arcy. Without her great kindness and understanding I cannot imagine how I could have survived the Noviceship. Never for a moment did I change my mind, but looking back, I see with painful clearness, how ignorant I was of even the elements of religious life and how wonderful was the patience of that dearest Mother.'

On September 28th, 1913, she received the habit and on the 29th made her vows. Until 1918 she taught drawing at Roehampton and then went for a year to Mount Anville where her old friend Mother Walpole was Superior. One who was a child at Mount Anville writes: 'I remember her chiefly for the encouragement she gave me…she worked on the principal that if we had done the appointed work for the day, then we could hear interesting reading. In this way we covered much during the year…this encouraging method allowed us ten to twenty minutes for enthralling reading and from this year I date my interest in good reading and history…' In September, 1919 she went to Probation and Profession at the Mother House, the Villa Lante in Rome. The following year saw her back at Roehampton where she taught until 1924 when she was transferred to West Hill as Mistress General of the day school. It must have been on leave from

Calcutta in 1924 that my parents took me to see Aunt Letty and I remember her taking me into a sort of pantry which seemed to a small child to be filled with shelves and shelves of square tins and out of one tin she gave me some quite the most delicious biscuits I have ever tasted! After a walk round the garden I pointed to the oval shaped lawn and remarked that I supposed that was her racecourse. 'Of course,' said my Aunt. On one occasion one of her brothers called at Roehampton and asked to see her only to be told she was in Retreat. 'What!' he exclaimed, 'A Burnett in retreat. Never!'

From 1931 to '39 Letty was back at Roehampton and was evacuated with them during the War. As Mistress General she was always ready to take a class if a nun fell ill, and no matter what the class was meant to be, it was always Scottish History if given by Mother Burnett, and very racy history at that! After the War when her heart was beginning to fail and she had to lead a very quiet life, she spent her time making lovely toys and painting on silk. Later, at Hammersmith, when her memory began to fail, she would still see hundreds of old friends annually until the queue had to be controlled. She was indeed a wonderful mixture and to many the greatest friend of their lives.

To return to her memoirs which end on a note so typical of her: 'And the last phase is Hammersmith, now nearing its end for I write in 1960. It is not possible for me to find words full enough of gratitude for all I owe the dear Society – for the patience of my Sisters and the kindness and love of my Superiors. Only the Lord can repay, and with all my heart I ask Him to do so – 'heaped up and flowing over of His own precious consolations on those who have been so kind to me and mine.' As she grew weaker and her mind became muddled one wish was foremost – to return to her beloved Scotland. This, with the help of her sister, Dorothy Irvine, she was able to do and she died in a home near Aberdeen in 1966.

When Aunt Letty became a Roman Catholic at the age of twenty-three she had no Roman Catholic relations, but she liked to remember that her Father at the same age had also wanted to become a Roman Catholic but her Mother's parents refused to allow her to marry a Catholic so it was only on his death bed at the age of eighty that he was received into the Church. It is ironic, isn't it – all those years earlier – he was the one who would have understood.

CHARLES STUART BURNETT, 1882–1945

ROBERT LINDSAY BURNETT, 1887–1959

There are extensive official records about my two famous uncles, Uncle Doodie, the Air Chief Marshal, and Uncle Robin, the Admiral, so I shall not embark on a history of their careers. I must, however, shed a little light on the many references to them in my Father's letters to his Mother and emphasise the affection with which they are remembered by the family.

Uncle Doodie, after several false starts found his rightful place in the Royal Flying Corps, and of course, later in the Royal Air Force. He had served with the Army in the South African War in 1900–01, and in West Africa in 1904–07. He had a most distinguished career in the Air Force but his youngest daughter, Ann, insists that no report has given him due credit for what she considers his greatest achievement – as A.O.C. Training Command before the last War he was responsible for the super-excellence of the pilots who helped to win the Battle of Britain. He shone in many roles, as a diplomat, administrator and commander. He, with Uncle Q (my Aunt Dorothy's husband, Quentin Irvine) were most vigilant trustees for my Father when he was in India. The most handsome of the four brothers, the only one who really looked a Burnett, Uncle Doodie was very disappointed that none of his four daughters had inherited their Grandmother's red hair. He once threatened to dye his daughter, Kate's, hair! I remember him as a very generous and likeable man.

Uncle Robin was always a great favourite. He was the fourth son, and, like his eldest brother, was born in Aberdeenshire. He wrote an account of his life, unfinished unfortunately, for his nieces and nephews in which he tells us that it was the sight of his brother Arthur's first uniform which started his thoughts on a naval career. He never wanted to be anything else but a sailor. It was as a boy at Bedford Grammar School that he first became absorbed with 'the seed of desire' for physical fitness and love of games, a desire and love that never left him. He became Staff Instructor of P.T. at H.M.S. Ganges II before the First World War. No devotee of naval history needs to be told about the Arctic Convoys when Uncle Robin became Bob Burnett of the Barents Sea, Officer Commanding the operation that sunk the Scharnhorst, and at the end of the War, C. in C. South

Arthur Burnett and his two famous brothers. Photograph by Aberdeen Journals Ltd.

Atlantic. A charming man, great sense of humour, a love of amateur theatricals and dressing up, on more than one occasion becoming a most attractive 'lady', he is remembered with love.

MY FATHER

Arthur Moubray Burnett missed Christmas Day by half an hour. He was born on Christmas Eve 1878 and ever since I can remember we always had the Christmas cake on the 24th as he regarded it as his birthday cake! Like many other families, we have made a custom of having our Christmas tree and presents on Christmas Eve and when we were small, we just thought it was because of Pop's birthday: one assumes things as a very young child without questioning. I remember discovering that my sister, three and a half years my junior, was quite convinced that Hymns A & M were in fact Hymns Arthur & Muriel.

After his initial instruction at the little school in Old Aberdeen, my father was sent to Rugby. Like his father, he was a keen sportsman and shone particularly on the rugger field. His ambition was to enter the Royal Navy and go to Dartmouth but he failed the medical examination on account of his eyes. Terribly disappointed, he chose the next best thing – the Merchant Navy. He always told us that he ran away from school, joined the Merchant Navy and sailed round the Cape in a windjammer! This story, attractive though it was, is not given credibility by the letter of recommendation from his house master!

Barby Road, Rugby.
Jan. 15th. 1894.

> Arthur Burnett was a member of my house during the years 1892, 1893 and during that time he gained uniformly good reports from those with whom he had to deal and was a steady and satisfactory member of my house.

Charles G. Steel

He was apprenticed to the Brocklebank Line in Liverpool and his "Ordinary Apprentice Indenture" was made on the 30th May 1894 whereby he, Arthur Moubray Burnett, aged 15 years, a native of Old Deer in the county of Aberdeenshire, was taken on a four year apprenticeship to the above Line. The document was signed by himself, his mother and father and "Thos. Brocklebank, Master" at Middlesborough in Lancashire. His wages over the four years were to be £22 divided up as follows: £4 for the first year, £5 for the second, £6 for the third and £7 for the final year. His first voyage was on the Sailing Ship "Holkar", Wm. Peterkins, Master, for Calcutta.

The Brocklebank Line plied between Liverpool and that city. They sailed in the June of 1894 and returned in March 1895, leaving again in the May and arriving home once more in April 1898. Long voyages they were but there would have been several ports of call and a time for re-fitting before setting sail again. His last journey on the "Holkar" was on the 19th May of that same year and they made Calcutta on 7th December. Here he bade farewell to the "Holkar" and his second skipper, a Captain William Peter Reid, and was transferred to the "Zemindar". After spending Christmas in Calcutta, they left in February 1897, arriving back in Liverpool on 13th June. It was on this initial trip in the "Zemindar" that there was a French sailor, Francois Guillou, who excelled in making models of boats in bottles. Pop got one of these from him and it really is a beautiful thing with a little tug in the neck of the bottle. Long days at sea across the Indian Ocean to the next port of call allowed time for such hobbies. On his final voyage as an apprentice, the "Zemindar" embarked from Liverpool on 30th July and returned on the 29th August 1898.

He left the Brocklebank Line with excellent references. His first Skipper, Peterkin had great pleasure "in stating that his conduct throughout the whole voyage has been very excellent. In fact it would have been impossible for his conduct to have been better. He has been at all times perfectly sober [and so I should hope, at that age]. For the time he has been at sea he is a splendid sailor. He is willing obedient extremely handy when put to do anything and shows every sign of taking a leading place in his profession." The second Master of the "Holkar" agreed and added "he is a smart intelligent willing obedient gentlemanly lad. I have not the faintest doubt that in a few years time he will make a very fine officer." Captain Frederickson, who was the Skipper of the "Zemindar", wrote from Hamburg on 10th September 1898: "This certifies that Arthur M Burnett has served his apprenticeship in the above ship and Sailing Ship "Holkar" belonging to Messrs. Thos. & Jno. Brocklebank of Liverpool. He has served me for a period of three years and three months in the above ship and has always conducted himself in a faithful, orderly and obliging manner. I have found him a competent seaman, a strictly sober one and he will in my opinion prove a reliable officer to any Master or Owner who may require his services. I have pleasure in handing him this testimonial on the completion of his apprenticeship." He got a similar one from the owners with a list of all the voyages he made.

In 1899 he joined the SS "Pindari" at Liverpool and sailed in her as Quarter Master. The following year, he graduated to 4th Mate and Officer in Charge of a Watch on SS "Ujina" of the British India Line, and that year Christmas was spent in Hong Kong. He wrote very regularly to his mother telling her details of the life on board ship and their various ports of call, always remembering to comment on the news in her letters and sending messages to those at home. I imagine she may have written as chatty and interesting letters as he did, and I certainly bless her for keeping so many of his. He was now twenty-two years old. The "Ujina" was one of the first transports up to China with troops bound for the Boxer Rebellion, and later, in 1903, he was awarded the China Medal for his participation in the troop transports. In 1901 he changed ships yet again, transferring to the "Warora" as a 3rd Officer. He complained in a letter to his mother that his main worry was that he kept leaving things behind when he changed ships![14] His second Christmas was spent in this vessel off Bombay and at the New Year he went down with fever. This was the occasion, when in much later years, he used to say he had had "a slight go of smallpox". He wrote next from St. George's Hospital, Bombay, where he remained for several months, all the while keeping his Mother up to date with his progress and what news he had. He had received "a letter from Daddy" and was so pleased that his youngest brother, Robin, had passed his medical and joined the 'Britannia'. He also wrote to Robin saying how glad he was that he had been accepted for the Royal Navy and telling him he must work very hard and maybe one day he would get his own ship and then "think how proud Mum and all of us will be!" Robin did as he was bid and became Admiral Bob Burnett of the Barents Sea, C in C Destroyer Squadron, Murmansk convoys and later C in C South Atlantic. The elder brother was always extremely proud of Robin's exploits in the service he himself had longed to join.

While he was still at the hospital in Bombay, he sent pictures and news of Delhi festivaties: "Some man from the Crystal Palace came out for the Delhi Durbar and on his way down gave a show of fireworks. We could see beautifully from up here and they were simply lovely. I have never seen such good ones." He is referring to the grand ceremony that took place on the great plains near Delhi when the Viceroy proclaimed Edward VII Emperor of India in front

14 *This habit has been passed down.*

of an enormous crowd of potentates and princes; not the actual Delhi Durbar.

When he was well enough to return to sea, he left Bombay for Calcutta where, in March, he joined the SS "Hindi" as "a proper 3rd Officer." Mail from home told him that his brother, Doodie, had taken up golf and that a Musical Evening was being arranged by Cousin Jack and Helen at Powis (in Aberdeen). Alice in Wonderland it was and his reply assures the reader that he thought "Robin will make a good Mad Hatter!" Another letter announcing yet another transfer, this time to the "Ethiopia", comments on the expected trouble with Russia over Manchuria.

In many of the envelopes there are still the snapshots he sent home. Some of them show them on board ship loading cargo and taking on coal – "dirty coal" – and pictures of himself and some of his friends and the crew. His Mother must have written about his sister, Lettie, who was contemplating becoming a Roman Catholic and for some reason he found this quite upsetting, and mentioned "Perhaps now that old Miss Hay is dead Lettie will not join the RCs." The Hays were family friends and in another screed he notes "Dreadful if Malcolm Hay sold Seaton and the Town bought it and built houses." There are frequent references to troop movements in the letters of this date; two hundred odd men of the West Kent Regiment were discharged and more troops loaded to return.In the August of 1903, he wrote and asked his mother to send out "all my RNR papers as I'm going up for 2nds. drill and exam. Have made up my mind to stay out here till 5 years up as the £5 a month is worth having" and another interesting remark. He was sorry to hear "Mrs. B.[15] very ill. Do you think if Mrs B died the old man would marry again?" He was very glad to learn that Mrs B was better in his mother's next letter!

When the ship docked at Tuticorin he sometimes managed to get a bit of shooting when he had time off. "The snipe here much bigger than ours at home." In the October of that year he had:

> ...everything arranged for a days shooting in Tuticorin, and the 2nd. was coming with me. However at the last moment he called off, I think the walking we did last time we were out rather frightened him. However I got the purser to come with me. He had never been out shooting before but enjoyed it very much as he got three pigeons. I got the loan of a

15 Mrs Burnett, AGB's third wife

much nicer gun than I had before, a hammerless one. Well we started away in two little pony carts to the jungle about five miles away. We took plenty of drinks and ice with us and a cold duck and some sandwiches. It was very heavy walking as it was all sandy soil, and very thick undergrowth, and every bush and tree almost was thorny, and when we finished the day my legs were full of thorns and scratches, my coat was all torn in forcing my way through thick places. In the morning we got six brace of pigeons and partridges and one quail. Then we had an hours rest for tiffin and started again, and had better sport, but lost two and a half brace of partridges you could not get through some places without wearing chain armour. All together we got two hares and 13 brace of birds so it was quite a good days sport. We were both pretty tired when we got back...Then I must tell you about a native wedding we went and saw. It was Kaitan's, the native I told you about[16]. Nearly all the natives here are Roman Cs. Well we went to the Church or rather we joined the procession first. First came some carriages with relations of the bride and bridegroom, then a band and people walking. Then a gorgeous "palkin" with the bridegroom who had a wonderful coat of gold thread and lace, with a hat to match, and a couple of young brothers or cousins beside him. Then the bride in another "Palkin" also covered with gold cloth and ornaments and then a few followers. I got one or two snapshots of them before they went into the church. It was a very long ceremony but interesting. Instead of using a ring, their hands are tied together, (I think it was the right hand of each). After it was over they came out of church, and some bridesmaids in front, and then there were a crowd of natives all around. We then went to the bridegroom's house, after the bride had been left at her own. And Kaitan gave us cake and champagne. He was very pleased at us coming to his wedding. I then took a group of the bridegroom and some of his relations. I could

16 *He had written and asked his mother to arrange for some money due him to be sent out as he wanted to go into business with Kaitan, but I think his mother may have thought it a bit unwise and no funds were forthcoming!*

not get the bride as she was not allowed to see him until the evening. They (the photographs) have all come out and I may be able to have them ready for this letter...Yes, I saw that the King had been expected to go to Cluny and that it had been put off, Lady G C must have been very disappointed I expect.

In November they left for Calcutta, Pop transferred to SS "Waronga" and Christmas that year was spent in Colombo. New Year saw them back at Tuticorin and he notes that Doodie has now taken up hockey and remarks that "Association Football is realy terrible now a days, no sport at all simply business. I hope Rugby will never go that way. I don't somehow think so." The Manchurian situation was becoming more acute: "I suppose there is bound to be a bit of a scrap sooner or later – the later it is the worse it will be for Japan, I think. I know one Company have stopped the fortnightly boats to Japan for some time. Touch of fever again. This time of year is unlucky for me, last year I had fever and a hurt knee and strained myself carrying one of the chaps up a ladder for a bet." A remark that amuses me in one of his January letters is: "a lot of small cyclones knocking about the Bay of Bengal lately." He was obviously concerned that "Lettie joins RCs." When they arrived in Colombo, they heard that war had been declared at last. It is interesting to note that on February 10th it was learned that a surprise night raid by Japanese torpedo boats had crippled the Russian fleet at Port Arthur and the two countries were plunged into an undeclared war. The Russians suffered enormous losses in their ship power and great was the rejoicing in Tokyo when the news broke. Only then did the Emperor declare war on Russia. A familiar ring to that story.

A letter written on 1st April – underlined – from SS "Chindwara" at sea. He was not playing April Fool when he let her know that he had been promoted to 2nd Officer. He had been very pleased to meet up with Captain Peterkin again while in port in Bombay.

Went ashore in Pondicherry, the French port, and got into one of those carriages there. 'Push Pushs' they are called. They are just the same as a motor car only you are pushed by a couple of men instead of an engine. You have a handle, just like the handle you steer with in a motor called the 'Oldsmobile'. You will see it in advertisements.

Sadly, the Merchant Navy days were nearly over. The eye weakness which had prevented my Father from being accepted by the Royal Navy had grown worse. In the April of 1904 he wrote: "I went yesterday to see about my eyes and I can't pass. I was almost sure of it, but will try again in Calcutta - I know this will disappoint you when you hear about my eyes, but I was almost sure of it for some time past. It is the glare and heat that has made them worse, I know. I am quite resigned to the idea of leaving the sea now, but I know you will be disappointed...Anyway I intend to stop the last year if only for the pay" And in another letter – "I have started wearing, or at least I did a month ago, blue goggles, lots of people wear them out here and they are a great rest to the eyes." As a matter of fact it was only one of his eyes that was weak, and later on he always wore a monocle. The only time one saw him wearing spectacles was when he was shooting. The good eye just had a plain glass lens and he was always regarded as an absolutely superb shot.

He stayed with the SS "Putiala", his last ship, until his time with the company was up and then returned to Britain for a spot of home leave. He went back to India, to Calcutta and to a job with the Continental Electrical Company. The letters to his mother for this period are missing but we hear from him again in 1906, up to something quite out of the ordinary.

II

The Government of India had decided to make a gift to the Tashi Lama of a beautiful motor car, an 8 hp Laurin Klement, and the British Political Agent in Gyantse, Tibet, was commissioned to deliver the vehicle. This was a certain Captain O'Connor. In his own little Peugeot, accompanied by a mechanic in the Laurin Klement, O'Connor set off to drive across 200 miles of incredibly difficult country across which car had never travelled before. Two passes, one of 12,500 feet and the other 15,700 feet had to be negotiated, for which porters were engaged. On a stretch of twenty miles the cars had to be hauled by mule and lifted bodily over the boulders which strewed the non-existent 'road'. Shortly after crossing the border into Tibet, the two men and their troop of porters halted for a cold and frosty night at Chumbi, 9,800 feet. The mechanic forgot to drain the radiators, which cracked. Aid was sought from Calcutta, history does not relate how, and a week later Arthur M. Burnett from the

Continental Electrical Company arrived by pony. He managed to patch up the radiators with a mixture of resin, powdered glass and white of egg! It worked! The expedition started off again with my father instead of the mechanic. He had, as was his wont, taken his camera with him, and took some lovely pictures of the cars, the 'roads' and the surrounding country. The little Peugeot, with my father at the wheel, was the first car to enter Gyantse, 13,000 feet, and Captain O'Connor at the wheel of the wonderful yellow striped Laurin Klement, drove in after him. The Tashi Lama was, I am sure, delighted with his gift and he took possession of it after he had built a fifty mile stretch of road for it. I love Pop's photograph of the road leading out of the Chumbi valley before coming to the Tang La Pass. Chumalari, the Sacred Mountain of Tibet[17], is in the distance.

III

My father did not remain with the Continental Electric for very long and the outbreak of the war in 1914 saw him back with the British India Company again in their offices in Calcutta. It was then that he joined the Calcutta Scottish, an auxiliary force (AF), and did training with them prior to the outbreak of hostilities. His letters to his mother resume in 1914. He enjoyed the drill and the route marches they undertook and felt much fitter for them. In the September he got leave from the Company and got away "to do his bit". A letter written from Calcutta on 3rd September: "We are very busy this morning and evening drilling etc. the Calcutta Scottish are about 460 strong now, and we are getting licked into shape, in fact I think we have done extremely well considering we have not been going a month...I got your letter last Saturday saying Bob was on the Laertes and on the Monday we heard that she had been in the thick of it and done so well...I am wondering where Doodie is, he is sure to have joined some regiment by now."

He managed to send off a very hurried pencilled note from Bombay on 18th September:

17 *Everest*

Dearest Mum,

Just a line to let you know that I and the rest of the Calcutta Battery (Volunteers) are off for East Africa. I had meant to write to you but we realy have not had a chance of any sort. Now I am in this Restaurant with about 10 men who got leave for an hour to get something to eat. We have had a very hard day today and nothing in the way of meat till just now 10PM. We move out of the dock tomorrow I believe. We are like ordinary Tommies, and I must say the accommodation we have been given is bad very very bad but, I have been trying to impress on the Sahibs of the Party that we must not grumble, on account of the others who are ready to already. All the same I must say they have run everything very badly indeed. I know as I had the same thing on the B I. when out in China. However we hope to have a good time. I only heard that they wanted men urgently on Saturday night and we left Calcutta for Bombay on Monday 2.30 p.m. pretty quick. I am very fit and very dirty. Your loving son Arthur M. Burnett. Written from Green' Restaurant, Bombay Apollo Bunder.

The next letter written on board the troop ship off Mombasa gives more details of the scramble to get away.

SS Bandra

Dearest Mum,

We will be off to Mombassa some time this evening, and with any luck should get into harbour as well. We have had a splendid run down, with realy fine weather all the way, and the crowd as a whole are very fit indeed. We went on ahead yesterday as the Dartmouth, our escort, had to go off to the assistance of one of her sisters who had gone ashore somewhere north of Mombassa. The beginning of the trip once we had all got out of Bombay Harbour and at sea was a fine sight, about 50 of us altogether one way and another – some going home and some for Egypt and three of us down here. We will be the first to arrive now, and will have to wait for the ship that is behind for the commanding officer.

> How long we shall be in Mombassa we have not the slightest idea, and when we shall be able to post letters or send them I don't know, so you must not worry if you don't hear for some time. I don't fancy we shall have very much in the way of fighting to do from all accounts but still you never know and we may see some after all. We have quite a nice crowd, and a great many of us knew each other in Calcutta which makes things cheerful. I fancy we shall be back in Calcutta again about March or April, but will possibly know more once we get to Mombassa. I am as fit as anything, the sea always bucks me up, and as I have not shaved since I left Bombay I have quite a beard on now, and look a terrible ruffian. The going away was such a rush, that I had not time to write properly before I left. I only knew on the Saturday evening that they wanted some more fellows as some had cried off, so I saw the Adj. in the Club and said I would go, if I could get leave and let him know at 10 am. Sunday. So I ran up to Donald's and just got him before dinner, went and had my own and then went on and saw Ramsay, one of the other partners and got him to ring up Bagley, and eventually fixed everything up in no time. Saw the Adj. who I knew and who I also knew was at the theatre, and got a fellow's kit on the Sunday morning, went and signed on and marched up to the Fort in the afternoon with the rest, and was addressed by the General - Monday we were on board the launch at 2 pm. and away in the train by 5 pm. Quick work I think. Now I must finish this off. All our letters are going back with the Captain to be posted in Bombay, so I have no idea when you will get it. I had not heard for two mails from you, and hope nothing is wrong or anything. All letters are being forwarded on to us but we have no idea when we shall get them of course. Must stop now. Best of love to yourself...

True to his usual form, my father took his camera with him to East Africa and his years with the KAR are well documented and illustrated.

From Mombasa they went up to Voi: "There is some talk of us making a move shortly. We got into marching order this morning, everything on the carts etc., just for practice." There is a good snapshot of the guns and gun carriages with oxen inspanned, and another one of the "fellows" of the CVB at riding exercise. They are pictured with a lot of camels as well as the mules and oxen. They marched on to Kiu where they had a bridge-building exercise and then on to Nairobi where they spent the first Christmas of the war. Pop wrote to his mother that he "was much pleased at getting into the K.A.R.s I am in the 1st. and at the moment am up in Nairobi learning all I can. I have to try to pick up as much of the language as I possibly can, and you know how bad I am at that game...They are all such real good fellows. My O.C. at the moment is an old Rugbean, Gifford is his name."

The Spring of 1915 saw them back at Kiu digging trenches. There was a Field Hospital there where there were more cases of fever and dysentery etc. than of wounded men, the climate and terrain turning out to be the greater enemy. They were often short of food too. Life had its lighter moments though and there are amusing snapshots of the Kiu Races and Gymkhana! You cannot have a Race Meeting without the ladies in their fine hats and there are pictures of "some of the chaps with 'Miss' Chalmers and 'Miss' Johnstone" and of course the Tout. My father is portrayed leading in the winner 'Jack Cooper up` and 'Miss' Chalmers assisting. Heaven knows where they got the hats and skirts.

In their pursuit of the elusive Paul von Lettow Vorbeck, C in C German Forces in East Africa, the KAR covered a lot of country, much of the time re-tracing their steps. They camped at Bura; they camped at Kilimabuza; they entrained for Maktau, formed a mule wagon and marched back to Kiu. Pop wrote to his mother from Nairobi on 28th December 1915:

> I heard from my friend Mrs. Langham last mail, a cheery kind letter and full of the Calcutta news. He lived, you remember, with me in the Chummery in 8 Pretoria Street for a long time. I am sure you would like her and him. Their kiddie is my God son.

This is the first mention of my mother and the "kiddie" is my eldest half-brother, Geoffrey. In a letter written on 2nd April 1916, my father describes some action: "The last big fight lasted about 6 hours, and the Germans after blowing up their big 4.1 gun (one of the Koeningburg's guns) cleared off down the line South. The fight is called the Ruwer River Fight and is quite close to their railway line and station, Kahe. We had a good many casualties, between 2 and 300, but I fancy we gave them more than they bargained for. We had a hot time of it, it was the first big thing I had been in, and I was very glad when it was all over, I must say."

In June he wrote, "I realy do think it splendid of my Father to have done all he has, and roughed it at his time of life, it is an example to all the slackers young and old, and he has never had to rough it to the extent he has to now, as a private. I quite agree with you I think it splendid of him, and I hope he comes through it none the worse."

A letter of 1st November that year tells his mother that he had been "told to put my third star up," and to tell Uncle Arthur "I am now a Capt. and much honoured by being so."

"14. 11. 16 I will get off a letter to-day to my Father. He in my mind has set an example to many by the way he has turned out and done his bit, and a good bit too – I have got another of those beastly veldt sores, but am getting rid of them by degrees. I want a rest for a couple of months..." and in another letter, "I should be glad of a real holiday but we can't think of those sort of things. That is one thing the fellows in France have the pull over us out here, they do get a bit of leave now and again, and do you know everyone I have met out here who has come out of France says the same thing 'Give us France any day to this.'" In August 1917 he says, "I don't know what they are going to do with me...I hope my Father has decided to chuck it, and stay now at Kemnay. He realy has done well I think and set an example to many."

First he refers to his own deteriorating health and secondly to the fact that his father had been gassed in France.

It is a well known fact that the East African Army was continually having to invalid men back to India and my father was sent back to Bombay at the end of 1917. After coming out of hospital he was stationed at one of the Prisoner of War camps in Bombay. In one of his letters home he had mentioned that "a lot of chaps" he had met who were "in jute" seemed to think there was quite a future in it and certainly better than shipping, so after he was discharged from the army he joined a Dundee firm of Jute Brokers for whom he worked until he retired. My mother used to tell a story about a rather pretentious lady who enquired, "What does your husband do?" to which my mother replied, "Oh, he sells sacks!"

In 1919 Seymour Langham, the friend of the old Chummery

days in Calcutta, died just a fortnight after his third son was born in Somerset. Two years later my father married his widow, Muriel, on 1st October. The following October I arrived on the scene in Calcutta and three and a half years later my sister, Jean, was born in Somerset. Now we were a family of five. We never did and never have thought of our half brothers as being 'half' brothers; we have always been very close, and I look back on a very happy childhood.

My father retired in 1934 and busied himself at Kemnay in various spheres. I can picture him quite clearly hoeing and raking the paths and drives and keeping the edges tidy. He served as a County Councillor for many years and became a Deputy Lieutenant of Aberdeenshire. At the outbreak of war in 1939 he joined the Local Defence Volunteers and then the Home Guard of which he commanded the Garioch Division. Towards the end of the war he was involved in the formation of the Cadet Force, became the Colonel of the Aberdeenshire force and gave it much of his time and energy. He was a lovely person, kind, full of humour and a wonderful father. Once he had given his word, he never broke it. He always said that if you promised something to a child, it was most important that you never went back on your word. He was one of the few men I have known, perhaps the only one, who never complained and made a fuss when he was ill. Perhaps if he had, they might have discovered his cancer before it was too late. He died in July 1948. One of the best of the Burnetts.

Well, there you are, Bunty, I hope you approve. Not a bad lot on the whole, one or two exceptions, of course, but —— we mustn't blow our own trumpet, must we?

View of Kemnay House from the Stables.
Pencil drawing by S.L.Burnett

THE SHADE OF THE PAST
By
Christina Leslie Burnett
1857

Could he appear—the grand majestic Spirit,
Telling the tale, so little prized before,
He, from the babbling present, did inherit—
All that our fathers heard, *yet* did not hear, of yore!

They who lived, acted, in the world's turmoil—
Who threw their passions'colouring o'er each scene—
Shone with may-flies, or with true sons of toil
Built up a life which tells that they have been.

Fragments they leave us of the world's old story
Fragments we muse and gaze upon and sigh—
Had we been there—in those bright days of glory!
Had we a faithful record 'neath our eye!

We sit and dim our eyes in vainly guessing—
In spelling olden letters half effaced—
All that thine eyes have watched in the progressing,
Seen every letter in succession traced!

Silent, still silent—never prayer hath moved thee
Calm look'st thou down on our laborious hours
Have ne'er thy votaries worn-out lives reproved thee,
Thou cruel miser, for thy hoarded powers?

One word of thine were worth ten thousand pages,
Brilliant, but doubtful, of historic guess
One living relic of those far-off ages
We vainly strive in fancy's robes to dress.

Ah! niggard sullen Ghost, where o'er thy treasures
Dost thou sit gloating, callous to all prayer?
While cruel Time, yielding to thee, outmeasures
Days, months and years all passing to thy care.

I know thou art even as I know God living
I know thou livest on, though seeming still to die
And all the treasure Time to thee is giving
Will it be ours then, in Eternity?

Like a spread map, may we unfold before us
The story of our earth from morn to night?
And shall a mightier power compel thee to restore us
The darkened page—all gleaming into light?

POTENTATES OF ENGLAND FROM THE CONQUEST

By Stuart Burnett 1887

William conquered at Hastings, where poor Harold fell;
And the Norman ruled England for years wondrous well,
But on Normandy's soil his life's journey was run,
And Tyrell's shaft pierced William Rufus his son.
King Henry the 1st died of lampreys and grief.
And Stephen his nephew came in like a thief.
King Henry the Second by Priests was well thwacked
Because, at his bidding, a priest's skull was cracked.
Richard Coeur de lion gave the Pagans no quarter
And his bad brother John, he signed the great Charter.
Henry IIIrd of his barons got many a Pinch,
But his son Edward Ist was a king every inch.
Poor Edward the Second knew little of luck,
But Edward the Third had abundance of pluck.
Richard IInd his grandson—was 'reft of his throne,
How and when he deceased, is not certainly known.
Henry IVth the Usurper, was well nigh undone
With mad Scots and Welsh and his riotous son.
King Henry the Fifth in his youth indiscreet,
Yet lived long enough to lay France at his feet.
Lost by Henry the Sixth, who, in civil war's strife,
Lost his realm, lost his son, and at length lost his life.
The morals of Edward the Fourth were .... so so,
Nor were Richard the Third's any better I trow:

For his nephews he slew, and made murder his sport
Till Bosworth's red field cut his villainies short.
King Henry the Seventh was a scrub and a bore
Yet he brought the realm peace, if he did nothing more.
The glory of Henry the Eighth still survives,
Tho' he lop't a few heads, and was wed to six wives
His son the sixth Edward, died early poor lad,
So ought all good boys, ere they live to be bad;
If bad ones lived on till they mended their ways,
What very old sinners we'd have in our days:
Ned's half-sister Mary of megrims was sick,
And nought could she relish but roast heretick.
Mary's half-sister Bess kept the Spaniards in awe,
Her word was command and her will was the law.
Three realms suffered patiently Scots Jamie's rule,
Too weak was the monarch, too learned the fool.
His son Charles the First by rebellion unmoved,
Died a martyr to truth and the church that he loved.
Old Noll, as Protector, held rule with stern sway,
He cleared out the House, and in storms passed away.
The Second King Charles was more merry than wise.
James the Second his brother, with Rome in his eyes,
Left three realms for a Mass when be fled in disguise.
Dutch William came here for no good; but Queen Anne,
Lets hope she meant well and she loved her weak man.
James the Third King by right, showed his face and away,
Led his friends to destruction—what more need I say?
The Elector, dark George, was a crusty old brute,
And his son George the Second, more brave than acute,
Whose grandson was George the Third worthy old King
Whose son, George the Fourth was by no means the thing.
Then came Sailor William, the soft soaking fool,
Whom the Whig's took in hand and they made him their tool.
Here's a health to our Queen in the year of her Jubilee
May she never take heed to the counsels of you, Billy!

KINTORE
By Stuart Burnett
September 2nd 1877

Tell me, in this world of changing,
Prince and peer and peasant ranging,
Evermore.
Rambling, scrambling, crowding, crushing,
Wrestling, jostling, panting, pushing
Like a foaming torrent rushing
With restless war.
What they're seeking, never getting,
From their fuming and their fretting
Tumbling, tossing and upsetting
And wrestling sore?
After phantom shadows flying,
That fleet on before
And with hungry hearts still crying
For something more.
While the preachers in their preachings,
And the teachers and their teachings,
Still anon are vainly screeching,
Whiles at your door
Is there then on land or ocean
Refuge from this wild commotion
This babel war?
Is there now in all the nation
Safe retreat from botheration
Where things sit as at creation?
—Yes—at Kintore.
There might hermit find abiding
Life like sleepy river gliding,
Here, where all things are abiding
As of yore.
As when valiant Bruce attended
By his faithful band descended
From the battle, won and ended
Near Kintore.
Which he made a borough royal
In reward for service loyal,

Done heretofore.
Gave them provost, gave them baillies,
Gave them lands whereon there kail is,
"Tofts" and crofts, for so the tale is
Told at Kintore.
And their sons, they sit like sages
Where their sires have sat for ages,
Think them not like birds in cages
There at Kintore.
Call not such a state stagnation,
Gladly deem that in the nation
Some find time for contemplation
Still as of yore.
And for harmless recreation,
Sit and snore.
Sit and smoke their pipes and wonder
At the hiss and clang and thunder
And the war.
As the railway trains do rattle
O'er the former fields of battle,
Startling oft the browsing cattle
On the moor.
And the porter at the station
Equal to each fresh occasion,
With a sleepy intonation
Calls out "Kintore".
Then the mutch-crowned wifie's, sitting,
Silently their stockings knitting,
Each at her door,
Thinks "Fat gars the folk be flitin', aye back an' fore?"
And the burghers, as they listen
Watching trains at distance glisten,
Growl, "What a bore".
Some who would be thought more clever
Say, "Let trains run on for ever
Small the chance to gain our shore
Here, at Kintore".
Till a bridge bestrides the river
From shore to shore.
"What! A bridge?" cry out the old ones,

“Furnish ye the funds then, bold ones
From your store!
What new fangled generation,
Hath the demon innovation
Come to our door ?”.
Perish such an imputation
On Kintore.
What, a bridge! Preposterous fancy
E’en to dream it, were unchancy
While a factor like our Francie
Rules at Kintore.
Surely then no vain delusion
Is the hope of bless’d seclusion
Safe from change’s rude intrusion
Here on the shore,
Of that smoothly flowing river
Finding what the vain world ever
Toiling, moiling findeth never
Rest—at Kintore.

QUEENSFERRY

By Dorothy Burnett

2nd June 1916

A wide expanse of water, cold and grey
A river widening as it reached the sea;
Hidden by blinding mist and driving spray
The ships that some would give their lives to see.

Under the bridge they come home one by one,
And none who saw will ere forget that sight.
The mist rolled back and God’s most glorious sun
Welcomed those heroes from that great sea fight.

But some who watched, I saw their eyes grow dim
Their ships would never more return from sea.
The cry went up “Oh God take care of him
And bring my best beloved back to me.”

And in that little town so small and grey,
Some say St. Margaret came to watch with them
To give courage, and the strength to pray
They would be worthy of their sailor men.

"The Dream Garden"
By Dorothy Burnett
1918

We shall have a garden with cherry trees in May;
The path shall be of flagstones and alternate all the way
A gooseberry and rose bush; there must be Bergamot
And all the sweet old fashioned flowers not one must be forgot.

There will be a gray wall, six feet high or so,
Every rose that rambles we'll plant and watch it grow,
All the little rock things will creep along the top,
Silvery clumps of saxifrage and yellow golden crop.

We shall have a border close against the wall,
Blue delphiniums at the back and annuals through it all;
But we won't be so modern as to have a colour scheme,
We'd rather have all colours in this garden of our dream,

Then just beneath the window, where the night wind can blow,
We'll have a bed of all the very sweetest things that grow.
Scented stock and mignionette with every kind of thyme,
'Tis a very perfect paradise, this garden dream of mine.

I can see my garden now, just turn towards the west,
Half close your eyes, remember, and I think God does the rest.
"Houses and smoke", you only see a dirty London Square,
My friend, it's plain you don't possess a garden in the air.

ACKNOWLEDGEMENTS

Fleur Houston for decyphering and translating Thomas Burnet's peculiar French.
Robert N. Smart, Keeper of Muniments University Library, St. Andrews for information regarding Dr George Lamont's degrees etc.
Professor Marlies Danziger and the Boswell Office at Yale University Library, for Permission to publish Alexander Burnet's letter to James Boswell.
City of Aberdeen Library Services – Reference and Local Studies Department.
John Menzies for the reproduction of the portraits.
Aberdeen Journals Ltd., for permission to use their photograph of my Father and his two brothers.
Nicholas Bogdan and Susan Edwards for their help in the early stages.
Philip Jacquet for the immense amount of work and research, with great attention to detail, to get this book camera ready.
My Family and Friends for their interest and encouragement.

BIBLIOGRAPHY

The Burnett of Kemnay Archives (NRA (S) survey 1368) have provided most of the information for this book.

Other sources were:

Aberdeen Almanac, Year 1773, J Chalmers & Co.

Banks, Mrs M. Macleod British Calendar Customs: Scotland, Vol. 1: Movable Festivals, Harvest, March Riding & Wapynshaws, Wells & Fairs. The Folk–Lore Society, 1937.

Burnett, George The Family of Burnett of Leys with collateral Branches edited by Colonel James Allardyce. New Spalding Club, 1901.

Cook, Chris & Stevenson, John British Historical Facts, 1760-1830. Macmillan, 1980.

Dinnie, Robert History of Kincardine O'Neil. Lewis Smith & Son, 1885.

Foster, Joseph Members of Parliament, Scotland, including the Minor Barons, The Commissioners for the Shires, and the Commissioners for the Burghs, 1357–1882. Hazell, Watson, and Viney, 1882.

Hellicur, Eileen Prime Ministers of Britain. David & Charles, 1978.

Mitford, Nancy Frederick the Great. Hamish Hamilton, 1970.

Namier, Sir Lewis & Brooke, John The House of Commons, 1754–1790. Her Majesty's Stationery Office, 1964

Pearson, Mowbray (editor) More Frost and Snow. The Diary of Janet Burnet. Canongate Academic, 1994.

Smith, Alexander (editor) A New History of Aberdeenshire. Lewis Smith and William Blackwood and Sons, 1875.

Smout, T C A History of the Scottish People 1560–1830. Collins, 1969.

Spence, James Ruined Castles, Monuments of Former Men in Vicinity of Banff. Edmonston and Douglas, 1873.